THE
WORLD
OF THE BIBLE

JOHN DRANE

D1369103

LION

Published by Lion Books
an imprint of
Lion Hudson plc
Wilkinson House, Jordan Hill Road,
Oxford OX2 8DR, England
www.lionhudson.com/lion
ISBN 978 0 7459 5645 9
e-ISBN 978 0 7459 5798 2

First hardback edition 2009
First paperback edition 2014

Acknowledgments
Scripture quotations are from the New Revised
Standard Version published by HarperCollins
Publishers, copyright © 1989 by the Division of
Christian Education of the National Council of the
Churches of Christ in the USA, and are used by
permission. All rights reserved.

A catalogue record for this book is available from the
British Library

Printed and bound in the UK, January 2014, LH26

Contents

Introduction

Thirty or forty years ago it would not have been at all unusual to hear politicians, academics, and even some religious leaders declaring that the time of religion's greatest influence on world culture lay in the past. Secularism seemed to be triumphant, atheism was widespread, and it looked as if the future for humankind would be a world without faith. Now in the second decade of the twenty-first century, that looks like wishful thinking of the most deluded kind. Religious concerns are driving the agenda of some of the biggest challenges facing the world, and those who imagined they would never need to engage with it are finding that it is still one of the most potent forces on the planet, with the capacity to inspire enormous good and to endorse horrendous evil. The one thing we cannot do is to ignore it.

The Bible has long been at the centre of Western civilization's self-understanding. Its teaching provided the underlying assumptions upon which that culture was established, and its precepts have had a formative influence in the evolution of the legal system, education, and morality – not to mention such concepts as "human rights" as well as ideas that might more narrowly be described as "religious". Moreover, while each one has its own distinctive emphasis, the Bible's contents are regarded with high esteem by the three great Abrahamic faiths: Judaism, Christianity, and Islam.

The Bible was not written in a vacuum. It reflects the social and cultural contexts in which its authors lived. Their interaction with the culture on the one hand and their faith in God on the other is what provides the connective tissue that unites what might otherwise seem to be a pretty disparate collection of writings. This is not a book about the Bible's message, nor indeed about its contents in any very specific way. Instead it is an invitation to begin to look at the Bible through the spectacles of the cultures in which it came to birth. It is a long journey, encompassing many different languages, styles of life, locations, and worldviews. Some parts of the story will be easier to grasp than others. Understanding this world is not the same thing as grasping its essential message, but to know something about the world of the Bible is to gain a fresh perspective on how its writers sought to contextualize their faith in God in ways that would both challenge and affirm the world as they experienced it. In the process of doing so, the message itself will be immeasurably enriched through being set in the times and places where it was first heard. Nuances that might otherwise be missed can be understood in a new light, and themes that seem arcane and irrelevant can take on fresh significance. More than that, by reflecting on how these ancient writers sought to adapt their essential message to different cultural circumstances, today's readers might be encouraged to discover new ways in which ancient wisdom can address the challenges of the very different world in which we live now.

1

The Bible and its Context

There can be no doubt about the Bible's status as one of the great classics of world literature. Its most recent parts were written something like 2,000 years ago, yet it is still a bestseller in the bookstores, while a search for the word "Bible" on the worldwide web highlights well over 100 million sites, and its entire text can be found online in more than fifty different versions. It has been translated into more languages than any other book, and has had a profound influence on the whole history of world civilization. Men and women have died for the privilege of being able to read it, and even today millions of people throughout the world avidly read it as a source of personal guidance for daily living.

The Bible has also been the inspiration behind many of the most radical social reforms of recent centuries. Inspired by what he read in its pages, the British politician William Wilberforce (1759–1833) embarked on a campaign that would eventually lead to the outlawing of slavery. Slightly later, another politician, Anthony Ashley Cooper, the seventh Earl of Shaftesbury (1801–85), committed himself to stopping the exploitation of women and children by their employers – again, inspired by what he read in the pages of the Bible. In the middle of the twentieth century, the African-American church leader Dr Martin Luther King Jr (1929–68) initiated a process that led to fundamental changes in relationships between the races in the USA, on the basis of what he knew of the Bible and its message. At the end of the twentieth century, much of the pressure that brought about the collapse of the system of apartheid that segregated the races in South Africa came from church groups that were fired by the vision of a better way of living which they read about in the Bible.

Moreover, Christians are not the only ones to have found inspiration in its pages. In his search for spiritual wisdom, Mahatma Gandhi (1869–1948) became an avid Bible student, and the teachings of Jesus on turning the other cheek and loving enemies[1] provided the operational model for his political campaigns. Though he lived an abstemious life, with few material goods, among his treasured possessions at the time of his assassination was a book entitled *The Life and Teachings of Jesus Christ*, along with a copy of John's Gospel, while a picture of Jesus adorned the wall of his home, carrying the inscription "He is our peace" (a quotation from Ephesians 2:14, which explicitly links Jesus with the breaking down of barriers between different races).

Yet although the Bible continues to be valued as a source of moral guidance and social inspiration, it also raises many questions, not least in relation to the truth of its message. The notion of "truth" is of course a slippery one in itself, and can be used to describe many different things, from historical or scientific veracity that can be studied in relation to other sources of knowledge, to the sort of truth about human life and its meaning that can only be tested by personal experience. This book is not designed to delve into such questions, but rather to examine the world of the Bible in a way that will enable serious searchers after truth to gain a better grasp of the social and cultural circumstances that called forth its various books, and to reflect for themselves on its relevance for life in the rather different social context that is the twenty-first century.

Even that modest aim is not as straightforward as it can be made to seem, because actually there is no such thing as "the world of the Bible" – for the simple reason that the Bible itself is not just a single book. A casual glance inside any Bible shows that it is divided into two main sections, usually called the Old and New Testaments – or, in terminology that better reflects its historical origins, the Hebrew Bible and the Second (or Christian) Testament. That is only the beginning of the story, however, for each of these major divisions also contains numerous shorter and self-contained books, thirty-nine of them in the first Testament and twenty-seven in the second. What we have here is an entire library of books that were written over a very considerable period of time. The Hebrew Bible consists of the literary archives of the ancient Israelites, starting with the beginning of time itself and then tracing the nation's early history through Abraham and his family, before eventually ending in the time of the Greek empire of Alexander the Great (356–323 BC) and his successors. The New Testament reflects a rather shorter historical period, and all of its writings were written in the course of the first century AD. Even here, there is considerable diversity among its various books, some of which reflect life in Palestine, at the eastern fringe of the Roman empire, while others refer to the rather different lifestyles and worldviews that characterized the urban citizens of countries such as Greece and Italy.

This diversity is even reflected in the languages in which the various parts of the Bible were originally written. As the name suggests, the books of the Hebrew Bible, the scriptures of the Jewish faith, were mostly written in Hebrew, though a handful of pages were in Aramaic, a language which achieved worldwide recognition during the period of the Persian empire (559–331 BC). The New Testament documents were written entirely in Greek, which, following the conquests of

Alexander the Great, had become the international language of the whole of the Mediterranean world.

In the light of all these facts, the world of the Bible turns out to be many worlds. Its earliest historical narratives are set in the Stone Age, while its latest documents reflect the life of the early Roman empire. In the process of telling this story, Bible readers are introduced to the cultures of ancient Mesopotamia and Egypt, as well as Greece and Rome. Even they are not homogeneous entities, for each of them underwent significant changes in the course of their own history. Then, interwoven through it all is the story of Abraham's family, the various people groups who traced their origins back to him, and their religious understandings of the world and its people. While it is perfectly possible to grasp the spiritual heart of the Bible's message without detailed knowledge of its historical background, placing its various books in the social contexts within which they were originally composed not only brings to life the characters who populate its pages, but also has the potential to illuminate many aspects of its message.

The value of such historical investigations can be illustrated by two stories, one from the nineteenth century and the other from the twentieth. They concern the search for original manuscripts of the Bible, and are worth including here as examples of how casual discoveries and professional investigations have both played their part in broadening our understanding of the Bible and its world. They also highlight how political intrigue and dealings in the criminal underworld can influence, and sometimes skew, how our knowledge of the Bible's world is obtained.

Discovering old Bibles

It can be disconcerting for modern readers to learn that there is no such thing as a first edition of the Bible, and that no-one knows what happened to the actual documents in which its books were first written down. Probably they did not last beyond the generation in which they were produced. Even in the time of Jesus (the first century AD), the Hebrew Bible was known only through copies of copies, stretching back in a continuous line into the dim and distant past. In this respect, the Bible is no worse off than any other literature from the ancient world. We have no originals of the classics of ancient Greece and Rome either. The works of Julius Caesar, for example, were written in the first century BC but there are fewer than a dozen surviving manuscripts, and the oldest date from as late as AD 800–900 – almost a thousand years after Caesar lived. The histories of the Roman historian Tacitus are the same. His books were written towards the end of the first century AD, but most of them have disappeared for good and our entire knowledge of what survives depends on only two manuscripts that date from the ninth and the eleventh centuries AD respectively. Things are exactly the same in the case of classical Greek writers. The earliest complete manuscript of the work of Thucydides (460–400 BC) dates from about AD 900, and there are fewer than ten manuscripts in all. In the ancient world no-one would have been surprised by this, but once people started to think more deeply about the Bible and its history it was both natural and inevitable to want to know where, exactly, these ancient books had come from, and more especially how we might be sure that the Bible in our hands is what its original authors intended it to be.

Searching for the New Testament

You would hardly expect words like "detective story" or "treasure hunt" to be used in connection with the Bible, yet once we begin to explore the way in which some of the ancient documents have come to light, that kind of language seems entirely appropriate. For me, the search began one cold winter afternoon in the University of Glasgow, Scotland – not the most obvious place to look, perhaps, but the library there contains a remarkable accumulation of books and papers gathered together by one of the world's most adventurous collectors of ancient manuscripts. Constantin von Tischendorf (1815–74) was a professor at the University of Leipzig in Germany, and when he died the trustees of Trinity Theological College in Glasgow got the chance to purchase his library. It cost them the grand sum of £460, an amount which they raised first from their own donations, and then by an appeal to the Free Church Assembly in May 1877. The Assembly commended the collection to its people in glowing terms:

> *For this most interesting acquisition the Glasgow college and the Free Church are especially indebted to the zeal and energy of Professor Lindsay. He has also collected a large part of the amount required: and it is hoped that wealthy friends in the west will not leave him in anxiety as to the balance. There is no respect in which a wise munificence may be better exercised than in enabling our college libraries to acquire rare and valuable books beyond the reach of private individuals, and scarcely to be found in any of our public libraries.*

No-one seems to know how Professor Lindsay came across the papers. But he obviously had no shortage of wealthy friends, for they raised the cash required to buy them in a remarkably short time, and the Tischendorf collection found a permanent home in his college. From the fine words of the General Assembly you might have expected that these books would have been given pride of place. In fact they were left locked away in a library cupboard, unlisted and all but forgotten, for the next hundred years. Then in 1974, when Trinity College had fallen into such a state of disrepair that it was almost collapsing, they were rediscovered and presented to the University of Glasgow.

They document a fascinating story that starts in 1839 with the young Tischendorf, who at the time was twenty-four years old. Five years earlier he had gone to the University of Leipzig, where he developed a keen fascination for the New Testament. He decided to try to reconstruct its text in the exact words that its authors had originally written. He started work with such materials as he could find in Leipzig, but soon realized that to make much progress he would have to travel a lot further afield. Many of the great libraries of Europe had lain undisturbed for centuries, and Tischendorf had a hunch that if he could get into some of them he would be able to unearth Bible manuscripts and other materials that had been ignored or forgotten for generations. As it turned out, his initial dreams were to be fulfilled beyond his greatest expectations. But like many great scholars and explorers, Tischendorf was not particularly well off, and so his first job was to persuade other, richer people that he was worth supporting. He started with his own government, and they gave him a grant of 100 thalers to cover his travel expenses. Considering that a mere 5 thalers would have bought a whole week's groceries for a family, this sounds like a very generous grant indeed. But Tischendorf was not impressed, and wrote in his diary:

> *What was such a sum as this with which to undertake a long journey? Full of faith, however, in the proverb that "God helps those who help themselves", and that what is right must prosper, I resolved, in 1840, to set out for Paris ... though I had not sufficient means to pay even for my traveling suit; and when I reached Paris I had only 50 thalers left. The other fifty had been spent on my journey.*

In Paris, Tischendorf soon found himself caught up in an argument that would ultimately win him fame and, more importantly, fortune. It all started with a document that he found in the National Library of Paris, which at first glance appeared to be a copy of the writings of St Ephraem, a fourth-century leader of the Syrian church. On closer examination, however, it turned out to have more than one layer of writing on it. Good writing material was very valuable in the ancient world, especially if it was made of leather as this was. Instead of buying new materials all the time, enterprising scribes made a habit of taking documents that were no longer needed, scrubbing them clean, and then using them over again. This is what had happened here, and the experts in Paris were trying to decipher the writing that had been there originally before it was scrubbed off. They had tried everything they could think of – strong lights, chemicals, and other novel inventions – but with no success, and eventually declared it would be impossible to read what was underneath.

But they had reckoned without Tischendorf's determination. Since he was interested in such documents, he thought he had nothing to lose by taking a look at this one, and after many hours of hard work – and, presumably, with the benefit of good eyesight – he had not only deciphered the original writing, but was also able to determine the document's history. It had, he said, originally been written in the fifth century, and then renovated in the seventh century and again in the ninth – finally to be scrubbed clean and inscribed with different material altogether in the twelfth century.

The scholars in Paris were bowled over by this extraordinary discovery. Tischendorf became a hero overnight, and with this success behind him he found it was now a simple matter to raise very substantial funds for his other projects. Well-to-do patrons of the arts were so impressed by his achievement that they were falling over themselves to have their names associated with his. But what interested Tischendorf most was that the writing he had uncovered on this manuscript was an ancient copy of parts of the Bible. He began to wonder if other documents like this existed elsewhere. He wrote in his journal:

> *The literary treasures which I have sought to explore*
> *have been drawn in most cases from the convents of the*
> *east where, for ages, the pens of industrious monks have*
> *copied the sacred writings, and collected manuscripts of*
> *all kinds. It therefore occurred to me whether it was not*
> *probable that in some recess of Greek or Coptic, Syrian*
> *or Armenian monasteries, there might be some precious*
> *manuscripts sheltering for ages in dust and darkness.*

With this possibility in mind, he set off on an epic journey to scour the monasteries of the eastern Mediterranean. Little did he realize what an astounding voyage of discovery it would turn out to be. He began by going round all the great European centres of learning – Venice, Modena, Milan, Verona, Turin, Rome – searching their libraries for ancient manuscripts. In the process, he made a number of significant discoveries. In Florence he came across a copy of the Bible translated into Latin by the fourth-century Italian scholar Jerome, allegedly while ensconced in a cave in Bethlehem. But it had travelled hundreds of miles before it found a home in northern Italy. Its journey had begun at Jarrow, in the north of England – a place which in the seventh and eighth centuries was one of the great cultural and religious centres of Western Europe.

It was here that the Venerable Bede (AD 673–735) wrote his *Ecclesiastical History of the English People*, and made a start on translating the Bible into Anglo-Saxon. He translated from Latin, and may conceivably have known the very manuscript which Tischendorf discovered: it was certainly during Bede's lifetime that the abbot of his monastery decided to make a pilgrimage to Rome, taking this document with him as a suitable gift for the Pope. Neither the abbot nor his gift ever arrived, for he died on the journey, and the manuscript found a home in the Italian monastery of Monte Amiata in the northern Alps. There it remained for a thousand years, until the monastery itself closed down in 1782, at which point the manuscript was taken to Florence, and that was where Tischendorf found it eighty years later, and told the world about it.

But it was on the second leg of his epic journey that he made his greatest find. In April 1844 he moved on to the Bible lands proper: Egypt, Libya, Arabia, and Palestine. Here, at the remote site of one of the central events of ancient Israelite history, Constantin von Tischendorf was to make history himself. Beneath the rocky crags of Mt Sinai, he came upon the stern walls of St Catherine's monastery, built in the days of the

Roman emperor Justinian (AD 482–565), and which is still a major pilgrimage site in the twenty-first century:

> *It was at the foot of Mount Sinai, in the convent of St Catherine, that I discovered the pearl of all my researches. In visiting the library of the monastery, in the month of May 1844, I perceived in the middle of the great hall a large and wide basket full of old parchments; and the librarian, who was a man of information, told me that two heaps of papers like these, mouldered by time, had already been committed to the flames.*

As Tischendorf thumbed through these pages, he recognized that they contained parts of the Hebrew scriptures but in a Greek translation, and as he compared them with the Greek Old Testament text with which he was already familiar, he realized that these were the most ancient copies he had ever seen. When he tried to persuade the monks to give him all the pages, they became suspicious of his motives and would allow him to have only those sheets that were about to be burned, forty-three of them in all. But at least he managed to persuade them not to destroy any more until he could return to study the whole manuscript in greater detail.

Once he got back to Europe, Tischendorf was kept busy sorting and cataloguing the many documents he had found on his travels, but he could not stop thinking about the manuscript at the foot of Mt Sinai. Through a friend at the Egyptian royal court, he stayed in contact with the monks, but even with friends in such high places he was unable to get his hands on the precious pages. In desperation, he decided that he would go back to the monastery, and if necessary would laboriously copy the entire document out by hand. So in 1853,

nine years after his first visit, he once more knocked on the
door of St Catherine's. He was well received by the monks,
and was shown many of their treasures, but he could find no
trace of the manuscript that had impressed him so much on his
previous visit. To his great disappointment, he was forced to
return to Europe empty-handed. Then he thought of a better
plan. The monks of St Catherine's belonged to the Orthodox
Church, and regarded the Russian emperor as the patron and
protector of their faith. So Tischendorf determined that this
time he would get the backing of the Russian government.
But there were other obstacles to overcome first:

> *This proposal only aroused a jealous and fanatical*
> *opposition in St Petersburg. People were astonished that*
> *a foreigner and a Protestant should presume to ask*
> *the support of the emperor of the Greek and Orthodox*
> *church for a mission to the east. But the good cause*
> *triumphed. The interest which my proposal excited, even*
> *within the imperial circle, inclined the emperor in my*
> *favour.*

In January 1859, with the backing of the Russian emperor,
Tischendorf set out once again for Mt Sinai. It turned out to
be a momentous journey, as this time he was warmly welcomed
by the monks and at last discovered the whereabouts of the
priceless manuscript he had first glimpsed fifteen years before:

> *Full of joy, which this time I had the self-command to*
> *conceal from the steward and the rest of the community,*
> *I asked, as if in a careless way, for permission to take*
> *the manuscript into my sleeping chamber to look over it*
> *more at leisure. There by myself I could give way to the*

*transport of joy which I felt. I knew that I held in my
hand the most precious biblical treasure in existence.*

After lengthy and delicate negotiations, which took him
all the way from Egypt to Constantinople and back, it was
agreed that Tischendorf should take the entire manuscript to
Russia, where it could be copied and examined by experts.
Finally, back in Russia on 19 November 1859, he presented
it to Tsar Alexander II, along with plans for its publication.
Tischendorf himself was the editor, and when the work was
completed his enterprise and scholarship was acclaimed by the
whole world. The emperor of Russia sent copies of it far and
wide, and Tischendorf received honours from the Pope and
other religious leaders, as well as degrees from the universities
of Oxford and Cambridge in England. His discovery turned
out to be so important that when he was presented to these
ancient universities, one British scholar commented somewhat
enviously: "I would rather have discovered this Sinaitic
manuscript than the crown jewels of the Queen of England."

He was not the only one to recognize its value, and in the
1930s, when the Communist government of Russia decided it
no longer had any use for Tischendorf's treasure, the British
government paid £100,000 to buy it, which was a huge sum
in those days. Its arrival in the British Museum at Christmas
1933 was one of the great events of that period:

*The queue of those desirous of passing in front of it was
continuous ... the crowd appeared to be drawn from all
sorts and conditions of men and women, and to be of
many nations and languages. As they appeared within
sight of the shining parchment sheets, not a few were
moved out of reverence to take off their hats. While none*

*could linger for more than a few seconds before the glass
case, some passed by quicker than others; for the majority
a look was enough, and they departed in peace.*

That was how *The Times* newspaper in London reported the
affair, and Tischendorf would have appreciated the mystical
overtones of its language – for he too was convinced that in
this document he had encountered more than just another old
Bible. Writing of it later, he reflected:

*While so much had been lost in the course of centuries, by
the tooth of time or by the carelessness of ignorant monks,
an invisible eye had watched over this treasure and when
it was on the point of perishing in the fire, the Lord had
decreed its deliverance.*

Today's historians would never admit to being moved to
this kind of mystical reverence for their discoveries, but
Tischendorf's hunches were correct, and his *Codex Sinaiticus*
(as it came to be known) was laying the foundation for the most
accurate text of the New Testament ever known. The train of
events that his discovery set in motion extended far beyond
his own time, and this manuscript is still the most complete
ancient Bible manuscript that we have. It was written in Greek
about the middle of the fourth century AD, and contains the
whole of the New Testament as well as a few sections of the
Hebrew Bible (in Greek).

But it is not the oldest Bible manuscript, not by a long
way. To discover that we must turn our attention to another
momentous find, this one much nearer to our own time.
Tischendorf went looking for ancient manuscripts: he knew
what he was searching for, and had a fair idea where to look. But

advances in knowledge just as often come about by accident, and this was what happened with the famous Dead Sea Scrolls.

Finding unknown texts

In spring 1947 a young Arab shepherd by the name of Jum'a Muhammed was wandering along the foot of the cliffs that overlook the north-eastern shore of the Dead Sea. To him and his companions it was just another day, and the only business in hand was to ensure that their flocks of sheep and goats managed to find enough grazing to satisfy their daily requirements. The people of their tribe – the Ta'amireh – had lived like this for centuries, and they knew all the nooks and crannies of the barren and forbidding landscape. Despite his familiarity with this place, as he clambered over the cliffs in pursuit of a wandering animal Jum'a noticed a couple of small holes in the sheer rock face, high above where he stood. With little else to do, he tossed a stone through one of the openings, and to his surprise, instead of a dull thud as the stone landed in the cave, he heard the sound of breaking pottery, and that could mean only one thing: some sort of treasure. This was not a spot where great towns and cities had ever stood. But precisely because of its remoteness, several legends attached to it. The Hebrew Bible had spoken of "the City of Salt"[2] that was located somewhere in this general area, and references like that had encouraged nineteenth-century archaeologists to search for the remains of the biblical cities of Sodom and Gomorrah in this area, because in the story of the escape of Lot and his family from Sodom and Gomorrah, Lot's wife was turned into a "pillar of salt".[3]

Jum'a resisted the temptation to enter the caves right away, for fear of getting stuck inside their small openings. But his two cousins were helping with the flocks, and one of them was only a teenager, smaller and therefore more able to get in and – more importantly – back out again. But no-one was in any great hurry, and it was two or three days before the three friends decided to settle their flocks overnight at the foot of the cliff just below the caves. At dawn on the next morning, the teenager was awake before the others. It was a long way up to the caves, but experience at chasing after wayward sheep and goats had taught him how to climb safely even over such major obstacles. In no time at all, he had lowered himself into the higher of the two openings. Jum'a had originally imagined that there might be coins, gold or jewels stacked up inside, but instead they found only a few stone jars. Most were empty, some others were just full of dirt, and one contained a roll of old leather. Then there were two other packages wrapped in rotted green cloth. These bundles also turned out to be documents of some kind, but in a script that none of them could understand, and their deteriorated condition hardly suggested they would be of much value to anyone. In fact, when they returned to their home base not far from Bethlehem, Jum'a casually hung them all up on the pole of his tent.

He soon had second thoughts, however, and over the next month or two various other items were removed from the caves, mostly more scrolls. They eventually found their way to the market in Bethlehem, where several traders had a regular business buying and selling such items. The dealers were initially suspicious, fearing that they had been stolen from a museum, but in due course their existence became public knowledge when they fell into the hands of Metropolitan Samuel of St Mark's Monastery in Jerusalem. The exact sequence of events by which they got there is still unclear, though they soon sparked off a lively debate among those who knew about such things. Some experts unhesitatingly dated them at least as early as the first century BC, while others insisted they were medieval, and one even declared them to be a modern forgery. But the people who unearthed them knew they were on to a good thing, and the caves above the Dead Sea soon became the place to go to search for more treasure.

By this time, the United Nations had announced the establishment of the modern state of Israel, and Palestine was thrown into disorder and conflict, which discouraged professional archaeologists from carrying out investigations in the area around the Dead Sea. By the beginning of 1949, the Arab Legion had posted a guard on the caves, but only after dozens of unauthorized explorers had already been inside and removed various items as well as leaving their own twentieth-century trash behind. Nevertheless, there were still many fragments of scrolls scattered about the caves, together with the various jars and bits of cloth in which they had originally been contained. Professional analysis of these confirmed beyond any doubt that these scrolls and jars were even earlier than anyone had imagined, and dated from about 200–250 BC, perhaps even earlier.

Down on the plateau and less than a mile away were some ruins that had been known for a long time: Kirbet Qumrân. These had been superficially explored by archaeologists in the middle of the nineteenth century, but in the light of the discovery of these scrolls they now assumed a new importance. Could these ruins be connected with the ancient documents that were gradually emerging from the caves? Thorough excavations in the early 1950s soon demonstrated that they were. The site had been occupied as long ago as the seventh and eighth centuries BC, but the major remains dated from the period immediately surrounding the beginning of the Christian era. Human occupation finally came to an end in AD 135, but all the signs were that the manuscripts must have been hidden just before AD 70, which was the year when the Romans devastated Jerusalem itself.

The ruins of Qumrân offer remarkable evidence of the engineering skills of those who lived here. To find enough water to drink in the middle of the desert was difficult enough in itself, but these people had constructed a complex system of aqueducts and cisterns that enabled them to gather water in enormous quantities, apparently for use in religious rituals as well as for more ordinary things like washing and drinking. Other remarkable finds included the remains of the tables at which the scrolls were first written, complete with ancient inkwells that even contained the dried up remnants of long-vanished ink.

After several decades of research, the consensus is that these people were probably related to the Essenes, who were a Jewish religious group mentioned by several ancient writers. Not all Essenes lived as part of an isolated monastic community, and in the time of Jesus it seems that they could be found throughout the country. But these particular people appear to have regarded themselves as a faithful remnant within what they believed to be a corrupt nation, and they lived at this isolated spot in order to keep themselves pure and separate from a culture which they regarded as hopelessly compromised through its connections with the Romans and their accomplices. The discovery of their monastery and the scrolls has led to many fascinating insights into the beliefs and way of life of this particular group, and more will be said about their lifestyle and beliefs in chapter 7.

Right now, though, our main interest in them concerns the scrolls themselves. In the years following the initial discoveries, other caves in the area were systematically explored, and dozens more texts came to light. Among them were the rules of the community and many religious commentaries. There were also texts containing excerpts from every book of the Hebrew Bible except one (the book of Esther). Very few of them were complete manuscripts, of course, but some could be dated back almost to the time of the events they record. Some scraps containing parts of the books of 1 and 2 Samuel are as old as the third century BC, while some of the texts of Daniel may have been written less than a hundred years after that book was first compiled. The most outstanding finds turned out to be very significant indeed. Typical of these is the Isaiah Scroll, which was probably among the first discoveries made by the three shepherds. It contains the complete Bible book of Isaiah and is an enormous document, made out of seventeen sheets of leather sewn together side by side to make a scroll measuring almost 8 metres in length by about 26 centimetres high. As well as this major find, there is also a second scroll of the book of Isaiah, though that is incomplete and has suffered considerable damage.

Before these momentous discoveries, the oldest known texts of the Hebrew Bible dated from the ninth and tenth centuries AD, supplemented by earlier copies in Greek translation that originated in Egypt in the first and second centuries before the time of Jesus, but which survive mostly in manuscripts from the third and fourth centuries AD. This is the same text as the one Tischendorf found in the Old Testament section of his *Codex Sinaiticus*. The chance discovery of the Dead Sea Scrolls unearthed manuscripts in Hebrew that were a thousand years older than any that had previously been known. They reveal what scholars had always suspected, that there were several editions of the Hebrew Bible in use at the time of

Jesus. But all the differences between them were in relatively minor details, corresponding to the sort of diversity of idiom and expression that can be found even between three or four English translations. The one thing that the Dead Sea Scrolls demonstrated beyond any doubt is that the text of the Bible has remained virtually unchanged for the last 2,000 years.

Varieties of Bible literature

As might be expected from a compilation of books that represents the archives of a nation (the ancient Hebrews), and then the foundational narrative of a spiritual community (the earliest church), many different literary genres are to be found in the Bible, and they will be reflected in later chapters of this book as we explore the diverse cultural contexts in which they were written.

The Hebrew Bible

The contents of the Hebrew Bible were traditionally arranged in three sections: the Law, the Prophets, and the Writings.

The Law consists of the first five books (Genesis, Exodus, Leviticus, Numbers, Deuteronomy), believed to be of special importance as they were traditionally regarded as the work of Moses, one of the earliest leaders of the nation. They are not all "law" in the sense that most of us would recognize today. Genesis, for example, contains nothing that even looks like rules or regulations, but consists instead of a collection of stories. Even the other four books in this section contain a lot of narrative materials, in addition to laws for various aspects of individual and community life. The understanding of "law" contained here was obviously more comprehensive and far-ranging than that of twenty-first-century secular states. The Hebrew word *Torah* is often used as a descriptive title for these five books, and is conventionally translated as "law", though a more accurate rendering would be a word like "guidance" or "instruction". That might easily include principles of justice, but also needed to incorporate stories that would serve as everyday illustrations and case studies of how people were intended to live. None of the stories were told in a vacuum, but all of them related to the historical circumstances in which the people found themselves at the time, which is why a knowledge of the cultural background in which the Bible was written can enrich our understanding of its essential message.

The Prophets is the largest section of the Hebrew Bible, and takes its name from a number of religious and political activists who sought to influence the life of the nation over a period of several centuries. This collection of books falls into two distinct sections, "the Former Prophets" and "the Latter Prophets". The books of the Latter Prophets consist of messages delivered by a series of religious and political activists who functioned as the moral and spiritual conscience of the nation – people such as Isaiah, Jeremiah, and Ezekiel (the so-called "major prophets" because of the length of the books containing their deeds and messages), along with Hosea, Joel, Amos, Obadiah, Jonah, Micah, Nahum, Habakkuk, Zephaniah, Haggai, Zechariah, and Malachi (called the "minor prophets" because their messages are preserved in much shorter books). The books of the Former Prophets are quite different in character, and consist of historical narratives: Joshua, Judges, 1–2 Samuel, and 1–2 Kings. They recount the story of the ancient Hebrews and their ancestors from the time when they first settled in Palestine to the destruction of the nation of Judah by the Babylonians in the sixth century BC – all of it interpreted in line with the moral and religious perspectives of the Latter Prophets, which explains why books of history-writing came to be regarded as also being prophetic in character.

The Writings include the remaining books of the Hebrew Bible. They are all poetry, but apart from that are quite different from one another in terms of their content and style. Psalms is a liturgical handbook designed for public worship and private devotion, while Proverbs offers traditional advice about how to live a good life, and Job offers a reflection on undeserved suffering, presented in dramatic form. Then there are those books known as the *Megilloth*, or "five scrolls": Ruth, Song of Solomon, Ecclesiastes, Lamentations, and Esther, each one different but gathered together because each one had a particular association with a significant religious festival. This section of the Hebrew Bible also contains the books of Ezra, Nehemiah, and 1–2 Chronicles, all of which relate to the situation in which the remnants of the people of Judah found themselves after they were allowed to return to their homeland after 538 BC by Cyrus, emperor of Persia. Last of all, there is the book of Daniel, containing visions and some stories, and relating to a later period still.

The New Testament

The New Testament is less complicated, reflecting the fact that all its books were written in the space of something like fifty years or so, rather than the centuries over which the Hebrew scriptures were collected.

The Gospels contain stories of the life of Jesus and accounts of his teaching. They were compiled for a variety of reasons, though all four of them (Matthew, Mark, Luke, and John) were intended to commend belief in Jesus to their original readers. Jesus himself lived in rural Palestine, but with the possible exception of Matthew these Gospels were compiled for people who were predominantly resident in the major cities of the Roman empire, which is why knowledge of life in that urban environment – as well as of rural Palestine – is so important for understanding all the nuances of their accounts. One reason for their writing was to preserve the reminiscences of those who had been Jesus' first followers, though Luke[4] and John[5] both explicitly claim to have written to commend the Christian message to a wider constituency, and invite others to join them in their new-found faith.

The Acts of the Apostles is unique in the New Testament, being an account of the life of some of the earliest church leaders ("apostles", from a Greek word meaning "those who have been sent out") and the communities that they founded. Written by the same individual as Luke's Gospel, it was based on personal diaries compiled by Luke himself (who was a participant and eye-witness of some of the events he records), as well as gathering together materials from other sources.

The Letters constitute a very important source of primary information about the earliest Christians, and were written by various church leaders to communities of Jesus' followers in different parts of the Roman empire during the first century AD. Most of them were written by Paul, but others are associated with the names of Peter and John, and also James the brother of Jesus and another lesser-known character, Jude.

Hebrews has the appearance of being a letter, as it contains greetings sent from Christians in one city to its recipients elsewhere,[6] but apart from that it reads much more like a philosophical reflection on various aspects of Jewish ritual practice in relation to Christian faith. The final book of the New Testament, Revelation, opens with a series of letters to churches in Asia Minor,[7] but then quickly invites the reader into an entirely different world with a series of visions dealing with themes of suffering, the power of evil and the triumph of goodness. This form of writing is known as "apocalyptic", from a Greek word that means "revelation" or "revealing". The book of Daniel is an apocalyptic book, and various sections of Ezekiel, Isaiah and Zechariah also share a similar outlook. The "revealing" in question was usually related to some divinely communicated insight into the meaning of history and its ultimate significance. Fascination with such matters was widespread in Jewish circles at the beginning of the Christian era, and similar concerns can be traced in some circles within classical Greek culture.

All these books – whether in the Old Testament or the New – were products of their own age, and the diverse contexts in which they were written can shed considerable light on their meaning and significance. Their message is no doubt distinctive, but their literary style and forms of expression owe a good deal to external influences from the wider cultures in which they took form. That, of course, is what ensured that they would be taken seriously. The New Testament books were written quite intentionally with the purpose of contextualizing the message of Jesus in a world that was quite different from his own original context – and in a slightly different way, many aspects of the Hebrew Bible also represent a deliberate reinterpretation of traditionally held views so as to infuse them with new meaning that was drawn not from the wider culture but from the Hebrews' own spiritual insights and experience.

Counting the books

One final topic is worth including in this introductory section, because it will come up later on. That is the question of how many books the Bible originally contained. If the Bible were just one single narrative from start to finish, that would seem like a very silly question. But it is actually quite an important one, arising precisely out of the fact that the Bible is an entire library of books and, like any other library of separate volumes, the number of writings that might be included was not always as fixed as it is today. This fact has occasionally been seized upon as evidence of some sort of conspiracy in the early days of the church, motivated by a desire on the part of church leaders to suppress ideas they disapproved of, or in other ways to bolster their own positions. The reality, however, is far more mundane and ordinary and can be traced back directly to the historical circumstances of the Bible's world.

What is in the Old Testament?
When Tischendorf discovered *Codex Sinaiticus* he noticed that it included two writings not found in today's Bibles: the *Epistle of Barnabas* and the *Shepherd of Hermas.* Another ancient manuscript, *Codex Alexandrinus* (a fifth-century AD document, so called because it originated in Alexandria in Egypt), also includes parts of two letters written by Clement of Rome, together with sections of a book known as the *Psalms of Solomon*. In addition, we know that the

Greek version of the Jewish scriptures that was most widely used by the early Christians also contained some additional books not apparently included in the Hebrew Bible. The scrolls discovered by the Dead Sea include some of the same works. So which are the books that really belong in the Bible? There has never been any argument over what comprises the contents of the New Testament, but there are various ways of looking at the extra books that are sometimes attached to the Hebrew scriptures. These include 1–2 Esdras, Tobit, Judith, Wisdom of Solomon, the Wisdom of Ben Sirach, the Letter of Jeremiah, Baruch, the Song of the Three Young Men, Susannah, Bel and the Dragon, the Prayer of Manasseh, and 1–2 Maccabees, together with additional material inserted in the books of Esther and Daniel.

Quite apart from these, the Hebrew Bible itself mentions yet other books that were never included among its number, nor do they exist in any other versions as far as anyone knows at the moment. These include the "Book of the Annals of the Kings of Israel",[8] the "Book of the Annals of the Kings of Judah",[9] the "Book of Jashar",[10] and the "Book of the Wars of the Lord".[11] There was clearly an impetus towards the recording of the nation's story from quite early times, and certainly long before any of the Bible books as we know them came into existence.

But it was only in the days following Nebuchadnezzar's destruction of Jerusalem and its temple in 586 BC that the intentional collection of the national archives became a pressing concern, as part of an effort to preserve the sense of corporate identity for the nation that was in danger of being lost at a time when its people were being scattered all over the world. Those who settled outside of Palestine soon became fluent in the everyday language of their new homelands, which, following the conquests of Alexander the Great, was Greek. Even in Palestine itself, Hebrew was no longer the spoken language, and as time passed, the number of people who understood it diminished significantly. There was a pressing need for a Greek translation of the Hebrew scriptures. This task was undertaken spontaneously all over the Mediterranean world, but it was the Jews of Alexandria in Egypt who apparently engaged in it most systematically. The translation they produced is often referred to nowadays as "the Septuagint", or LXX (the Roman numeral for seventy), and in chapter 3 we will explore how and why it got this name. For now, we will note that this Septuagint was more than just a Greek version of the Hebrew Bible. It was not actually one single volume at all, in the first place for the simple reason that no-one then knew how to bind writing materials together in large enough quantities to contain such a large body of literature in one document. Possession of a Greek (or Hebrew) Bible involved many separate books, with each one being written on a separate roll of material. There were also a number of different translations to choose from.

When the Christians eventually produced a single-volume version of the Old Testament in Greek, they generally included some or all of the books that are now referred to as "deuterocanonical" or "apocryphal". This could happen quite easily, as an ancient library was not like a modern one. In the nature of things, rolls could not be kept on a shelf, but were stored in boxes. A library consisted of a large number of these boxes, which were made in a standard size and served not just as storage but also as a classification system. But rolls came in different sizes, depending on what was written on them. After the main scroll had been stored in a particular box there would often be surplus space, and that space might easily be filled with another scroll whose contents dealt with a similar subject. This was probably how the deuterocanonical books came to be associated with the original writings of the Hebrew Bible. By virtue of them all being kept together, they came to be accepted as part of the national archive even though they had never been a part of the original Hebrew scriptures. Following the destruction of Jerusalem by the Romans in AD 70, Jewish religious experts found it necessary to gather together the traditions of their nation in a more definitive way, and at a meeting in Jamnia in about AD 90 the rabbis formally decided to recognize the books of the Hebrew Bible, as used in Palestine itself, as being of special authority, and these are the books that are now contained in the Christian Old Testament.

So why do some Christians include the extra books in their Old Testament? This again has a simple historical explanation. There were probably no Christians who ever spoke or wrote Hebrew as an everyday language, and in the first generations their Old Testament was invariably a Greek translation. They subsequently gathered together a complete Greek Bible consisting of both Testaments, and when they produced translations into other languages their most natural starting-point was Greek. One of the most influential of the ancient translations was the Latin version of Jerome, produced in the fourth century. He actually based much of his work on the Hebrew Bible, in consultation with some Jewish religious scholars whom he knew, and was aware of the fact that the Hebrew Bible contained fewer books than the Greek versions used by most Christians. Nevertheless, he decided to include the extra books simply because they were so well known. His Latin Vulgate became the Bible of the Western church, and through this formed the scriptural canon of the medieval church. At the time of the Protestant

Reformation in the fifteenth century, Martin Luther (1483–1546) reverted to the Hebrew Bible as being the only authoritative version of the Christian Old Testament, though he recognized that some of these other books could be useful in offering practical guidance on matters of morality. The Calvinist Reformers, on the other hand, whose opinions are represented by the Westminster Confession of Faith (1646), denounced them as being perversions of the truth, and insisted that their people should accept only the books of the original Hebrew Bible.

Confirming the New Testament

The compilation of a list of New Testament books was more straightforward. In the earliest days of the church, of course, no-one ever stopped to think about which of their writings might carry special authority. From the very start, the scriptures of the Jewish faith were given a special place, but the sayings of Jesus and the stories of his life were also bound to be highly regarded as well, though there was never any aim to make a comprehensive collection of them. The New Testament itself occasionally refers to sayings of Jesus that are not now contained in any of the four Gospels. Acts 20:35 offers one such example, when Paul encouraged his hearers to remember "the words of the Lord Jesus, for he himself said, 'It is more blessed to give than to receive.'" It is perhaps surprising that since he knew of that saying Luke chose not to include it in his own Gospel, though both he[12] and John[13] readily acknowledge the existence of other sayings of Jesus without any suggestion that their own narratives are inadequate for not including them. Nor do they imply that such sayings might be inferior to those which they did include in their own compilations.

As the leaders of the church (people like Peter and Paul) gave advice and guidance to their converts, it was natural that their words and writings should also come to be highly respected. They themselves seem to have felt that a special authority attached to what they wrote,[14] and by the time some of the latest books were written, the earlier New Testament documents could already be regarded as "scripture".[15] Among the next generation of church leaders, in the early years of the second century AD, we find Ignatius, Clement of Rome, Polycarp, and others referring to most of the New Testament books as scripture, while also continuing to use and value other Jewish and Christian writings.

The Christians could probably have lived with this kind of pragmatic flexibility for a long time, had it not been for one particular episode. In about AD 150 a man called Marcion left the church at Rome and announced that he had unearthed a new message – a message which he alleged was not actually new but had been given in secret by Jesus to his disciples. They had failed to preserve it adequately and so its secret was subsequently entrusted to Paul. To back up this claim, Marcion compiled a list of those books that allegedly provided proof, including only one "Gospel" (similar to Luke, but not identical to it), along with ten of Paul's letters. At about the same time, there was a proliferation of other sectarian groups, all of which were busy compiling their own lists of inspired writings, some of which are considered in more detail in chapter 9. In the nature of things, the books they each included were those that best served to back up their own distinctive ideas.

In the face of arguments like this, what could the leaders of the mainstream church do in order to present what they believed to be the authentic Christian message? Since everyone else seemed to be trying to prove their case by reference to lists of sacred texts, that was an obvious place to begin. The sectarians were saying, in effect, "Here are the books that prove our claims: what proof have you got for your position?" By the end of the second century, Irenaeus, leader of the church at Lyons in France, had compiled such a list himself. He also set out guidelines for deciding on the relative usefulness of the various Christian books that were then in circulation. Those of most value, he argued, must be the ones that had a clear connection with the apostles themselves, for they were the people who had been the close associates of Jesus and therefore must have known and understood his teachings at first hand.

In the years that followed, this principle was refined more precisely so that in the third century the historian Eusebius (AD 264–340) could list three different categories of Christian writings. He mentions those that were certainly authoritative (the four Gospels, Acts, the letters of Paul, 1 Peter, 1 John, and Revelation); those that were certainly not (the *Acts of Paul*, the *Shepherd of Hermas*, the *Apocalypse of Peter*, the *Epistle of Barnabas*, the *Didache,* and the *Gospel according to the Hebrews*); and those whose status was disputed (James, Jude, 2 Peter, 2 and 3 John). Eventually in the fourth century we find people drawing up comprehensive lists of authoritative books, one from Athanasius in the Eastern section of the church (AD 367), and the other from the Council of Carthage in the Western church (AD 397). The books they list are the twenty-seven books of the New Testament as we know it.

These books did not suddenly become authoritative overnight. They had already been widely used and highly regarded for centuries, and the decisions made in the fourth century were simply the formal recognition of a state of affairs that had existed for a very long time before that. Far from trying to suppress beliefs that they disliked, the church leaders were reaffirming what most Christians already believed and practised. If they had not been doing so, history would certainly have recorded it, and their opinions would soon have been rejected.

2

The Beginning of History

The Hebrew Bible is, as its name suggests, mostly concerned with the history of the ancient Hebrew and Israelite people. But in its opening pages (Genesis 1–11), it invites its readers into a different world altogether, with a narrative that goes even further back in time than the start of Israelite history – to the very beginning of all things, with the story of creation and of humankind's earliest ancestors. In that respect, it is no different from the national literature of many peoples in different parts of the world. Curiosity about the world and its origins, and a desire to understand what makes people tick, seem to be an integral aspect of being human and alive. Who are we? Why are we? Where did we come from, and where might we be going? And what does it all mean? These questions, and others like them, are as old as time, and are still the subject of much speculation in the twenty-first century.

The Bible's creation narratives have always been a source of fascination, and their interpretation has occasionally spilled over into acrimony and disagreement in relation to the nature of the stories and their integration with other ways of understanding human life. In the years following the publication of Charles Darwin's ground-breaking book *On the Origin of Species* in 1859, these passages in Genesis were subjected to ever closer scrutiny as devoted Bible readers endeavoured to reconcile what they thought they knew of the Bible with what looked to be the assured conclusions of palaeographic evidence in relation to the origins of the world and the development of its people. The arguments were frequently divisive, and when the American state of Tennessee passed a law forbidding the teaching of Darwin's ideas in its schools, the ensuing controversy ended up in one of the most high-profile legal battles of the twentieth century – the Scopes Monkey Trial, in which a high-school teacher named John Scopes was accused of abandoning what was regarded as a biblical account of creation in favour of the scientific opinions of Darwin and his followers. That was back in 1925, but in some places the same arguments continue in a different form even today.

Going back in time

Our knowledge of the earliest period of Mesopotamian history is largely dependent on the findings of archaeologists, though much of the primary evidence is no longer readily accessible. The invasion of Iraq at the beginning of the twenty-first century led to the substantial destruction of many of the surviving sites along with the disappearance of large numbers of artefacts that had been previously uncovered and which were preserved in museums in the area – as well as curtailing further investigations that would no doubt have shed more light on the earliest inhabitants of this region, whose customs and lifestyles exerted an influence that has extended well beyond their own time and place.

The existence of ancient remains in these lands had been known long before the development of formal methods of investigation. From the Middle Ages onwards, rich Europeans had developed a fascination with countries that not only had a longer history than their own but also seemed to belong to an entirely different world, which was all the more fascinating because of its apparently mysterious and mystical past. Such affluent visitors regularly went back home laden down with souvenirs that they had collected along the way. Blocks of stone, carvings, an inscription or two, as well as jewellery – they all found their way into the rich houses and castles of Europe at this period. By the sixteenth century, professional explorers were turning their attention to even further-flung places, as they became aware of the existence of the southern hemisphere and developed the ability to get there. But the possession of ancient artefacts that could stand by the fireplace was still regarded as a status symbol in many upper-class European homes, and a steady stream of treasure-hunters ransacked the area covered by ancient Mesopotamia during this time. In the early eighteenth century, scholars were beginning to take a more systematic approach to the understanding of these antiquities, though it was only at the end of the nineteenth century that rigorous procedures began to be applied to investigating the sites of ancient cities.

A typical ancient site in this region often takes the form of a large mound, or *tell*. On the surface it might appear to be just a large hill covered with trees or grass, but buried deep inside a tell will be the remains of an ancient city. Settlements were often built on a natural hill, to provide a good view of the surrounding countryside and make them easier to defend against marauders. But that was not universally the case, and many of these tells actually started at ground level, and have been raised to their present height by the normal processes of building over many years. In the ancient world most buildings were made of mud and wood, and when a place fell into decay for some reason the inhabitants would gather together any available materials that could be recycled, and then set to work building their own new town on the ruins of the old. Inevitably, the new level would always be higher than the one that preceded it, so that over time the ground level was gradually raised. If it were possible to take an x-ray image of one of these mounds it would look a bit like a giant gateau with many different layers superimposed one on top of the other.

To make the most sense out of what is contained in a site of this sort, it is of fundamental importance to try and distinguish the contents of the various layers. If the remains of one city were to become jumbled up with debris from another, that would give a very misleading picture, because each layer represents the remains of a different settlement that might easily have been separated from the others by a time of several hundreds of years. In theory, the ideal way to accomplish this would be to start at the top and slice off the entirety of each layer in turn. However desirable in theory, that would never have been a practical possibility because of the amount of time (and therefore cost) that would be involved. As a way around that, archaeologists have developed a compromise that involves cutting into a mound in much the same way as a slice might be cut from a cake, in a process known as "stratigraphic excavation". This technique makes it possible to uncover a cross-section of the entire contents of a mound at the particular point where the excavation takes place. To be worthwhile, it requires a careful judgment by the archaeologists as to where might be the best place to start digging.

A typical excavation will almost always unearth more pottery than anything else. Being in widespread everyday use, and easy to break, there was always going to be a lot of it in the first place. But pottery is also virtually impossible to destroy completely, and even the tiniest fragments can yield valuable information about the time when it was made and the use to which it was put. Fashions in pottery changed with remarkable frequency and varied from one place to another. While some styles were in use for longer than others, fashions in size, shape, texture and decoration generally lasted for only a limited period, which means that when the same types are discovered at several different locations it is reasonable to conclude that the layers in which they are found were occupied at about the same time. This has become one of the main methods by which dates are assigned to objects that may be found in any particular site. After examining pottery styles that were excavated across many different locations, archaeologist Sir Flinders Petrie (1853–1942) came up with the idea of what he called a "Ceramic Index". This consisted of a catalogue of typical pottery types that could be accurately dated, and since his day it has been refined with such accuracy that it is possible to assign very precise dates to a particular layer of almost any excavation by reference to the type of pottery that is found there.

From hunter-gatherers to city-dwellers

From what we know, it is clear that a key milestone in the emergence of urban environments was the development of agriculture. Prior to that, the lifestyle of the hunter-gatherer meant that people collected whatever food was to be found in their local environment, and then when the supply was exhausted they moved on to somewhere else. This particular region always appears to have been blessed with rich resources of wild cereals, nuts, fruits and so on, along with a plentiful supply of fish and meat, and there is no particularly obvious explanation for the move into more settled communities where crops could be cultivated and animals domesticated. Indeed, some evidence indicates that the earliest agriculturalists may well have had a harder life overall than their hunter-gatherer forbears, so presumably the move to a less nomadic lifestyle did not happen in direct response to any particular issues of environment or food supply but came about through greater social awareness and a preference for life in more diverse groups of people. It was of course a shift that took place over a long period of time, with evidence of increasing urbanization between 9000 and 7000 BC in those areas where the natural climate made agriculture relatively straightforward. But it was only a matter of time before artificially constructed irrigation systems began to appear in the form of canals that drew water from the major rivers and distributed it through an elaborate system of trenches and pipes into the fields, thereby enabling crops to be cultivated on land that might otherwise have been agriculturally unproductive.

On the basis of archaeological remains, it is conventional to identify several cultural developments in the period from 7000 to about 3500 BC, each of them being named for the sites where their settlements have been found: the Hassuna/Samarra period, followed by the Halaf period (roughly 6500–5500 BC), which in turn was succeeded by the Ubaid period (5500–4000 BC). Evidence for the first two comes from the northern extremities of Mesopotamia (Halaf takes its name from *Tell Halaf* in north-eastern Syria), and is characterized by distinctive pottery designs, as well as the development of private housing in the villages and, in at least one place, the remains of something approximating to streets. There is also extensive evidence of highly skilled craftspeople making jewellery in this period and using materials that were not local – something that suggests that these individual communities were not isolated, but were developing significant trading relationships with other people, which must also have entailed the emergence of recognized routes by which it was possible to travel from one place to another.

By the end of this period there is evidence not only of an increasingly complex system of trade, but also the construction of buildings that appear to have had religious as well as commercial connotations. The site of Tepe Gawra in the north has several temple buildings alongside each other, suggesting that many divinities were probably recognized, while a seal discovered in the remains of a house there also provides the earliest evidence of beer-drinking ever to be uncovered anywhere in the world. In the south, the city of Eridu, just to the south-west of Ur, had a particularly important temple that came to be associated with a deity later known as Enki or Ea. In line with the customary use of temples at a slightly later date, it is likely that such buildings had a commercial as well as a narrowly religious purpose, serving as warehouses and marketplaces as well as places of worship. Large numbers of fish bones have been unearthed in some parts of the Eridu temple, suggesting that they may be the remains of sacrificial offerings left there for the deities. The city itself was subsequently named as one of five cities to be established before an extensive flood occurred in the area, something that is reported and reflected upon in many ancient sources, including the Hebrew Bible.[1]

The development of writing

The period between about 3500 and 2700 BC saw several notable developments in human interaction and culture, and has often been called the proto-literate period because it was at this time that the first evidence of anything like writing started to appear. It also marked the emergence of the first communities that might reasonably be regarded as a state, as distinct from the self-contained local settlements of the earlier period. Our knowledge of this era is still largely derived from discoveries at particular sites, and Uruk in particular has provided so much information about city life at this time that the early years of the period are regularly referred to simply as the Uruk period. Such evidence as there is for cities further to the north seems to suggest that life continued more or less as it had been previously.

Various theories have been advanced to try to explain why this development started in the south, but the most likely factor was probably related to the physical environment. The city of Uruk was located right at the point where the rivers run into the Persian Gulf, providing the opportunity for the development of a wide variety of agricultural lifestyles – fishing in the marshes and hunting in the surrounding countryside – while the proximity of a ready supply of fresh water flowing into the sea made the irrigation of organized crop-growing areas relatively straightforward. Moreover, the need for all these different activities to integrate with one another led to the emergence of new relational networks between workers, and opportunities for even greater collaboration in the development of an urban lifestyle.

One of the other features of life in this environment is marked by the discovery of large quantities of everyday pottery that was made in a mould or on a potter's wheel, as distinct from the specialized handmade pieces of a previous era. This is one of the earliest examples of mass production, which in turn offers a further indication of a fast-growing population in which employment was becoming increasingly specialized as one section of the workforce supplied another with its own distinctive products.

In earlier times each family will most likely have been capable of producing all the goods it needed, whether that was food, clothing, shelter or tools. But as soon as workers' skills became more narrowly focused, the exchange of one's own goods for other necessities of life became an indispensable part of life, and in order for that to work with fairness the development of formal structures and systems was inevitable. The temples played an important role in this, and an alabaster vessel of the period shows goods being carried into a temple, where they were symbolically given into the care of the deity, whose responsibility it would then be to ensure their fair distribution.

Of course, all this in turn required the development of other new skills in counting and measuring, and then some way of recording what had been received – requirements that in turn brought into being other specialized jobs for those who were able to create the systems that would facilitate the accomplishment of all these tasks. The region itself offered a ready supply of natural materials that could support the development of writing and record-keeping, in the form of mud that was easy to shape into portable tablets that could be inscribed while still soft, and then left to bake hard in the heat of the sun. Even before the period of concentrated urbanization, this method had been used to produce distinctive stamps that were attached to containers or jars as a way of identifying their contents, and by the time centralized distribution methods emerged these had been developed into cylinder seals consisting of hardened clay rollers with designs impressed in them that could then be used as a template to produce multiple seals easily and quickly. Like pottery, such items were exceedingly difficult to destroy completely, and this ensured that many thousands of records embossed on clay tablets have survived up to the present day. They include the traditional stories of the people, handed down over many generations, as well as records of everyday transactions and even rudimentary dictionaries. It is clear that there was a rapid expansion of spoken language as new terminology was developed to describe the transactions that would come to dominate this new style of market economy. The form of writing that emerged at this time eventually developed into a sophisticated style known as "cuneiform", which means "wedge-shaped" – so called because it was made by inscribing mud tablets with the end of reeds, which tended to have a triangular or wedge shape to them. At first, picture symbols were used to represent words, but it was not long before these were simplified so as to represent sounds, which made the entire system much more flexible.

While the most comprehensive evidence for all these developments comes from Uruk, by the beginning of the third millennium BC similar trends were appearing in other places as well. It is impossible to trace a direct connection on the basis of the information available to us, but it seems highly likely that the expansion into other localities of what started as a southern Mesopotamia lifestyle probably came about through direct interactions between the people of Uruk – especially the growing ruling class – and the inhabitants of other cities. Explanations for this development vary, and in the initial stages it may have been motivated by a simple need to obtain materials that were available in larger quantities elsewhere – things like stone and wood. But it was also probably inspired by a growing confidence in this new way of life, driven by a desire among the new upper classes to obtain luxury goods that would serve to mark them off from the rest of the population – and also, according to some, a growing belief that the deities of their own city may have had more than a merely local jurisdiction, with influence extending to other, more distant places as well.

Ancient Mesopotamia: birthplace of civilization

In relation to the early chapters of the book of Genesis, there can be no doubt that its stories were rooted in traditions that can be traced back to an altogether different world, that of ancient Mesopotamia. The term "Mesopotamia" literally means "between the rivers", and is a reference to the rivers Tigris and Euphrates, which begin in the mountains of Turkey and then wind their way southwards through various countries of what is now referred to as the Middle East before emerging into the Persian Gulf. The ancient inhabitants of this region never referred to their homeland by that name, and it appears to have been first used by Greek historians in the centuries immediately preceding the Christian era. The territory generally designated as Mesopotamia covered an area that includes land now located in Iraq and Iran, along with parts of Syria and Turkey. Insofar as any part of the world can be regarded as the birthplace of civilization as we know it, this region has more of a claim than most. As far as anyone can tell, there were no towns or villages anywhere in the world before about 9000 BC (the start of the Neolithic or New Stone Age), but some of the earliest settlements ever known were located here in Mesopotamia, where genuinely urban communities were starting to develop in the form of localized city-states from about 3500 BC. The first evidence of real writing also comes from this period, as city administrators developed new ways of keeping track of their citizens.

The Ubaid people were based in southern Mesopotamia, and developed communal living into a more complex pattern, with larger cities soon being established. Two of these – Ur and Uruk – both feature in the narratives of the Hebrew Bible. Ur is identified as the original home of Abraham and his family (Genesis 11:28–32), while Uruk (called Erech in the

Bible) is listed as one of the places associated with "a mighty hunter" named Nimrod in Genesis 10:10, and also features in stories from many centuries later (Ezra 4:9). Excavations at Uruk suggest that the population there might have been as many as 10,000 by about 3200 BC. The varied shapes and sizes of buildings in this culture indicate the development of a stratified society, with the emergence of ruling bureaucrats who controlled the community's resources and were responsible for the organization of a substantial labour force that contributed to the growing prosperity of the region.

Origins and meanings in Sumerian culture

Uruk was not the only city-state to develop in southern Mesopotamia at this time, but it was soon to become the capital of a more extensive dynasty under the Sumerians, who between about 2900 and 2350 BC brought together a loose-knit coalition of city-states that were willing to work together under the governance of a series of kings, whose exploits are recorded on the monument known as the Weld-Blundell Prism. Now kept at the Ashmolean Museum in Oxford, England, this consists of a block of mud that was inscribed with cuneiform script on all four sides in the city of Larsa about 1800 BC, and then baked hard to preserve it. It has a hole up the middle, which suggests it may have originally been mounted on to a shaft of some kind, presumably to enable a reader to turn it round from one face to another. This Sumerian King List is of importance for a number of reasons, the most obvious being the fact that it actually names the early rulers of Mesopotamia, predominantly in the south, though including the important city of Mari to the west, as well as some on the north and east, beginning in about 3200

BC and ending in the time when the list was drawn up. Though all these individuals were probably rulers only of their own autonomous city-states, the way the list is compiled implies that they followed after one another, almost like a continuous dynasty. It is widely supposed that this was a literary device adopted by the scribe who compiled the list in about 1800 BC, designed to bolster the position of the king of Larsa at the time, who would have been his own patron.

Of particular interest in relation to the Bible is the way that the list divides these rulers into two categories: those who lived before the flood, and those who reigned after it. The mention of a great flood reflects a natural phenomenon of the region (the Tigris and Euphrates regularly flooded between February and May, bringing considerable devastation at what was the traditional time of harvest). But in the context of the Hebrew Bible, it is natural to wonder how the information contained in this list of kings relates to the stories in the early chapters of Genesis. In the Sumerian account, events described as being before the great flood are placed in primeval time, a period so far beyond human memory that it could only be described in the language of traditional mythological accounts of a world that was populated as much by gods as by people. Indeed, it makes the point that the notion of kingship itself was something that descended from heaven, thereby endowing the kings with a divine authority that they might not otherwise have enjoyed. In contrast, the period after the flood is described in a more down-to-earth way, and describes events and people that can readily be documented from other historical sources. The book of Genesis has a similar division, with chapters 1–11 being presented as an account of primeval events, and the actual history of the Hebrews beginning only from chapter 12 onwards with the story of Abraham.

Moreover, the flood is not the only feature that these two narratives have in common. On the Sumerian King List, those kings who are said to have lived before the flood reigned for extraordinarily long periods of time, whereas those who came after it enjoyed more conventional life spans. Much the same pattern is reflected in the book of Genesis, though Methuselah, who lived for 969 years,[2] was only a youth by comparison with the Sumerian Dumuzi, whose reign is recorded as having lasted for well over 3,000 years. He was identified as the husband of the goddess Inanna, a notion that also finds echoes in an obscure story in Genesis in which divine and human beings commingled to produce a hybrid race of giants.[3] Another intriguing connection is to be found in the way that many of the names on the Sumerian King List echo those found in the genealogical lists in Genesis 5:1–32 and 10:1–32. In addition to such details, however, there are some traditional Sumerian stories that look as if they might have even more extensive connections to the stories of Genesis. One of them (the story of creation) has even been dubbed "the Babylonian Genesis".

The creation of the world

Like the other stories that will be discussed here, this traditional account is known from records that were collected by Ashurbanipal, the Assyrian emperor from 669 to 627 BC, who was an indifferent ruler but was responsible for the assembling of a massive library bringing together the traditions of the various ethnic groups who collectively made up the population of ancient Mesopotamia. Like the evidence from earlier periods, it comprises many thousands of clay tablets inscribed with cuneiform script.

It should surprise no-one that the stories of primeval events that were familiar to the Hebrew people would have parallels with similar stories that were told elsewhere in their world. The events of history are always the unique story of the people whose narrative they encapsulate, but stories about primeval origins are a part of the common heritage of all humankind. When the ancient Hebrews described the creation of the world, they did so in what were the conventional terms of the region, though in the process of doing so the book of Genesis put its own stamp on these traditional ideas in such a way that they became a means of articulating a quite different understanding of relationships between the natural world, its people and God.

The Mesopotamian text that invites most comparison with the account in Genesis 1:1–2:4 is an old Akkadian tale called *Enuma Elish*. In the time of Ashurbanipal, this was recited in the temple at Babylon on the occasion of the annual New Year Festival, and was a hymn in praise of the god Marduk. It tells how at the beginning nothing existed except the dark waters of primeval chaos, personified as Apsu and Tiamat. In their turn they reproduced a series of other deities representing the various elements of the universe. Later, a revolt against these forces of chaos led by the younger and more active gods brought into existence the ordered world. Apsu was killed by magic, Tiamat was cut in two, and Marduk used one half of her body to make the solid sky (firmament), and the other to make the flat earth. The story can be found in various forms, with the main difference being the names given to the gods and goddesses. The version just summarized is the one used at a later period in Babylon, where Marduk was the patron god of the city, but in an earlier Sumerian version the deities are named as Anu, Enlil, and Ninurta. The fundamental themes are always the same, though, with light emerging from a watery chaos, followed by the sky, dry land, sun, moon and stars, and finally people, and after all this the creator or creators taking a rest. Human beings are typically described as originating in one of two ways, both of which connect them firmly with the soil of the earth. One way of depicting this has them growing out of the ground, in much the same way as plants sprout from seeds, while another regards them as having been moulded like pottery, using clay that consisted of a mixture of earth and divine blood or spittle. Once people had been created, the gods could relax, because humans were now expected to do the gods' work for them – until they became too numerous, at which point a great flood occurred to keep the population in check.

The similarities between this and the stories in Genesis are so obvious and detailed that it is clear they must both have originated from within the same cultural matrix. The way in which Genesis adopts traditional metaphors that would be widely understood and then puts a different spin on them is an early example of how the Bible's message has always been capable of being contextualized in many different circumstances. For while the general outline of the Genesis story closely follows the Sumerian and Babylonian creation accounts, it is used in the Hebrew Bible to present a very distinctive understanding of the nature of the cosmos.

When the Mesopotamian stories were first deciphered in the late nineteenth century, there was a tendency for scholars to suppose that the Bible's account was just a variant on the Babylonian texts. But closer examination has shown that an altogether more sophisticated process was going on, as the traditional accounts were given a completely different meaning. For example, in the *Enuma Elish*, order emerges out of watery chaos as a result of a conflict between the gods and the wild waves of the ocean, with giant sea monsters challenging the deities in a battle between the forces of chaos and order that was still ongoing, and in which the chaos could be held at bay only through the ritual of the annual New Year Festival. Genesis reiterates the themes of chaos and order, though there is no sign of a battle between sea monsters and God. Instead, the power of God was moving over the waters of chaos from the very beginning,[4] and the "great sea monsters" are explicitly said to have been only a part of what God created.[5] Interestingly, the Hebrew word used to describe their creation is carefully chosen, to indicate that God's control over these creatures was quite effortless and in no way the outcome of some cosmic battle. In the wider traditional culture, the sun, moon, and stars were regularly regarded as having power over people, and astrology was widespread as a way of trying to comprehend their influence – but that idea also is undermined in Genesis by the description of the heavenly bodies as being nothing more than "lights",[6] and certainly not in any way divine. Though the name of the first person in the Genesis account (Adam) means something like "earth", the underlying significance accorded to people is also quite different, and far from being created as an afterthought to serve the deities, women and men are made in God's image[7] and rather than making them to be servants of the gods, God in effect serves them by providing plants for their food.[8] In a few carefully chosen sentences, a traditional story that depicts the lives of people being controlled by the unpredictable forces of nature and unknowable and capricious deities has been turned into a story that affirms that the destiny of people is in the hands of a loving and powerful personal God – something that for the ancient Hebrews was rooted in the details of their own history, and which could then be applied to the understanding of matters that by definition lay outside of and beyond normal everyday experience.

The great flood: stories from the Bible and Mesopotamia

The story of a great flood marks a major turning-point in the early chapters of Genesis (Genesis 6:9–9:17), and this also has its counterpart in ancient Sumerian mythology in the shape of the Epic of Gilgamesh. This is another traditional story found in various versions, the most complete of which was also preserved in the library of Ashurbanipal, written in cuneiform script on twelve clay tablets. This particular version of it is one of the earliest known pieces of literature to bear the name of its author, a scribe called Sin-liqe-unninni, who is said to have composed it between about 1300 and 1000 BC, though he certainly consulted existing sources, and the oldest Sumerian version of the story can be traced as far back as the period between 2150 and 2000 BC.

Gilgamesh is identified as the king of Uruk, reigning somewhere between about 2750 and 2500 BC. At one time he was assumed to be an entirely fictitious character, though the existence of Enmebaragesi of Kish, who appears as one of the characters in the story, has been confirmed through archaeological finds that date him to about 2600 BC, which makes it entirely possible that Gilgamesh also was indeed a real person. The recounting of the story of the flood is almost incidental, as the main purpose of the narrative is to offer a set of philosophical reflections on the nature of death and the possibility of securing eternal life.

Following the death of his friend Enkidu, Gilgamesh comes to the realization that he himself must soon die, and decides to try and find the secret of eternal life. He seeks out his own ancestor Ut-napishtim, who had himself gained immortality, and asks him about it. He is advised that he must first get a plant from the bottom of the ocean that will renew his youth. But at this point in the story, the dialogue is interrupted as

Ut-napishtim goes on to tell Gilgamesh how he himself had escaped from a great flood. He had been warned by Ea, the god of magic wisdom, that the other gods, especially Enlil, had decided to send the flood. Ut-napishtim was advised to build a boat, which he did. This was not really a boat at all, but was more like a large cube, and was therefore rather different from Noah's "ark" in the Bible story. After coating this cube inside and out with bitumen, he stocked it with food and brought all his family and belongings into it, together with animals and skilled craft-workers. The storm raged for seven days, at the end of which nothing but water was visible. Twelve days later, Ut-napishtim's "boat" ran aground on a mountain, whereupon he sent out a dove and a swallow in turn, both of which came back. Then he sent out a raven, which did not return, as the waters had subsided and the bird presumably found somewhere to nest. When he left the "boat", he made a sacrifice to the gods, who crowded round like flies to smell it and promised that never again would they send a flood. They then bestowed immortality upon Ut-napishtim and his wife.

This is another example of an ancient Mesopotamian story that is so similar to a familiar Bible story that it would be hard to deny they both originated in the same stock of folk memories of primeval times. But, like the creation stories of the day, it was used by the writer of Genesis in such a way as to empty it of its original significance and infuse it with values that reflected a rather different understanding of the world and its people. The Gilgamesh epic offers no explanation for the flood, which is perhaps unsurprising as this was not the main purpose of the story in that context. But in another Akkadian source that tells much the same story (the Atrahasis Epic), the flood is said to occur when the gods decide they need to take action because people are making too much noise. The Genesis version, in contrast, depicts an entirely different image of God as one who sends the flood as a judgment on human extravagance, and the recurring theme is that there is only one God, who (unlike the Babylonian deities) is not afraid of the flood but is in complete control of it. Nor are people dealt with in an arbitrary way, for the deliverance of Noah is the outcome of his own good behaviour, while the destruction of others is traced to their own misbehaviour. Just as the traditional creation stories were contextualized in such a way as to promote ancient Israel's distinctive understanding of the world, so in this case also the character of God is described as one whose dealings with men and women depend on predictable moral standards rather than on capricious self-interest.

Immortality and language

There are two other references in Sumerian tradition that are worth mentioning here as providing a possible background to ideas also found in the book of Genesis. One is the story of Adapa (also called Adamu), who was a son of Enki (otherwise known as Ea), the god of wisdom, and patron of the city-state of Eridu. As a result of misbehaviour, he was called to appear before Anu, one of the oldest gods in the Sumerian pantheon. Enki advised Adapa to be appropriately repentant, but warned him that on no account should he accept any food that he may be offered, as it would lead to his death. In the event, Anu was so impressed by Adapa's honesty that he offered him food that had the power to make him immortal. This story hardly offers an exact parallel to the story of the Garden of Eden, but they have several elements in common, which might suggest that here again is a common stock of ideas that the Hebrew Bible takes for granted as an appropriate vehicle through which the rather different faith of ancient Israel can be contextualized so as to be more widely understood. The theme of eating food being connected in some way to the possibility of immortality features in the Genesis narrative,[9] though once again it has been taken out of the realm of myth, as it were, and the prospect of living for ever is no longer linked to the unpredictable behaviour of a deity, but is grounded in a strong sense of morality and justice.

Another example of a story that offers a minor parallel to a biblical account is found in the Sumerian text known as *Enmerkar and the Lord of Aratta*, which tells how people all spoke one common language, which Enki changed so that they could no longer understand one another. This particular story appears without any descriptive framework, which suggests it may originally have been more extensive than the fragment we now have. The book of Genesis, though, adopts this theme and once again utilizes it in such a way as to promote its own distinctive understanding of the God of Israel, whose operations are based not on a whim but on well-founded ethical principles – and so the Tower of Babel story explains the confusion of languages as the outcome of human pride.[10]

Religion, politics, and law

Reference has already been made to the connection between various deities and life in the burgeoning settlements of this period. As with most cultures of the ancient world, differentiating between religious beliefs and social structures introduces an artificial distinction that would not have been understood by the people of the time. The idea that it is possible to draw a line between the sacred and the secular has developed only through the influence of Enlightenment thinking in the emergence of Western culture, which means that in order to come anywhere close to understanding the world of the Bible most of us need to suspend our natural assumptions in the effort to comprehend these ancient people on their own terms. As long as we recognize that, though, it is still useful to separate out the various elements of the ancient mindset in order to come to a better understanding of the culture of the time.

Priests and kings

The underlying belief from the earliest times was that each city had its own deity, indeed that the cities had been constructed as dwelling-places for their celestial patrons in primeval times. So, for example, Uruk was the domain of Inanna, Nippur belonged to Enlil, Ur was the province of Nanna, and so on. Since the city was thought of in this way, it was only natural that the deity who was its patron would have a grand residence there in the form of a temple. In the earliest times, Mesopotamians had no sense of any personal identity attaching to the supernatural influences that were believed to control things. Natural forces such as fire, water, wind, and so on were regarded as powerful, though essentially unknowable. In the course of the fourth millennium BC, the natural cycle of the seasons became a matter of some interest, and as the alternation of the birth and death of nature was studied more closely it became apparent that, if these forces were indeed divine in some way, then their life must be running in parallel with that of human beings. Out of this in turn emerged a consensus that projected the patterns of human relationships onto the gods and goddesses. This development coincided with the rise of the Akkadians to power. Unlike the Sumerians, who were native to southern Mesopotamia, the Akkadians were of Semitic origin, and as their influence spread so the character of Sumerian beliefs gradually changed. Their connection with the forces of nature was weakened, and they were assimilated to Semitic deities, most of whom were male. An extensive pantheon of deities was identified, and one source lists almost 4,000 of them.

The temple of a city was not only regarded as the dwelling-place of a deity, but as we have already seen it also occupied a central position in relation to trade and social interactions, in which the exchange of goods always took place through the agency of the gods and their representatives the priests. The theory was that the city deity received goods from those who produced them, and was then responsible for their equitable distribution. This invested the guardians of the temples with a particular authority in relation to the smooth running of the entire community, which meant that the role of priest and the role of king were essentially different aspects of the same thing. The Sumerian King List mentioned previously opens with the words 'After the kingship descended from heaven ...', and this sense of divine appointment continued to permeate the world of the Bible for many centuries. Insofar as the office of king existed at all, it had been a local phenomenon during the Sumerian period, with each city having its own ruler whose power base was in the temple. But with the arrival of the Akkadians, competition for land and resources increased, and an individual's military prowess came to be as important as his perceived divine connections. Or, rather, the two went hand in hand. Military leaders were typically granted authority only on a temporary basis, to galvanize the community and help defend their position in the face of a particular threat.

This pattern is reflected in the stories of the judges in early Israel, all of whom were essentially local leaders appointed for a specific task, and directly accountable to their own people. In Sumeria, such local leaders soon developed their own dynasties, building palaces and establishing a more permanent form of rule. The tension between these two forms of kingship appears centuries later in the biblical story of the appointment of Saul as the first king of Israel. Like these ancient Mesopotamian rulers, he was initially appointed on the basis of his personal charisma and military accomplishments, backed up by the conviction that he was God's chosen one.[11] He was acclaimed as king by a popular gathering of the people, in much the same way as the military leaders of the Sumerian city-states, and with the same expectation that he would be accountable to this people's assembly. When he then adopted the style of a dynastic monarch, he was disowned by the prophet Samuel, who argued for the preservation of the old order and was subsequently responsible for appointing David in his place, again emphasizing the two aspects of popular acclaim and divine approval. This connection between ancient kings and the temples has led to a good deal of speculation as to whether the later kings of Israel were themselves priests as well as political rulers. It is certainly the case that Solomon acted as high priest when the temple in Jerusalem was dedicated,[12] though there is insufficient evidence to demonstrate that the kings of Israel and Judah ever occupied quite the same sacral position as their counterparts in Mesopotamian culture.

Power struggles and social evolution

The desirability of wider coalitions between city-states became a more pressing concern with the emergence of an Akkadian empire, when Sargon conquered the Sumerian cities in 2340 BC and consolidated his power over an area extending from the Persian Gulf in the south to Lebanon in the north. His capital city was Akkad (hence the term "Akkadian"), a city that was later known as Babylon, and which then dominated the region for almost the next 2,000 years. His reign lasted for only a short time, and by 2125 BC his empire was finished. But Sumerian culture was never to be the same. Even before Sargon's victories, the structure of the various cities had become increasingly centralized.

Before the third millennium BC, society had been based on units similar to what would now be described as the nuclear family; but now these groups started to combine into more extensive structures so as to form households that constituted a larger economic unit and offered the possibility of being self-sufficient, while also being of a large enough size to be in a good bargaining position with other households for those items that could not be produced internally. Life in these households inevitably developed their own social structures, with a majority of members working at menial tasks while others supervised operations. But they also provided a social security net for individuals who could otherwise have found themselves as outcasts. Widows and orphans were able to join these households, which would provide them with food and shelter in exchange for their labour. This pattern appears throughout the whole of Mesopotamia, and may well have spread even further afield. The family units of the Hebrew Bible all reflect a similar organizational structure. Abraham's household was not just a nuclear family, but included Lot (who was still regarded as a permanent member even after he parted company for a time[13]). It also included the Egyptian woman Hagar, with whom Abraham had a son. She and her son were subsequently expelled and left to find a home for themselves, highlighting the essentially patriarchal and hierarchical nature of these arrangements.[14] But the later example of how such a household took care of Ruth and her mother-in-law Naomi displays a more benevolent aspect of this lifestyle.

By the end of the third millennium BC, Mesopotamia had two major centres of power: Akkad in the north and Ur in the south. Under Sargon, Akkad was at the forefront of initiating new forms of relationship between the originally independent city-states. Though their indigenous leaders generally remained in office, they were no longer free to run their own affairs but acted as provincial governors for the Akkadian empire. A centralized taxation system was developed, along with the rationalization of methods of weighing and measuring things and the introduction of a single language through which official business would be conducted: Akkadian. Like the people who first used it, this was a Semitic language, quite different from Sumerian and more akin to Hebrew (another Semitic language). This strategy of imposing a single language for use in inter-state relationships would be continued by later empires, with the Persians using Aramaic and the Romans' Latin for their official communications – though it was Alexander the Great's vigorous promotion of Greek that ensured its position as the only truly international language that would survive the demise of the empire that imposed it. Documentation from the time shows that at its height the Akkadian empire's influence extended into Syria in the west and Turkey in the north, as well as into other places such as Elam and Simurrum, whose exact location is not at all certain but probably lay to the east in the general area of what is now Iran. The dominance of Akkad was short lived, but its success as an empire that was able to acquire territory well beyond its own boundaries changed the thinking of Mesopotamian people. Sargon and his successors may not have been at all popular during their lifetimes, but later folklore hailed them as great heroes. The accounts of their accomplishments came to provide a powerful inspiration for the Assyrians and Babylonians, who later established their own empires from a base in the same region.

Nomads and city-dwellers

In the years following the collapse of the Akkadian empire, the city of Ur became the driving force in Mesopotamian life. Urbanization continued apace, with large-scale building projects constructing everything from irrigation canals to royal palaces and grand temples. The taxation systems introduced from Akkad were extended and co-ordinated so as to form a solid economic base for the extension of Ur's influence. At the same time, previously subservient cities were able to break free, suggesting that the dominance of a centralized bureaucracy was far from established. When Ur's power diminished in 2004 BC it did so almost overnight, and for no very obvious reason, having lasted for only a little over a hundred years. Records compiled shortly afterwards seem to suggest that a key role was played by invaders from two directions: Amorites coming in from the west, and Elamites from the east. There are periodic references to Elamites in the Bible, though little of a specific nature is said about them.[15] But the Amorites are mentioned much more frequently, because they are identified as being among the original inhabitants of Canaan, the land in which the Hebrews first emerged into nationhood.[16]

Archives from the time of Sargon connect the Amorites to a place called Amurru, which is generally thought to have been located somewhere in Syria and possibly included the north of Palestine. But their influence undoubtedly spread much wider than that, as they are mentioned in documents from places as far apart as Egypt in the west and Mari in the east. The reason for this is simple: they were not settled city-dwellers, but semi-nomadic people who moved from one place to another in search of pasture for their flocks of sheep and goats. The climate of the region meant that during summer it was almost essential for them to stay close to the permanent settlements, because that tended to be where water was most likely to be found. In effect, therefore, they became urban residents during summer and nomadic wanderers in winter. By definition, people who are always on the move tend to leave little evidence behind them. All the references to them in monuments and inscriptions derive from the city-dwellers, and therefore offer an outsider's understanding of their lifestyle. Although they could occasionally come under suspicion as thieves and vagabonds, on the whole their presence was valued by others whose lifestyle was more sedentary. There was clearly a symbiotic relationship between nomadic tribes and city-dwellers, with mutually beneficial arrangements that ensured the fair exchange of goods and services between the two groups. There is also some evidence of the nomads being taxed and providing military assistance to the city rulers from time to time. As their wealth and influence expanded, and their herds grew to a size that made them hard to handle effectively, some of the more successful nomads began to adopt a settled lifestyle by investing in land rather than animals. A similar process of settlement often occurred at the opposite end of the social scale, as those who were unable to sustain herds that might grow large enough to offer a secure income looked for employment among the city-states, quite often as mercenaries in the local militias.

This is the cultural environment in which the stories of Abraham are set, and insofar as it is possible to offer any sort of date for the Bible narratives at this point, they appear to fit into the same period, which was between about 2000 and 1600 BC. By the time w¹ en the material of the Hebrew Bible was collated and written up in its final form, ancient Israel had been a settled farming community for as long as anyone could remember. But the liturgy for the annual celebration of the harvest festival preserved the memory of a different time and place, with its opening declaration that "A wandering Aramean was my ancestor".[17] Insofar as this statement was intended to refer to a specific individual, it appears to have been Jacob,[18] though all the major characters in the book of Genesis had an itinerant lifestyle. It is not altogether clear why any of them should have been referred to as "Aramean", as this was a group that rose to prominence only after about the eleventh century BC, when they established a small empire based in Syria. But like the Israelites, who also emerged as an identifiable nation at about the same time, their origins must go further back than that, and many experts believe that the groups later known as Israelites, Canaanites, and Arameans all shared some common ancestry through the Amorites, who in turn roughly corresponded to the wandering nomadic pastoralists of the early second millennium.

The stories of Genesis certainly suggest that there was some close ethnic connection between all these groups, though the precise relationships are never clearly spelled out. The conviction that the ancestors of the nation consisted of a collection of somewhat disparate nomadic tribes is fundamental to the entire biblical story. But it is not the only aspect that connects it to what is known of Mesopotamian culture at this time. When Joshua addressed the people towards the end of his life, he began his speech with the words "Long ago your ancestors lived on the other side of the River Euphrates and worshipped other gods".[19] The story shows him continuing to repeat that theme, as he invites the somewhat disparate tribal elements he was leading to commit themselves to a shared future that would be characterized by the abandonment of the local deities who had previously held their allegiance, in favour of the worship of the God who had been revealed to Moses as "Yahweh", the one whose very name implied control of the whole of history.[20]

Closer examination of the stories about Abraham reveals a pattern of life that reflects this semi-nomadic pastoral existence that is so well documented elsewhere. Abraham is clearly represented as one of the more successful nomads: he is the owner of large flocks and has considerable wealth at his disposal. Even the food he eats provides evidence for his prosperity: when a meal has to be prepared in haste to feed some unexpected visitors, it includes "cakes ... a calf ... curds and milk".[21] This menu is remarkably similar to the sort of food that was expected by Sinuhe, an Egyptian aristocrat who lived in Canaan for a while:

> *Bread was made for me as daily fare, wine as daily provision, cooked meat and roast fowl, beside the wild beasts of the desert ... and milk in every kind of cooking.*

Tale of Sinuhe

Like other well-to-do semi-nomads, Abraham and later members of his clan generally camped near to smallish settlements,[22] sometimes staying for long enough to become farmers,[23] and at times of particular stringency they could even become city-dwellers for a while.[24] As the story unfolds, his descendants Isaac and Jacob gradually adopt a more settled existence until Jacob is persuaded to migrate permanently to

Egypt[25] and adopt a far more urbanized lifestyle altogether. Abraham could also command large numbers of men, and was able to call on the services of what was in effect a private army, which he used to great effect in rescuing his nephew Lot from captivity.[26] The many kings mentioned in that connection correlate well with the description of the political organization described in a letter from Mari (a north Mesopotamian city-state) dating from shortly after 1800 BC:

> *No king is truly powerful on his own. Ten to fifteen kings follow Hammurabi of Babylon, Rim-Sin of Larsa, Ibal-pi-El of Eshnunna, or Amut-pi-El of Watna; but twenty kings follow Yarim-Lim of Yamkhad.*

The names given to the kings who feature in the Abraham story are typical of the sort of names people had at the time, and the same thing is true of the names given to members of Abraham's immediate family, all of which have linguistic forms that seem to connect them with names that were popular among the Amorite peoples living in various parts of northern Mesopotamia in the early second millennium BC.

There may be other connecting points between the book of Genesis and north Mesopotamian legal practices, and some experts believe that discoveries at the town of Nuzi provide evidence for this. A central feature of the Abraham story concerns the way in which his childless wife Sarah presented him with a female slave by whom to have a child.[27] In one text from Nuzi, certain marriage contracts obliged a childless wife to provide her husband with just such a substitute, though if a child was subsequently born to the slave, Nuzi law prohibited her expulsion from the household – something that could provide a cultural context to explain why Abraham was so reluctant to dismiss Hagar and Ishmael from his household, though he did eventually do so.[28]

Another way in which childless couples at Nuzi could ensure the continuation of their family line was by adopting a slave who would take the place of a son. Such an individual would then inherit their property, though if a natural son was eventually born, the slave-son would lose his rights. When Abraham expressed a fear that his slave Eliezer might succeed him,[29] some such custom could be implied. The evidence does not allow us to claim that there was any direct connection here, as if Abraham was following Mesopotamian legal precedence, but it suggests that the general ethos of these stories is to be located within this cultural context. The behaviour of these early Hebrew ancestors is certainly closer to what we know of Mesopotamian culture than it would have been to later Israelite standards, which prohibited a man from being married to two sisters at once,[30] as Jacob certainly was[31] – while Abraham's own marriage to Sarah would also have been banned under later regulations, because she was his half-sister.[32]

Kings and lawmakers

We cannot leave this period without some mention of Hammurabi, who is arguably the best-known of all the early Mesopotamian rulers. He was born into a family who had ruled Babylon for several generations before him, and when he came to power in 1792 BC the city was one of three major power centres in the region (the others being Larsa and Eshnunna). By the time his reign drew to a close in 1750 BC, he had established a lasting legacy that was to prove inspirational for all future rulers of Babylon, despite the fact that his kingdom outlived him only by little more than ten years.

Hammurabi's fame comes from a large column of basalt that is generally referred to as the Code of Hammurabi. It stands more than 2 metres high and has a carving in which Hammurabi is depicted receiving the laws of his kingdom from Shamash, the god of justice. After that, the various laws are set out in Akkadian, the everyday language of Babylon. The monument itself (known as a *stele*, a Greek word meaning "pillar") was damaged when it was seized by the Elamites in about 1165 BC, but it is well enough preserved for its inscriptions to be read quite easily. It was also repeatedly copied, and many other versions of its contents have been unearthed, including some later ones that incorporate a running commentary on it. Though it is usually referred to as a law code, it is quite unlikely that it ever functioned as a handbook for judicial decisions in the regular courts.

Many thousands of cuneiform tablets are known that record proceedings in the courts at this time, and to date there is only one clear example of a standard referred to on the stele being implemented in an actual judgment. This occurs in a case from four or five years after the end of Hammurabi's reign, relating to a dispute over the ownership and cultivation of a piece of land, and which concluded with the plaintiff being judged "according to the wording of the stele". There is actually a fair amount of evidence from legal records to show not only that Hammurabi's code was not a regular point of reference, but that everyday judgments could often go against ideas that were expressed there. As a consequence, it is now thought that the 282 cases described on the stele were never intended as laws that would inform the workings of the courts, but are to be interpreted in the context of the way kingship was understood at the time. The king was regarded as both ruler and protector of his people, and in this latter role it was important for the people to have confidence that he would always act with fairness and justice. The epilogue to the code clearly identifies this aspect of kingship:

> *The great gods have called me; I am the salvation-bearing shepherd, whose staff is straight, the good shadow that is spread over my city; on my breast I cherish the inhabitants of the land of Sumer and Akkad; in my shelter I have let them repose in peace; in my deep wisdom have I enclosed them. That the strong might not injure the weak, in order to protect the widows and orphans ...*

Viewed in this light, Hammurabi's code can be seen to offer a series of case studies showing how he operated in an even-handed manner, and thereby providing reassurance about the moral basis of his rule, as well as preserving a model to serve as an example for future rulers. The fact that all this was recorded onto a stele rather than being preserved in palace archives tends to support this understanding. It was no doubt intended to stand in a prominent place on public display as a testimony to Hammurabi's accomplishments and an inspiration to his successors, as well as to the ordinary citizens of Babylon, to embrace the same high standards in their own dealings with one another.

From time to time, efforts have been made to draw direct comparisons between the standards of justice exemplified by Hammurabi's stele and the many legal prescriptions contained in the Hebrew Bible. There are indeed some similarities, though they almost certainly represent a more widespread general understanding of matters of justice, rather than embodying any direct connections. The Ten Commandments, for example,[33] are presented in a way that clearly identifies their divine origin, just as Hammurabi asserted the divine origin of his own standards of justice – but every other king of the time believed the same thing, so there is nothing especially distinctive about that. Some of the provisions of the Hammurabi Code are also similar to biblical stipulations, and the terminology occasionally sounds similar, but again the parallels all relate to very common situations such as telling lies, assault and kidnapping, or damaging another person's property, together with various aspects of marriage and kinship. The nearest to a close correspondence, in both terminology and concept, would be the place occupied by the *lex talionis* (law of retaliation), as stated in paragraph 196 of Hammurabi's judgments ("If a man put out the eye of another man, his eye shall be put out") and in Leviticus 24:19–20 ("Anyone who maims another shall suffer the same injury in return ... eye for eye, tooth for tooth"). That sort of justice can sound extreme to modern ears, but in a culture where Lamech could boast that "I have killed a young man because he struck me",[34] a law that limited retribution to only an eye for an eye might be regarded as an improvement.

The three centuries following the end of Hammurabi's reign saw the demise of many previously strong city-states, and a gradual shift of power and influence away from the old Sumerian areas of southern Mesopotamia towards the north. Babylon retained some influence for a while, and consolidated its ongoing position by adopting many of the cultural practices of the earlier Sumerian city-states, including the integration of its own patron deity Marduk into the Sumerian pantheon. But by 1595 BC Babylon itself had been overrun by the Hittites (whose origins were somewhere in Syria and Palestine), and for the next hundred years they, along with other marauders such as the Hurrians (also from further north) and Kassites, dominated the scene. Hard evidence from this period is very limited, and little is known of the Kassites in particular. The Hurrians seem to have been innovative people in many ways, and may have been the first group to develop the use of horses and chariots. But during the same period the urbanization of the preceding 2,000 years went into reverse, and those cities which survived operated at a much lower level of sophistication than had previously been the case. All this was but the precursor of much more extensive changes in the entire region, as Mesopotamia began to interact more directly with other nations and competition for control of the burgeoning international trade routes changed the power dynamic of the area for good.

3

By the Banks of The Nile

Though the Bible's story begins in the cultures of Mesopotamia, the focus soon shifts in a more westerly direction, which brings it into contact with another major power of the ancient world: Egypt. This civilization, its rulers and its people, was to have a significant and long-lasting impact on the emerging national consciousness of the Hebrew people, and even today Judaism looks back to the story of a group of slaves who managed to escape from Egypt as the central formative episode in the entire history of the faith.[1] Joseph was a later member of Abraham's family who was sold into slavery by his brothers and then rose to a position of prominence in the Egyptian court. His rags-to-riches story has captured the imagination of many generations, and is so well known that it hardly needs to be recounted here.[2] For some, it is entertainment, as they encounter it first through one of the most enduring musicals of the last forty years, *Joseph and the Amazing Technicolor Dreamcoat* by Andrew Lloyd Webber and Tim Rice. For others, its life-and-death storyline has inspired them to challenge oppression and exploitation in their own backyard. The enslavement of Joseph's successors and their subsequent escape from the power of the Egyptian king sustained the spirit of African slaves in the American deep south, and provided the imagery that was to inspire Dr Martin Luther King Jr in the civil rights movement that led to the abolition of segregation in the 1960s. By an ironic coincidence, his final speech happened to be delivered in Memphis, Tennessee, a city that had been named after one of the capitals of ancient Egypt. As he concluded his address at Mason Temple on 3 April 1968 he encouraged his listeners with these words:

> *I've been to the mountaintop ... I just want to do God's will. And he's allowed me to go up to the mountain. And I've looked over. And I've seen the promised land ... and I'm happy, tonight. I'm not worried about anything. I'm not fearing any man. Mine eyes have seen the glory of the coming of the Lord.*

The reference is to the biblical story of Moses, who led his people out of slavery in Egypt and to the threshold of their own promised land,[3] something that was so deeply ingrained into the psyche of African Americans at the time that the allusion required no further explanation. Knowing the background to this story not only opens up new angles on the Bible, but illuminates some of the most significant events of the late twentieth century.

Politics and society in ancient Egypt

The story of Egyptian culture can be traced back at least as far as that of Mesopotamia, and periodic contacts between the two took place from the late fourth millennium BC onwards. Egypt, of course, is on the extreme north-west corner of Africa, so its population was rooted in quite different ethnic stock than the various people groups who were discussed in the last chapter. Its social structure was also very different from that of Mesopotamia, for while it followed the same pattern of expanding urbanization over the centuries, the Egyptian cities never developed into independent city-states. As far back as its history can reliably be traced, Egypt seems always to have been a territorial nation-state, and its development is usually described by reference to the various ruling dynasties that controlled it.

The early pharaohs

The founder of the first dynasty was Narmer, also called Menes in some sources, and his reign lasted from about 3100 to 3050 BC. The kings of Egypt were always known as the pharaoh, a word which in its original Egyptian form meant "great house", and therefore presumably referred in the first place to the palaces in which the rulers lived – though it was soon transferred to the most important person in the great house and subsequently came to be used as a generic term to refer to all the Egyptian kings of ancient times.

Paintings and sculptures from the time display similar signs of remarkable creativity and skill, though in retrospect it can be seen that this period during the fourth dynasty marked the high point of cultural and artistic endeavour in the earliest phase of Egyptian history. The dynasties immediately following witnessed a diminution of the power of the pharaohs, which later developed into large-scale political upheaval and led to a period of social instability that was not resolved until the time of the twelfth dynasty under Amenhemhat I (1991–1962 BC). In addition to restoring order to what had been a fragmented kingdom, his rule also inaugurated a great age of learning and literature, including what might be regarded as some of the earliest examples of the work of spin doctors who were employed specifically to strengthen his own position. The *Prophecy of Neferti* refers in glowing terms to a ruler whose achievements are described in almost messianic terms, and though this ruler is given the name "Ameny", this seems too close to "Amenhemhat" to be dismissed as a coincidence. Much of the literature of the period was in the form of short tales with a moralistic intention, but the Egyptian court had encouraged the production of quality literature long before this. *The Maxims of Ptah-hotep* from the time of the fifth dynasty (2498–2345 BC) is only the best-known example of a literary genre that soon became widespread, and which finds its parallel in the Hebrew Bible's wisdom literature (the book of Proverbs in particular). There is no suggestion that there might be any direct connection between Proverbs and these early Egyptian writings, just that their presentation and subject matter demonstrate a shared concern with living the good life, and an expectation that one function of a king was to offer such advice to ordinary citizens. (The book of Proverbs was also traditionally associated with the royal court, in that case of Solomon.)

This is not the only aspect of this period of Egyptian history that illustrates some aspects of the Bible stories. In describing the ideal ruler, the *Prophecy of Neferti* also praised him because

> *Asiatics will fall to his sword and Libyans will fall to his flame ... [and he] will build majestic walls to prevent Asiatics from entering Egypt.*

One of Amenhemet's accomplishments was the construction of a series of fortresses on the eastern edge of his kingdom, for the express purpose of safeguarding it against incursions by semi-nomadic groups such as were commonplace elsewhere in the region at the time, and of whom the biblical character Abraham was a typical example. There is of course an account of Abraham migrating temporarily to Egypt at a time of famine, which reveals one of the more despicable aspects of his personality as he tries to obtain food in exchange for allowing the pharaoh of the day to have sex with Sarah his wife (Genesis 12:10–20). While it is quite impossible to relate this to any particular pharaoh, or indeed to any specifically identifiable period in Egyptian history, it provides a good example of the reasons why control of Egypt's eastern border was so important for the twelfth dynasty.

Whether intentionally or not, the royal protocols mentioned in Genesis bear a remarkable similarity to the formalities documented in the *Tale of Sinuhe* (mentioned in the previous chapter), which was set in the aftermath of the death of Amenhemet I. There is also a painting from the tomb of Khnum-hotep in Beni Hasan that provides a visual account of such migrant traders from the east arriving in Egypt in about 1890 BC. This painting shows the men carrying what look like metalworking tools in their hands, while the women appear to be bearing eye makeup to trade with the Egyptians – something that itself offers an indication of the sophistication of Egyptian society at this time, and makes it all the more understandable why semi-nomadic pastoralists might find it an attractive destination.

The pyramids of Egypt

Whenever ancient Egypt is mentioned, the first thing that most people would instinctively think of is the pyramids, but it was not until the time of the third dynasty that the earliest pyramid was constructed, designed for the pharaoh Djoser in around 2650 BC by an architect named Imhotep. Its construction was rather different from the later pyramids. They had smooth triangular-shaped sides, whereas these early ones were constructed in such a way that each side was like a flight of steps – hence the reason that this style is often described as a step pyramid. Similar-shaped monuments have also been found in Mesopotamia, where they were known as ziggurats, though there is no obvious connection between the two. Unlike the Mesopotamian versions, which were constructed out of sun-baked clay bricks, Djoser's pyramid was built of stone, which makes it the earliest known large public structure to be constructed from this material, something that itself is eloquent testimony to the advanced technological knowledge of these early Egyptians, which not only enabled them to cut the stone into regular shapes but also to transport it from the quarry and then lift it into place.

The rapid development of sophisticated engineering skills at this period can be gauged from the fact that by the time of the next dynasty (the fourth), the builders were already experimenting with the construction of smooth-sided pyramids. They started by adding extra stones to fill out the spaces on a step pyramid, but very soon they worked out how to carve the stones into a shape that would ensure smooth sides from the outset. The Red Pyramid of Pharaoh Sneferu (2613–2589 BC) not only was the first perfectly aligned smooth pyramid, but is still one of the biggest to survive in Egypt to the present day. Sneferu's successor, Cheops (2589–2566 BC), went one better, and presided over the construction of the Great Pyramid of Giza, which held the record as the largest structure in the world for more than 3,000 years, and is the only one of the seven wonders of the ancient world to survive more or less intact to the present day. Its sheer size is remarkable, consisting of some 2.5 million cubic metres of stone (mostly limestone, supplemented by granite) – more than enough stone to construct all the cathedrals in England,

and equivalent to something like thirty of New York's famed Empire State Building. Its complex mathematical and geometric design was so cleverly arranged that it still engenders both spiritual and architectural curiosity even today. Not only is the system of measurement used in its construction believed to be the first example of a linear system based on an accurate understanding of the size of the earth, but its alignment means that lines drawn through its north–south and east–west axes and projected round the globe would divide the earth exactly into four quarters.

Uncertain times

The twelfth dynasty came to an end in 1786 BC, and what had been a time of energetic cultural innovation ground to a halt as a series of weak rulers followed one another in quick succession. As a result, the all-important eastern border was neglected and migrants found it easier to gain access to the country. Though there is no obvious connection between events in different parts of the region, the political strength of many states was diminished at this time. Between about 1650 and 1500 BC urban life in Syria and Palestine – and throughout much of Mesopotamia – was in decline, with a corresponding increase in the number of semi-nomadic groups who were constantly moving from one place to another in search of the necessities of daily life. By the middle of the seventeenth century BC, Semitic migrants had entered Egypt unhindered, and were even powerful enough to establish themselves as rulers of the country, choosing to establish their capital at Avaris, a site that was not far from the north-eastern border through which they had entered the land. They became the fifteenth dynasty (and maybe also the sixteenth). They were known as the Hyksos pharaohs (meaning "foreigners"), though colloquially they were often referred to in a phrase reflecting their origins as "shepherd kings". Their rule lasted for almost 200 years. They introduced some significant innovations that included a new design of chariot, along with different types of weaponry as well as knowledge of irrigation systems. There is also evidence to show that they tended to favour the appointment of individuals with a Semitic background to run the country.

While it is virtually impossible to connect any of the stories of the book of Genesis with either events or people mentioned in the annals of Egypt itself, the Bible accounts of the life of Joseph[4] are often thought to reflect this period. On being sold as a slave into Egypt, Joseph found himself working in the household of a rich Egyptian named Potiphar, but subsequently rose to a position of considerable power in the royal household. This narrative is one of the most carefully crafted pieces of literature in the entire Hebrew Bible, offering the sort of psychological insights into the characters' thinking and behaviour that is rarely found elsewhere in the Bible. The entire sequence of stories has obviously been well polished by storytellers, as it was repeated and handed on from one generation to another. So it is all the more surprising to discover that it contains a number of detailed descriptions of practices that were unique to Egyptian life at this period but which would have been quite different from the habits of the Hebrew population among whom the stories were later preserved. When Joseph was summoned from prison to appear before the (unnamed) pharaoh, he "shaved himself and changed his clothes".[5] Shaving was an Egyptian practice, as illustrated by many paintings of the day, which also invariably depict Semitic men wearing beards. At a later stage, when his brothers had arrived in the land and appeared before him in a formal audience before being given a meal, Joseph and his officials followed Egyptian custom by eating "by themselves, because the Egyptians could not eat with the Hebrews".[6] And after his death he was embalmed and interred in Egyptian fashion.[7]

By the mid-fifteenth century BC, the Hyksos had been chased out of the country and replaced by a dynasty of native-born Egyptian rulers. The first-century AD Jewish historian Josephus identified their banishment with the exodus story as told in the Hebrew Bible (Josephus, *Against Apion* 1.16). Though the exit of the Hyksos is certainly the only well-documented large-scale population movement of ethnically Asiatic peoples from Egypt in roughly the direction of Canaan, it is impossible to make that link. On any reckoning, the Hebrew exodus involved nothing like the numbers that must have moved out at the end of the Hyksos dynasty, and in any case such evidence as there is cannot be made to fit a date in the sixteenth century BC. The enslavement of the Hebrew people that led up to the exodus is attributed to the accession of a "new king, who knew nothing about Joseph",[8] which could easily have been an appropriate description of a native Egyptian ruler coming to power after the Hyksos had been removed from office.

The pharaohs of the eighteenth dynasty were certainly determined to make sure that it would never again be possible for something like the Hyksos invasion to take place in the future, and they embarked on a deliberate policy of territorial expansion so as to protect their borders. Tuthmosis I was the third pharaoh of this dynasty, and in spite of the fact that his rule lasted only from 1525 to 1512 BC, he turned out to be one of the most accomplished. He not only secured the north-eastern boundary, but pushed it well back from the heartlands of Egypt itself by invading Palestine and forcing the rulers of its various independent city-states to swear allegiance to him. He was also the creator of the Valley of the Kings, which was to become the burial site of the pharaohs for generations to come. The subjugation of Canaanite cities did not last for long, though, and by the middle of the thirteenth century BC things were back to where they had been before, with marauding groups jostling for power in the region.

In the late nineteenth century AD, a chance find by a group of peasants led to the discovery of a collection of cuneiform tablets whose content illustrates some of the things that were going on at this time. They are known as the Amarna Letters, from the place where they were found: Tell el Amarna, which is the site of a new capital that had been established by Amenophis IV, who was pharaoh from 1369 to 1353 BC. He was fanatical in his worship of the sun god Aten, and not only denounced the worship of other traditional deities, but even changed his own name to Akhen-aten, and gave his new capital the name Akhet-Aten.

It has occasionally been suggested that there might have been some connection between this primitive form of monotheism (belief in only a single deity) and the faith to which Moses introduced the escaping Hebrew slaves. There are certainly some resemblances between Atenism and the worship of Israel's God, Yahweh: like Moses' God, Aten was described as "the god beside whom there is none other", and there was a heavy emphasis on teaching in Atenism, just as the Torah later came to be associated with Moses. Parts of Psalm 104 praise the wonders of Yahweh's creation in language similar to an Egyptian hymn to the sun that was attributed to Akhen-aten. Such similarities demonstrate nothing specific about either Egyptian spirituality or the faith of the Hebrews, for this common use of language and imagery in worship was fairly widespread throughout the ancient world. But it is probably another example of the way in which the faith of Israel was consciously contextualized within the wider culture of the day, though invariably with subtle additions and alterations that in the end portrayed a rather different view of God, the world and people.

Nomads, slaves, and the story of the exodus

The Amarna Letters consist of a series of pillar-shaped tablets written in cuneiform script, mostly in a form of Akkadian, which seems to have been widely adopted as the diplomatic language of the time. They comprise an extensive collection of some 350 letters in all, dating from the early fourteenth century, and were written to Akhen-aten and his predecessor Amenhotep III (1398–1361 BC). They have nothing to say about the religious reforms that were taking place at the time, but consist of official diplomatic correspondence from the rulers of various other states. A small number of them came from the kings of other large territories, including Babylon and Assyria, and they reveal a considerable degree of respect among them: they address one another as "brother" and discuss as equals matters to do with trade and royal weddings, which were seen as a good way to maintain friendly relationships between these various superpowers. But the majority of the letters were written by rulers of smaller city-states in Canaan and Syria, and have a quite different style that demonstrates their dependence on Egypt, and declares their desire to maintain the security which that bestowed on them.

They contrast their own subservience with the activities of other groups of people, who are referred to as *apiru* (also variously spelled *hapiru*, *habiru* and *aperu*) and who were clearly regarded as a danger to good order, with the potential for creating disturbance throughout the whole area. The names *apiru* and "Hebrew" sound alike, and probably have some linguistic connection, though it is not possible to make a simple identification between these groups and the stories of Israel's early life in Canaan. At least one letter refers to them as former slaves, while the general picture is of a significant underclass existing on the fringes of Canaanite society, who, if they succeeded in their aims, might serve as some sort of rallying-point around which other disadvantaged people might gather and instigate a social revolution. While this was not the entire story as depicted in the biblical books of Joshua and Judges, some such social revolution is widely believed to have been one aspect of the complex series of events that led to the emergence of Israel as a discrete nation within the land of Canaan. These Amarna Letters were all written over a relatively short timescale between about 1365 and 1335 BC, but the sort of social tensions that they indicate on the borders of Egypt and Palestine were typical of life in the region for several centuries, and certainly serve to illustrate the political context within which the stories of the emergence of a Hebrew state can best be understood.

Akhen-aten had been so idiosyncratic in his style of governance that things were always going to change on his death, and within less than a hundred years the eighteenth dynasty of which he was a part had been superseded by the nineteenth. The first pharaoh of this period, Rameses I, reigned for only a year, but his son Sethos I (1291–1278 BC) set about re-establishing Egyptian influence in the wider region. One of his first actions was a military campaign that took him through much of Palestine and Syria in a move that was designed to remind the local city kings that their survival depended on loyalty to their more powerful neighbour to the south. He is best known, though, as the instigator of a massive building programme in the north-east of the country around the delta of the River Nile, where it runs into the Mediterranean Sea. He supervised the construction of some magnificent temples, and the inscriptions and paintings on their walls reveal much information about the way he perceived his place in Egyptian history, with extensive lists of pharaohs going back to the earliest times, but with no reference at all to his immediate predecessors with their capital at Amarna and their devotion to the god Aten. Many of his projects were so ambitious that they were never going to be completed in his own lifetime. His son, who succeeded him as Rameses II, was the one who finished them and consequently went down in history as one of the greatest pharaohs of all time – so great, in fact, that no fewer than nine later pharaohs took his name for themselves. When he came to the throne in 1279 BC, he had already been co-regent alongside his father for some considerable time, and his reign was one of the longest of any of the pharaohs, lasting for some sixty-six years. He consolidated Egypt's position as one of the premier empires of the day, though he was unable to prevent the Hittites seizing control of territory in the south of Syria that had formerly been held by Egypt. As part of his regeneration and celebration of Egyptian culture, he built a new capital, which he named after himself, and which was the city that is identified in Exodus 1:11 as one of the construction sites where the Hebrew slaves were forced into hard labour.

This is the period in which the Bible sets the story of Moses, the child born to Hebrew slaves who was brought up and educated as an Egyptian and subsequently confronted pharaoh, demanding an end to their slavery and, when this was refused, leading them out of Egypt and across the desert into Canaan.[9] This is another example of a Bible story that reflects conditions in the time of which it speaks, but which is impossible to place in relation to the documented history as it can be discerned from Egyptian sources. The existence of gangs of slave labourers who were mostly drawn from what Egyptians called "Asiatics" is well documented, and, given the sheer scale of the building programmes undertaken by Rameses II, it is not surprising that large numbers of such slaves would be in the area of the Nile Delta at this time. The making of bricks with straw, which the Hebrew slaves were forced to do, is known both from Egyptian accounts and from the remains of bricks that survive, and was a regular practice especially during the thirteenth and twelfth centuries BC. The withdrawal of a ready supply of straw, coupled with the insistence that the slaves go and gather their own instead of having it already available on site, would have added to their burden in more ways than one.[10] Not only were they forced to go further afield to scavenge for straw, but its absence would have made the bricks much harder to fashion into appropriate shapes for building. Contrary to the popular image, the incorporation of straw into the mud was not designed to give greater internal strength to the finished articles, but was the catalyst for a complex chemical process as enzymes released by the straw reacted with the clay so as to create a consistency that was then easier to mould.

Other incidental details of the story also reflect aspects of Egyptian life as we know it in this period. The description of the princess who found the abandoned Moses as a baby, and of his subsequent upbringing at the hands of a slave woman who turns out to have been his birth mother, reflects practices in the many harems that were kept by the pharaohs, as also does his easy access to the royal courts as an adult. Foreigners of Asiatic and Semitic origin were commonly employed as attendants in the palace, though they rarely rose to the positions of power that had been available to their forebears during the ascendancy of the Hyksos dynasty. Any effort to make more specific connections between the biblical story and life in Egypt at this time is bound to be frustrated by the complete absence of even a brief mention of either Moses or the exodus in the Egyptian records. This is hardly surprising, for whereas Moses is the hero of the biblical narrative, he might well have been one of hundreds, if not thousands, of Semitic people working in the royal courts. A similar comment might be made in relation to the escape of the slaves themselves. The actual numbers involved were not all that great when compared with the enormous numbers of slaves in the country, and even the Bible itself describes them as a rag-bag of somewhat disparate individuals.[11]

The one thing we do know for certain is that by the time Rameses' son Merneptah reached the throne in 1213 BC there was a group of people in Palestine who were known by the name "Israel". Evidence for this comes from a stele made of granite that had originally been put in place by Amenhotep III. In its original form, one face had been left blank, and on this Merneptah carved his own inscription. Among other battles, he describes a military campaign that he had previously led into various areas of Palestine and Syria, and in the catalogue of his victories there is this line:

> *Canaan is captive with all woe. Ashkelon is conquered, Gezer seized, Yanoam made non-existent; Israel is wasted, bare of seed.*

The reference to Israel is quite coincidental, and nothing more is said about it. But the statement that it is "bare of seed" is taken to be an indication that at the time an entity known by that name was living an agricultural lifestyle in Palestine, and that Merneptah had destroyed the seed necessary for the next season's crops. Since the various battles that are listed were all in the past when the record was inscribed, it appears to imply that, whatever "Israel" may have been understood to be at the time, it was sufficiently well established that it could be distinguished from the cities and cultures mentioned alongside it. But it may be significant that although the others who are mentioned in this inscription are clearly identified as fortified city-states, Israel is described somewhat more vaguely as a people group, with the possible implication that they may not have had fixed territorial boundaries at this period. Various calculations appear to indicate that this can all be dated somewhere between about 1240 and 1220 BC. Even if this mention of "Israel" raises at least as many questions as it answers, Merneptah's stele is an important reference point for dating the emergence of "Israel" as a recognizable designation for people living in the land just to the north east of Egypt.

Culture, religion, and lifestyles

The most obvious evidence of ancient Egyptian culture is to be found in the many monuments and buildings – not least the pyramids – that still draw visitors from all over the world, amazed by the technological sophistication that made possible the construction of such grand designs with what must have been relatively primitive tools and equipment. But there was much more to this ancient civilization than that, and these physical remains are only one small aspect of the splendour that characterized Egyptian life.

Literature

We have already noted several significant pieces of literature that are known from as early as the beginning of the second millennium BC, but that was by no means the beginning of writing in this culture. One thing that did dominate literature at every period, though, was the production of forms of wisdom literature, consisting of wise sayings of sages and kings, offering advice on everything from everyday matters such as relationships between family members to reflections on some of life's most imponderable questions such as the suffering of good people and the apparent power of evil. Many stories are also found, and include novels as well as moralistic stories and others that are obviously intended to be fairytales. Even the titles of some of them give a flavour of the sort of stories represented here: from the late second millennium BC we have *The Story of the Foredoomed Prince*, and *The Misadventures of Wenamum*, as well as *The Capture of Joppa*, which is more a tale of plotting and intrigue than a straightforward military account. In addition to items that would readily be identified as literature today, the many inscriptions in temples and other buildings also serve a literary purpose, recounting the deeds of the pharaohs as well as preserving traditional stories of deities, and hymns and prayers composed in their honour.

All this was written in hieroglyphics, which was a form of picture language based either on the sound of a word or some concept associated with whatever was being described. This required a very large number of characters, and more than 2,000 of them have been identified in ancient Egyptian writing. The earliest known writing of this sort dates back to the fourth millennium BC. As time passed, the actual shape and structure of hieroglyphs developed and changed, and simplified forms eventually emerged, including some characters that functioned almost like the letters of an alphabet. But hieroglyphics never entirely disappeared, and survived well into the time of the Roman empire. They still survive even today in a residual form through Coptic, which is written in a script that derives mostly from Greek, but with some additional symbols and characters that are directly descended from Egyptian hieroglyphics.

From the time of the European Renaissance onwards, there were several efforts to decipher the inscriptions on Egyptian monuments, but it was not until Napoleon's invasion that any real progress was made. Napoleon's primary purpose for visiting Egypt was military conquest, though he also took an interest in the history of the place and invited a team of 167 scholars to accompany him for the express purpose of exploring it. But it was a casual discovery that enabled real progress to be made. In 1799, and purely by chance, an officer in the French army came across a stone that was inscribed in three languages: Greek, together with two forms of Egyptian. It came to be called the Rosetta Stone, after the harbour where it was found, and turned out to have been inscribed in 196 BC to record various decrees of the pharaoh at the time, Ptolemy V (204–181 BC). Not long after this, the British invaded Egypt and defeated the French, in the process of which they seized the stone and took it back to London, where some preliminary work on deciphering it was carried out. But it was not until the French scholar Jean François Champollion set to work on it that the secrets of ancient Egyptian writing were finally unlocked, thereby enabling the pyramid inscriptions to be deciphered for the first time in modern history and in the process opening up a whole new world to European eyes.

Papyrus production

One aspect of Egyptian literary culture that is worth special mention is the material on which much of it was recorded. In many parts of the ancient world, the skins of animals were often used as writing material, but in Egypt the most commonly used medium was papyrus (from which the English word "paper" is derived). The use of papyrus can be traced as far back as 4000 BC. The papyrus reed *Cyperus papyrus* grew in vast quantities on the banks of the River Nile, and could be harvested quite easily. On collection, its outer skin was peeled off to reveal the pith inside, which was then cut into thin strips. After being soaked in water for a few days, the strips were laid on absorbent cotton cloths and arranged alongside one another in two layers crossing at right angles, so as to produce a sheet with the fibres horizontal on one side and vertical on the other. Each sheet was then piled up with others and pressed with weights so that the strips began to glue together. The cotton sheets were taken out after a day or two and the hot sun did the rest, making a brittle, though almost indestructible, writing material. Papyrus became one of Egypt's most valuable exports, and sheets of it were sent all over the known world. But it was in Egypt that they were able to survive the vicissitudes of the centuries. Even when they were discarded, papyrus sheets tended to be preserved by the hot dry sand, whereas in other countries around the Mediterranean Sea the damp weather and colder temperatures meant that it easily disintegrated unless it was carefully looked after. In later times, papyrus sheets would be stitched together so as to make a longer piece of material that could then be rolled up. Some of the oldest known copies of Bible books are written on papyrus, though early in the Christian era scribes discovered a way to fold sheets down the middle and then stitch them together into the shape of a modern book, known as a codex.

Religion

Many of the most impressive monuments of ancient Egypt were temples – and of course the pyramids themselves also offer an insight into the religious beliefs and practices of the people. With very many variations, Egyptian spirituality was centred on the life of nature, and especially the cycle of birth and death as it was reflected in the seasons of the agricultural year. The fertility of the land was of extreme importance, for though the soil of the Nile Valley was very fertile, it would also have been extremely dry had it not been for the annual rise and fall of the river floods, which provided sufficient moisture for successful agriculture. With the exception of the brief rule of Akhen-aten, who insisted on the worship of only one god, Egyptian religion recognized a large number of deities. Some of them were acknowledged throughout the whole country and had a sort of national status, while others were predominantly local gods and goddesses. But they all had some connection with the life of nature and the cycles of the seasons – even the single god whose worship Akhen-aten promoted, for Aten represented the disk of the sun. Crocodiles, cats, and other animals were regarded as sacred, and some deities could be represented in ways that portrayed those birds and animals that identified with them. So, for example, the sky god Horus was depicted as a hawk, though with a human body. Other gods represented the sun, moon, and stars.

One of the most important deities was Osiris. His story encapsulated the eternal theme of a good person who was done to death by his enemy (in this case his brother Seth), but who subsequently managed to turn the tables by becoming master of the underworld, while his son Horus and wife Isis avenged his death, with Horus inheriting the regal position of which Osiris had been robbed. He was also recognized as a god of vegetation, manifested in the annual flooding of the Nile, as well as playing a major role in the complex funeral rites of the time. Much later, Osiris, Horus, and Isis also commanded a considerable following well beyond the shores of Egypt, and the advocates of several mystery religions of the New Testament period (on which see later, in chapter 9) fashioned their initiation ceremonies after the primeval stories of these characters in the Egyptian pantheon.

This story also offered hope for a life after death that would be even more glorious than this life, if that were possible. The magnificence of the pharaohs' pyramid tombs, and their more secretive resting-places in the Valley of the Kings, is one of the most obvious signs of this expectation. Such apparent extravagance derived from the belief that the pharaohs were themselves divine beings who needed to have in their tombs all that would be necessary to ensure that they enjoyed a comfortable existence in the next world. Just as the pharaohs were cosseted in death, so worship in the temples was designed to look after the gods on a daily basis. In other parts of the ancient world, temples were public buildings, often (as in Mesopotamia, and later in Jerusalem) serving as marketplaces and gathering-spaces for the community as well as a place for the performance of rituals and devotions. But in Egypt, only the priests were allowed to enter the temples, and many of them were surrounded by high walls to prevent other people even peeping inside. Just as the kings were the embodiment of the gods, so the daily life of the gods was patterned on life in the royal palace, with the role of the priests being to ensure that the deity was properly cared for by being woken up in the morning, fed throughout the day with various offerings, and enabled to carry out business between mealtimes before being laid to rest at night. There were of course regular festivals, when the gods (in the form of their statues) would come forth from the temples and process around the neighbourhood in grand style, but that would be the only occasion when ordinary people ever got to see them or even offer them worship. Daily devotions would, of course, take place in the home, but they tended to be directed to local deities rather than the national gods.

This pattern of religious practice continued right up to the time of the Roman empire. When Alexander the Great invaded Egypt, he consulted an oracle which declared him to be the son of Re, the traditional Egyptian sun god, and set a precedent that is almost certainly the origin of the claims to divinity made by later Roman emperors.

Later Egyptian history

Rameses II was succeeded as pharaoh by his son, who ruled from 1186 to 1155 BC under the name Rameses III. But Egypt's influence was already beginning to decline, and a whole variety of other groups started to expand their influence in the area. One group that attempted an invasion of Egypt itself was the so-called "sea peoples", which was a term used to denote marauders who – unlike more traditional invaders of the region – travelled by sea rather than over land. Rameses III managed to repel them from his shores, but other evidence suggests that at least some of them settled in the south of Canaan, and there is good reason to think that the Philistines of the Hebrew Bible were one component within these sea peoples. There has been a good deal of unresolved speculation about where they actually came from, though the early designs of their pottery suggest some connection with Greece and Asia Minor (other areas where there was considerable political upheaval taking place at this same period). In relation to their ethnic origins, they have been variously identified as Manoans and Trojans, though once they settled in Palestine they soon developed their own distinctive culture and way of life.

They were not the only ones with whom Rameses III had to contend, and his kingdom was attacked on its western flank by insurgent tribes from Libya. His power was also weakened as a result of natural disasters that led to food shortages, and eventually members of his own immediate family conspired with court officials to have him assassinated. It is not known whether or not the plot succeeded, and his mummy certainly shows no outward signs of a violent end. The existence of the plot itself is known from court transcripts written on papyrus which document the trial of those who were accused of conspiring against him. However he met his death, he was succeeded by his son, who became Rameses IV. But by now the heyday of Egyptian power was well and truly past.

Despite its own internal weakness, Egypt still had aspirations to maintain its position as one of the major power-brokers of the region, and in the centuries following the demise of the twentieth dynasty, Egyptian rulers continued to embark on occasional military expeditions into Palestine and Syria. A much easier way to secure a place among the superpowers was by maintaining the sort of fraternal international relationships that are illustrated in the Amarna Letters, and marriage alliances between the various royal houses formed a key part of this strategy. An illustration of this can be found in the Bible account of the reign of Solomon, king of Israel from 971 to 931 BC, who came to be renowned for his very many wives, all of whom played a part in his own strategy for securing the borders of his kingdom. A throwaway remark in the Hebrew Bible records how "Pharaoh king of Egypt had gone up and captured Gezer and burned it down, had killed the Canaanites who lived in the city, and had given it as a dowry to his daughter, Solomon's wife".[12] This not only offers an insight into the Egyptian approach to international relations at this time, but also provides some indication of the strength of Solomon's kingdom. Egypt still had the military capability to mount a successful attack on a place like Gezer, which was quite a distance from the Egyptian border, but its real security was dependent on forging alliances with other powerful states in the neighbourhood, of which Israel was obviously now one of the more significant. Evidence from the site of ancient Gezer not only confirms the Egyptian attack but also indicates that Solomon subsequently rebuilt the city in a distinctive style.

Greeks and Jews

Egypt continued to take an interest in events in Palestine for some considerable time after this, but only on an occasional basis, and usually in response to initiatives from elsewhere. But even as late as the time of the Roman empire, Egypt still had some influence in international affairs, and by the beginning of the Christian era it was home to one of the largest Jewish populations anywhere in the world. The political events in Israel and Judah that had led to this will be discussed in chapter 5.

Before leaving Egypt here, however, we will jump forward in time by a thousand years or more to the centuries just before the birth of Jesus. By now, Egypt had briefly been incorporated into the Persian empire, before being liberated by Alexander the Great in 332 BC. Though Alexander was himself a considerable empire-builder, he preferred to allow conquered nations a large measure of self-determination, and on his untimely death in 323 BC Egypt fell into the hands of Ptolemy, who was one of Alexander's generals. He and his successors liked to think of themselves as heirs to the great pharaohs of the distant past, and set about restoring the fortunes of Egypt by reinstating its influence in what by this time was a very different world from that of its earlier history. Alexandria became the capital, and the Ptolemaic pharaohs set about validating their own little empire with the construction of many new temples on the traditional pattern of Egyptian spirituality. Under Alexander's influence, Greek had become the universal language of the entire Mediterranean region, but these new Egyptian rulers went to great pains to identify themselves with Egypt's past glories, and even arranged for their own exploits to be described in hieroglyphic script and preserved for posterity on the walls of their grand new public buildings. This was the period when the Rosetta Stone, briefly mentioned already, was inscribed, and these new Greek rulers went to considerable pains to gather together traditional stories of the kingdom that was now theirs.

Even before the Greeks arrived, considerable numbers of Jewish people had already settled in Egypt. Evidence of this is contained in a series of papyrus documents written in Aramaic (the official language of the Persian empire) which show that during the period of Persian occupation of Egypt there was a garrison of Jewish soldiers stationed on the island of Elephantine, which was known in classical times as Abu or Yebu, and is located near Aswan on the River Nile. It was famous for many reasons. In much earlier times its quarries had supplied much of the stone that was used for public buildings, but more recently it had achieved fame as the place where the first documented measurements of the earth's size were calculated by the Greek mathematician Eratosthenes of

Cyrene in about 240 BC. The reason for the presence of Jewish troops was more mundane: this was a strategic location on the southern borders of Egypt and close to the important trading-post of Syene, where traders from further south in Africa met the ships of Egyptian traders on the Nile. They may well have arrived there long before the Persian Cambyses first invaded Egypt in 525 BC, but the Elephantine Letters date from a period between 495 and 399 BC.

There are many different kinds of document in this collection, including deeds for property, marriage contracts, and other legal transactions, but the most interesting ones are those that describe the religious observances of this group. It is clear from them that the kind of Judaism being practised in this Egyptian garrison had its own distinctive characteristics, many of which were derived from traditional Egyptian beliefs. They even had a temple, the only one known outside of Jerusalem, which is hardly surprising as the Hebrew Bible specifically prohibited sacrificial worship taking place anywhere outside the Jerusalem temple. Very little is known about the building itself, except that it had pillars of stone, five gateways made of carved stone, and a roof of cedar wood. Some experts have speculated that there may be a veiled reference to its construction in Isaiah 19:19, which declares that "on that day there will be an altar to the Lord in the centre of the land of Egypt, and a pillar dedicated to the Lord at its border".

Whatever its origins, its destruction in 410 BC is well documented in the various letters found there, and seems to have been instigated by elements of the local population who disapproved of the sort of worship that was carried on in this temple. Some of these letters contain instructions sent from Palestinian authorities advising the Egyptian Jews to restrict their worship to the offering of agricultural produce and the burning of incense. That would no doubt have pleased the Egyptians, for whom animals were regarded as divine beings, and therefore the idea of sacrificing them was always going to be especially abhorrent (and may explain why they attacked the temple in the first place). For centuries, Elephantine had also been home to the Egyptian god Khnum, who was depicted as a ram, though with a human body, and was patron of the river itself and, by extension, of potters (for whom the river clay provided their basic material). The Jewish temple shows no sign of having incorporated elements of this Egyptian tradition, but it does appear to have been a place where more deities than just Yahweh, the God of Israel, were revered. Yahweh (or Yaho, as he is called here) was definitely the leading figure to whom the temple was dedicated, but some evidence points to the worship of others, though there is disagreement as to exactly how many: some experts believe there were five deities, represented by the five gates of the temple, while others can find evidence for only two or three. Most of the others mentioned in the texts have no Egyptian connections, but are more likely to have been of Canaanite origin. At an earlier period, the Hebrew prophet Jeremiah had dealings with Jewish exiles in Egypt, whose practices reflected something similar, and who justified their worship of "the Queen of Heaven" by reminding him that this was "just as we and our ancestors, our king and our leaders, used to do in the towns of Judah and in the streets of Jerusalem".[13]

Translating the Hebrew Bible

Finally, we come to the Bible itself, for one of its most important early versions has a good claim to have been translated in Egypt. This is the Greek version of the Hebrew scriptures, the Septuagint, already referred to in chapter 1, where its composition and contents were discussed. The question of its origin was deliberately omitted there, because it is part of the story of Egypt.

An ancient narrative sets out to address that most intriguing of questions. Known as the *Letter of Aristeas*, it contains the reminiscences of a court official of that name who served in Egypt during the reign of the Greek pharaoh Ptolemy II Philadelphus (285–247 BC). Alexandria was already home to a thriving Jewish community, which had adapted well to a new way of life and a new language: Greek. In that environment it was inevitable that sooner or later the Hebrew scriptures would need to be translated into this everyday language so that future generations of Jews could have easy access to the traditional faith of their nation. Unlike some of his predecessors, Ptolemy Philadelphus was a peaceful ruler who loved culture, and he was determined that his land would become a great storehouse for all the wisdom of the ancient world. He already had a head start, with the monuments left behind by previous generations of Egyptian pharaohs, and so he put much of his own energies into the establishment of a library. He scoured the world looking for books to include in his collection, and soon amassed almost a quarter of a million volumes. Though he cannot possibly have read them all, he still wanted more. Naturally, all the classics of Greek literature were there, but his collection was cosmopolitan and international in scope. He and his librarian, Demetrius, began to search for other suitable literature wherever it might be found, and with such a large Jewish element in the population it was only a matter of time before their attention focused on the Hebrew Bible. A large body of literature like this certainly deserved to be given a place in the royal library – but it would first have to be translated into Greek.

The story goes that the king sought the advice of the leaders of the Jewish community in Alexandria, who were highly flattered that anyone would take such an interest in their faith, and readily agreed to co-operate in the work of translation from Hebrew into Greek. It was decided that a letter would be sent to the high priest in Jerusalem, asking for his help in supplying reliable copies of the sacred text along with language scholars who could be trusted to undertake the work. Aristeas took the letter, accompanied by another Egyptian courtier by the name of Andreas. To ensure that they were well received, Philadelphus ordered the release of more than 100,000 Jewish slaves in Egypt, and sent to Jerusalem 100 talents of silver as well as many sacrifices. Eleazer, the Jewish high priest, responded favourably, and appointed seventy-two men for the task, six from each of the traditional twelve tribes of ancient Israel. All of them had impeccable moral and religious credentials, as well as being experts in the two languages, Hebrew and Greek. They made the journey back to Egypt, taking with them the scrolls on which the scriptures of their nation were inscribed in golden letters.

On their arrival, they were warmly received by Philadelphus himself, who duly acknowledged the value of their scrolls by bowing down before them seven times. He then spent a full week feasting and asking questions of the Jewish scholars – one for each of them every evening – before they were finally packed off to the island of Pharos to begin their work. According to one version of the story, each translator was shut up in an individual room, so that they would all work independently of each other. There they stayed for precisely seventy-two days. When the time was up, the seventy-two scholars emerged from their seventy-two rooms, and to everyone's amazement their seventy-two translations were word for word identical! The Jewish people in Egypt were naturally delighted, and so was Philadelphus, who at once recognized this marvel as a sign that the work must be divinely inspired:

> *When the whole work was read to the king, he was greatly astonished at the spirit of the lawgiver. And he said to Demetrius, "How is it that none of the [Greek] historians or poets ever thought of mentioning such great achievements?" He replied, "Because the Law is holy and has been given by God – and some of those who did think to mention it were smitten by God and desisted from the attempt." He said that he had heard Theopompus tell how when he was too rashly intending to introduce into his history some of the incidents from the Law which had previously been translated, his mind was deranged for more than thirty days ... "I have been informed too," he added, "by Theodectes, the tragic poet, that when he was intending to introduce into one of his plays something recorded in the Book, he was afflicted with cataract of the eyes; and, suspecting that this was the reason for his mishap, he besought God's mercy and after many days recovered his sight."*

When he heard these extraordinary tales, Philadelphus must have wondered what mishap might possibly befall him, which no doubt explains why he played safe and "made obeisance, and ordered that great care should be taken of the books, and that they should be guarded with proper awe". So he gave the new translation pride of place in his library, and sent the translators back to Jerusalem with extravagant rewards. Not everyone believed that sort of story, even in the ancient world, but it does explain why the Greek Old Testament came to be referred to by the abbreviation LXX, the Roman numeral for seventy (based on the number of scholars who translated it). In the story, of course, there were seventy-two translators, which would be LXXII in Roman figures, but presumably LXX came into common use simply because it was easier to say and remember.

The process of translating the Hebrew Bible into Greek almost certainly took place in a far less dramatic fashion, with different books being translated at different times and by different people. It all happened sometime between the third and first centuries BC. By the time of the New Testament the Septuagint (or LXX) was in widespread use throughout the Mediterranean world and beyond, for though Greek political power was at an end, Greek survived as the international language of the day and was readily understood everywhere. Though Egypt was by now a spent force politically (and would soon become a part of the Roman empire), its significant contribution to the story of the Bible continued through the influence of this translation, and it turned out to be the one ever-present influence that can be traced in the world of the Bible from its beginning in the Stone Age to its end in the Roman empire.

4

Life in the Promised Land

After wandering in the desert that lies between Egypt and Palestine, the descendants of those Hebrews who had escaped from slavery in Egypt eventually settled in a land that the Bible calls Canaan, and its inhabitants Canaanites. This terminology is also found in the Amarna Letters and in various Greek sources, where the designation is applied predominantly to those people groups who occupied the coastal areas of Syria and Palestine. The Phoenicians, who were one of these groups, referred to themselves as Canaanites. But it was never a narrowly ethnic designation and could be used much more broadly to include the inhabitants of inland areas more to the east, so that in some texts the Amorites could also be described as Canaanites.

Documents discovered at Ebla in north Syria testify to the fact that as early as the third millennium BC the political organization of this land followed a similar pattern to the rest of the region, with many independent city-states. For much of the second millennium BC the Egyptians were the most influential power, though they were generally happy to rule through local kings rather than trying to govern the country directly themselves by integrating it into a consolidated imperial structure. They did, however, insist on forging direct relationships with every local ruler individually, and went to considerable lengths to discourage any sense of interdependence or collaboration among the city-states, even though in some cases there might be as little as 2 or 3 miles between them. This policy was designed to minimize the possibility that local alliances might emerge and be strong enough to challenge Egyptian rule, and as a consequence there was a fierce sense of competitiveness between the various cities and their rulers – a situation that is clearly reflected in the biblical books of Joshua and Judges. Egyptian records and archaeological discoveries from various sites provide evidence of a complex system of urbanized city-states, particularly in the centre of the country, which is where the most fertile agricultural land could be found. Access to agricultural land was always going to be of vital importance, for the life of a city depended on the ability of its people to grow enough food to sustain their expanding populations.

But the land also had another strategic importance, because it was criss-crossed by the major trade routes that connected Egypt and Mesopotamia. It was always going to be a major priority to ensure that the city-states with control of the roads would be ruled by kings who could be trusted to maintain Egypt's own security. This necessity was the one thing that ensured that throughout the biblical period, Canaan (or Palestine, as it later came to be called) would always be regarded as an important prize for whatever superpower dominated the region. There was never a power vacuum for very long, and the story of this small strip of land and its conquerors reads like a roll-call of major empires throughout history: Egyptians, Syrians, Assyrians, Babylonians, Persians, Greeks, and Romans all recognized the strategic significance of this land. Little has changed, of course, and the conflicts being played out in the Middle East today centre on the very same issues, of landless people seeking a safe home for themselves and of control of the trade in natural resources that provide the region's source of wealth.

Canaanites and Israelites

No matter which source we look to, one of the big unsolved mysteries of early Israelite history is the question of when and how Canaanite culture became Israelite culture. Egyptian records from the reign of Merneptah (1213–1203 BC) identify Israel as a discrete entity, but also seem to regard the Israelites as just one element of the Canaanites. As well as the stele mentioned in the previous chapter, there is also a series of four battle reliefs in the temple at Karnak that go back to Merneptah's reign, showing the same three city-states as are mentioned in the inscription (Ashkelon, Gezer, and Yanoam), plus the people group known as "Israel". These Egyptian paintings regularly used dress as a stylistic indication of the identity of different people groups, and semi-nomadic individuals were always depicted wearing clothing different from that of the indigenous Canaanite city-dwellers. In this particular inscription (which is the earliest known visual representation of any Israelite people), they are indistinguishable in appearance from the inhabitants of the Canaanite city-states.

Origins and ethnicity

By the time of Rameses III (1198–1167 BC), the whole of Canaan was in a state of upheaval as a result of the incursion of multiple groups of migrants who were vying with each other to settle in the land. Egyptian records mention the arrival of at least two separate waves of "sea peoples" during the thirteenth and twelfth centuries BC, with a group that is identified as the Philistines playing a prominent part in the second wave of invasion. They were not the only ones to be called "sea peoples", and others who are specifically named include the Tjeker, Shekelesh, Denyen, and Weshnesh. None of these are mentioned in the Bible narratives, though the Philistines appear repeatedly as one of the most feared enemies of the Hebrew settlers. These "sea peoples" appear to have originated in Crete and the area around the Aegean Sea, to the east of Greece. They had originally been recruited as mercenaries by the Egyptians to help fortify and defend the Canaanite city-states, though a temple inscription of Rameses III shows women and children among them as well as soldiers, which suggests that this was part of a sustained mass migration of people who were looking for a new land in which to live. The Philistines settled mainly along the sea coast, adopting the same kind of political structure that the Egyptians had imposed on the rest of the land and establishing five city-states of their own: Gaza, Ashkelon, Ashdod, Ekron, and Gath. In time, they also gave their name to the whole country ("Palestine" being a derivative of "Philistine").

They were not the only ones trying to establish a foothold in Canaan. The invasion of these "sea peoples" from the west was paralleled by the incursion of semi-nomadic groups from the east, who found it relatively easy to settle in the hill country, where the terrain was less hospitable and therefore less attractive as a place to live. In the midst of all this movement of peoples and cultures, we can trace the emergence of a national entity called "Israel". But what exactly does that mean? This is not the place to engage in any extensive discussion of that question, as it would take us well away from our main focus here. The Bible itself suggests that Canaanites and Israelites – not to mention Amorites, and others who are found in the literature of the day – were not entirely unique ethnic designations, but had a complex interrelationship with one another. The book of Exodus indicates that the group of slaves who escaped from Egypt were not all of the same racial background, but included a motley group who are described as a "mixed multitude".[1] Then in the book of Joshua, which tells the story of selected aspects of the Israelite settlement in the land, there is more than one occasion when Joshua seeks to unify the people he leads by inviting them to pledge allegiance to the Ten Commandments and other laws associated with the name of Moses. In describing this, there is specific mention of "alien as well as citizen" making this commitment.[2] Later the people are given a choice to continue either the worship of "the gods that your ancestors served beyond the River [Euphrates] and in Egypt ... or the gods of the Amorites", or the worship of Yahweh, the God revealed to Moses.[3] Other indications in some of the stories of Joshua point in the same direction, implying that "Israel" was a cultural designation that included people of quite diverse origins. The family of Rahab, a prostitute in the city-state of Jericho, not only became Israelites,[4] but they were later recognized as one of the leading families of the nation, and Rahab herself found fame as one of the ancestors of Jesus.[5] There is also the account of how Joshua made a treaty with the Gibeonites, a group that again came to occupy an important niche in Israelite life, this time as attendants in the temple.[6] At a much later period, when there was a tendency to identify "Israel" by reference to a narrow definition of ethnicity, the book of Jonah protested that this was not an authentic reflection of what its nationhood was ever intended to be.

When all these things are put together, we end up with a complex picture of the emergence of the Israelite nation that is also supported by the archaeological evidence from Canaan at this time, which shows the relatively advanced culture of the original city-states gradually being replaced by a different lifestyle that came to be identified as "Israel". The one distinguishing feature of the state that eventually emerged as "Israel" seems to have been its concept of statehood, based on a shared story of its origins in the exodus and subsequent events, and the monotheistic faith promulgated in the Ten Commandments and the Torah.

The religion of Canaan

The distinctiveness of this approach to faith becomes obvious when it is compared to what is known of the general religious traditions of Canaan. Knowledge of this is quite extensive, thanks to a large amount of evidence from the site of the ancient city of Ugarit. Like many significant archaeological discoveries, this one was made more or less by accident at Ras esh-Shamra, which is near the Syrian seaport of Latakia and just opposite Cyprus. Nowadays it is a popular tourist resort, with a restaurant at the site and a fully equipped resort hotel just down the road alongside another important excavation at Ras Ibn Hani.

Early in 1928, a local farmer by the name of Mahmoud Mella az-Zir was ploughing a field overlooking the sea when he unearthed a large flat stone. Carefully prising it loose from the ground, he soon identified it as the entrance to an ancient tomb. He quietly removed a few items and took them to a local antique dealer, but it was inevitable that news of his discovery would leak out. At the time, this area was ruled by the French and they kept a staff of professional archaeologists there for the sole purpose of checking out such finds. According to local legends, the mound of Ras esh-Shamra had once been the site of a great city, and at the deserted bay where Mahmoud Mella az-Zir lived a prosperous harbour had flourished.

Local officials immediately recognized that this site would repay closer attention, and within a year a professional archaeologist had arrived from Strasbourg. This was Claude F. A. Schaeffer, and he began work in March 1929 not far from the shore at the bay of Minet el-Beida. This was some distance away from the large mound, but he realized that this was a discovery of major significance. Purely by accident, he had started digging in the middle of an ancient cemetery, and important objects soon came to light. He could have spent many weeks here, but his curiosity got the better of him and he switched his attention to the remains at Ras esh-Shamra, just a short distance away. When he started work on the mound itself there was very little to be seen, apart from a great crop of fennel (the Arabic name simply means "Head of Fennel"). It was certainly not easy to decide where to start digging, so he began at the highest point, which looked as if it might contain the remains of ancient walls, and which was the place where some locals claimed to have found valuable objects.

In no time at all Schaeffer was unearthing scores of fascinating objects, as well as the remains of ruined buildings. Among the finds were vast numbers of clay tablets inscribed with cuneiform writing. This gave him no cause for surprise, for by the early years of the twentieth century thousands of them had already been unearthed all over the area comprising ancient Mesopotamia and the Egyptian borders. But the writing on these was quite different from anything he had previously encountered. Other texts used hundreds of symbols to record their messages, but these seemed to be written using what looked like an alphabet with not more than about twenty or thirty letters. Charles Virolleaud, who was the director of the Antiquities Service of Syria and Lebanon, and a gifted linguist, was fascinated by these new discoveries and in a remarkably short time he began to decipher the script on the texts. He shared his findings with other scholars in Europe, and by the end of 1930 they had cracked the code of what turned out to be an entirely new language. Quite apart from whatever light these texts may shine on ancient history and culture, they were an important find in relation to understanding how writing had evolved, with their type of cuneiform script written using an alphabetic structure.

By now, Schaeffer was really excited about his discoveries, and in early 1930 he made his way back to the site. This time he had more backup resources, including thirty French soldiers to guard both the site and the experts. Safety could not be taken for granted, as just the previous year another French archaeologist had been murdered in the same area. Once more, he started work around the cemetery, reviewing what he had found the year before and also identifying a large building with many rooms, which subsequently turned out to be part of a tomb for the kings of the nearby city. But the mound held an inexorable fascination for him, especially the area where the tablets were unearthed. By digging a deep pit right through the mound, Schaeffer established that people had lived there as far back as the third millennium BC. In the meantime still more tablets kept turning up, and in several languages that used different types of writing. As well as bearing testimony to the high level of education of the scribes who compiled the texts, the diversity of languages found among them indicated that this had been a city with very extensive international connections. The civic leaders seemed to have been equally at home communicating in Akkadian, Sumerian, or Hurritic, as well as in their own language, which came to be known as Ugaritic. Since these languages all operated with rather different scripts, this level of competence would be the equivalent of someone today being equally at home in English, Arabic, Chinese, and Russian.

As excavations continued, a picture of life in this ancient city was gradually pieced together. But it was the American archaeologist W. F. Albri ht who first speculated that this place may be Ugarit, a city that was mentioned in other sources but up to that time had not been identified. His intuition was soon confirmed as Virolleaud found the name "Ugarit" in many of the texts. With the outbreak of the Second World War in 1939, work came to a standstill when Schaeffer was drafted into the French Navy, though he did return after the war ended and stayed until 1969. The excavations of Ras esh-Shamra are among the most extensive of any town or city related to the Bible, and after almost a century of work at the site a great deal is now known about the life of ancient Ugarit. The most prosperous time for this city was from about 1500 to 1200 BC, and this is the age about which we are best informed.

The city was actually the capital of a small kingdom, with about 200 associated villages scattered over an area of 1,300 square miles. Most of the people were farmers, but with three sea ports there must have been a fishing industry as well. Rich traders from Ugarit certainly owned fleets of ships, and to judge from the size of some of their anchors they must have been large vessels, estimated to have been up to 30 metres long and weighing almost 200 tonnes. Timber was one important product of the area, along with cloth and various metal objects that included carefully crafted jewellery as well as domestic implements and agricultural tools. These were all sold in world markets, transported by sea under the protection of a large Ugaritic navy. The city itself had many large and impressive houses, some of which contain the remains of substantial libraries. The documents discovered here show it to have been a community with great wealth, but it was also a culture with a strong sense of social responsibility. The king took a personal interest in the welfare of the citizens, displaying special concern for widows and orphans and other marginalized people. Religion was important as well, and, next to the royal palace, the temples of Dagan and Ba'al were the largest buildings; the priests who superintended them played an important part in the life of the nation.

All this seems to have disappeared virtually overnight towards the end of the thirteenth century BC. Though Ugarit had survived invasions before (notably by the Hittites in about 1360 BC), when the 'sea peoples' came on the scene they were too powerful to be resisted, and the city and its inhabitants were wiped out not long after 1200 BC. It all happened so swiftly that when they were excavated the ovens in the royal palace turned out to contain the remains of cuneiform tablets that had been in the process of being baked hard when the end came.

Stories of Ba'al from the libraries of Ugarit

In relation to the Bible and its world, the most significant finds at the site of Ugarit are the texts. They were all written in the last hundred years of Ugarit's known history, between about 1300 and 1200 BC, and in a previously unknown language that is now called Ugaritic. Though in appearance Ugaritic is quite different from Hebrew, the two languages have many underlying similarities, not only in relation to particular expressions that are used, but also in terms of their general structure. The similarities are so close that through the study of Ugaritic it has been possible to shed light on some otherwise ambiguous turns of phrase found in the Hebrew Bible, especially in its poetic books such as Psalms, Proverbs, Job, and others. There are some 1,400 texts in all, many of which contain stories of the deities that were worshipped in

Ugarit. In addition, the many religious objects that have also been found here (altars, statues, and so on) provide added insights into how these deities were worshipped. Some of them appear in the Bible, including Ba'al, who was one of the leading characters of the Canaanite pantheon. Others who feature here include El, the chief of the gods, and his female companion Asherah. But Ba'al, the weather god, is undoubtedly the most important, along with his lover Anat, the goddess of love and war.

One of the most important stories about Ba'al recounts an occasion when he was attacked by Mût, the god of barrenness and sterility, who overcame Ba'al and the powers of life and virility, and scattered his body to the four corners of the earth. While El, the father god, was leading the heavenly mourning for his lost son, Anat, the goddess of fertility, went out to take her revenge:

> *She seizes Mût, the son of El,*
> *with the knife she cuts him,*
> *with the shovel she winnows him,*
> *with fire she burns him,*
> *with millstones she grinds him,*
> *on the field she throws him.*
> *The birds eat his remains,*
> *the feathered ones make an end to what is left over.*

Mût subsequently came back to life and fought Ba'al himself in a conflict that was interrupted by the intervention of El, who banished Mût so that Ba'al could once more reign supreme. Ba'al's power was then renewed through his sexual relationship with Anat, and that in turn ensured the fertility of the earth and its inhabitants for another season.

Themes such as power and fertility are familiar from nature-based fertility religions throughout the world. They were of particular importance in Canaan, where agriculture was the mainstay of life, and everything depended on the rains that fell from October to April. When the rains stopped in May, it seemed as if Ba'al was dead and needed to be revived. Some experts have suggested that the story of Ba'al's revival by Anat could have been the high point of an annual autumnal Canaanite New Year festival at which the king and a female temple official acted out the story of Ba'al and Anat, along the lines of the very similar festival in ancient Babylon. There is certainly plenty of evidence to show that sexual activity played a prominent role in Canaanite religious observances, and to engage in it at the right time and place was as much a part of the job of a farmer as the actual operations of sowing the seed and reaping the crops.

Faiths in conflict

Religious practices tend to remain the same over many generations, and though Ugarit had already been destroyed by the time Israel emerged as a separate kingdom in the land, it is likely that the cultural matrix within which the Bible narratives are set was very similar, if not identical, to the sort of lifestyle that can be documented in this city-state. The influence of Canaanite religion is a recurring theme throughout the Hebrew Bible, where it is generally regarded as one of the most subtle threats to the self-identity of the emerging state. The book of Judges makes a direct connection between military defeat and the adoption of Canaanite spirituality, and this is used as an explanation for both success and failure throughout the historical books that follow:

> *The Israelites did what was evil in the sight of the*
> *Lord and worshipped the Ba'als; and they abandoned*
> *the Lord, the God of their ancestors, who had brought*
> *them out of the land of Egypt ... They worshipped Ba'al*
> *and the Astartes. So the anger of the Lord was kindled*
> *against Israel, and he gave them over to plunderers who*
> *plundered them ... and they were in great distress.*
> Judges 2:11–15

All the prophets, from Elijah to Jeremiah, echo the same message: that whenever the people of Israel were defeated it was due to their love for the fertility deities of Palestine.

To people with deep roots in Canaanite culture, it would never have looked like that, of course. We have already noticed how local deities were regularly honoured alongside national gods in both Mesopotamia and Egypt without any perceived conflict of interest. In that sort of environment, it would have seemed only prudent to recognize the importance of the local divinities of Canaan, for they had long experience of controlling the weather and fertility of the fields. The Canaanite city-states had developed an impressive level of economic prosperity through successful agriculture, and if that was a consequence of maintaining the traditional religious observances, then the wise course of action would obviously be to leave well alone by continuing along the same lines. That need not have precluded worship of Yahweh, the God of Moses, as a national patron – but his power was apparently demonstrated through historical events such as the exodus, something that required skills quite different from knowing how to grow crops successfully. To be all-powerful in relation to the semi-nomadic life of the desert provided no guarantee that such power would automatically extend to the rather different style of settled agricultural life in Canaan.

This is exactly the scenario that is depicted throughout the historical accounts of the Hebrew Bible, as the people sought to hold these two religious belief systems in tandem, by recognizing Yahweh as all-powerful but at the same time playing safe and using Canaanite shrines and Canaanite ritual with which to worship him. The extent to which this ambivalence was engrained in Israelite culture can be seen in the way that even leading families, who were otherwise praised as faithful to the worship of Yahweh, could give their children names that would invoke the protection of traditional Canaanite deities. One of the sons of Saul was named Jonathan (meaning "Gift of Yahweh"), while another was Ish-Ba'al (meaning "Man of Ba'al"). In much the same way, the names of Ba'al and Anat were attached to many Israelite towns and villages.

The Bible also offers evidence of the adoption of other distinctive Canaanite religious practices. For example, two stelai discovered at Ugarit provide evidence of ancestor worship. This also features in some Old Testament books, where it is condemned, most notably in the case of King Saul, who made contact with the dead prophet Samuel.[7] But in spite of the disastrous outcome it had for him, the practice must have continued for some considerable time, because Isaiah mentions it and also adds the information that the dead ancestors were referred to as *rephaim*, "shades", which is the same word as was used in Canaanite mythology.[8] Another tradition associated with the dead is something that is described as "weeping for the dead", which was not so much an expression of grief at bereavement as an effort to persuade the gods to bring the dead back to life again. Traces of this can be found in various prophetic books, where again the practice is condemned.[9]

Popular religious practice rarely reflects a pure ideological understanding of a faith, and the history of Christianity offers plenty of examples of local beliefs that in theory cannot be reconciled with Christian theology but which nevertheless have been incorporated into mainstream forms of Christian worship. In many parts of South America, Christian devotion owes more to ancient Inca practices than to anything found in the Bible – just as, in the sixteenth century, some Protestant Reformers based their theology of the church not on the New Testament but on the civic organization of European cities at the time. Some dismiss such developments as syncretism, while others regard them as an essential contextualization of faith into circumstances that are quite different from those originally envisaged in the Bible. The history of ancient Israel displays exactly the same sort of tension between the prophets on the one hand and ordinary worshippers on the other, with the prophets insisting that Yahweh was a God who acted in history and in personal relationships with people and communities, and could therefore never be understood as a nature deity – and indeed was to be regarded as beyond both gender and sexuality. Unlike the traditional Canaanite deities, who tended to act in unpredictable and sometimes capricious ways, they believed that Yahweh acted on the basis of morally established principles that were unchanging, and that appropriate forms of worship therefore had nothing to do with any sort of magical procedure that might be intended to change God's mind about things.

The classic example of this is the story of how Elijah challenged the prophets of Ba'al to a contest that would demonstrate which of these divinities – Yahweh or Ba'al – was truly powerful and could send the rain that was essential for successful crops. Though the Old Testament does not spell out all the details of what might have been involved in this, its description is not at odds with what is known from Canaanite culture, in which drunkenness and sexual activity both played a prominent part. In the ancient world, rain and semen were regarded as similar substances, as both of them produced fruit, and so in the effort to persuade the gods to send the rain that would grow crops it made sense for humans to cajole them into action by their own parallel activity. Many biblical passages condemn such behaviour, and this is also the background against which restrictions on priests drinking alcohol in the course of their duties are to be understood.[10] The Elijah story offers a particularly striking contrast with all this, with its portrayal of the dissolute behaviour of the Ba'al devotees in stark contrast to Elijah's appeal to the ethical faithfulness of Yahweh's commitment to his people.[11]

In a previous chapter we noted how traditional stories from Mesopotamian culture could be used in the Hebrew Bible but then given a meaning different from the ones they originally had. There are many passages in which traditional Canaanite beliefs are given a similar treatment. When Ba'al was revived each spring, his banishment of death was celebrated as his enthronement over the other gods, and in much the same way various psalms use enthronement language to celebrate the power of Yahweh.[12] Moreover, in some passages God's enthronement is specifically connected with the stability and renewal of the natural world. But at this point, a subtle distinction is drawn between Ba'al's accomplishments and the work of Yahweh, who unlike his Canaanite counterpart does not die and revive on a seasonal basis. On the contrary:

The Lord sits enthroned over the flood;
The Lord sits enthroned as king for ever.
Psalm 29:10

Some other aspects of the relationship between Canaanite and Israelite religious practice are less clear cut. For example, the book of Leviticus lays out regulations for an annual ceremony that involves two goats, one of which is sacrificed while the other is sent out into the desert "for Azazel".[13] The precise meaning of "Azazel" is disputed: the word occurs nowhere else in the Hewbrew Bible, and the context here gives no specific indication as to who or what it might be. But later Jewish literature identifies it as some kind of desert demon, and if that is the case this ceremony of the sending of the scapegoat finds an interesting parallel in Ugarit, where two such goats were sent out each year, one for a god and the other for a demon. There is a difference, though, because at Ugarit the process was sexualized through the introduction of a female priest in the ritual.

Everyday life in Israel and Judah

The story of Israel in Canaan is a long one, beginning with the Bible books of Joshua and Judges and ending with Ezra and Nehemiah. More than 700 years separate these two epochs, and the nation underwent many social and political traumas and transformations during that period. The earliest leaders – the judges, whose stories are told in the book of that name – were essentially local heroes who galvanized their people in the face of military threats from other groups who were also trying to establish themselves in the land at the time, most notably the "sea peoples". Their influence lasted only for as long as the military emergency, after which the judges disappear from the narratives.

Saul was the first person to be appointed to a permanent office of king, though not without some dissension and argument between those who wanted "a king to govern us, like the other nations",[14] and those such as Samuel, who would have preferred to perpetuate the old ways. In many respects, Saul continued to operate on the same *ad hoc* basis that the judges had established before him, and in most of the stories he is fully occupied in defending the people against other invaders. His rule lasted for some forty years (1050–1010 BC), but it was only with the accession of his successor David (1010–970 BC) that the trappings of a state began to emerge.

Unlike Saul, David understood the need to consolidate a sense of national unity that would be based on something more substantial than just the popular appeal of a military hero who could mobilize volunteers to fight when the need arose. He established a permanent army, and captured a new city that would be his capital (Jerusalem), which he started to transform through the construction of civic buildings, and drew up plans for a grand temple that would serve to unite the people in one common religious faith. He also created an environment in which his own son would be the most obvious person to succeed him as king. This son was Solomon, and during his reign (970–930 BC) he built up a sophisticated state apparatus that enabled him to extend Israelite control over virtually the whole of Palestine.

The magnificence of Solomon's royal court was legendary, and he also completed the building of the temple. But in order to fund it all, he levied high taxes and even forced some of his own people into a form of slavery. These things, together with his own extravagant lifestyle, created an atmosphere of discontent that boiled over on his death. Though his own son Rehoboam succeeded him on the throne, he was unable to maintain the sense of national unity that had been the secret of his father and grandfather before him, and what had been built up into a significant territorial state was soon weakened as it fractured into two separate kingdoms: Judah (which Rehoboam continued to rule, and which included Jerusalem and its temple) and Israel (the northern part of the original kingdom, where Jeroboam I established his own capital in Samaria).

The two kingdoms soon drifted apart, and some Bible passages imply that they even spoke different languages.[15] Each kingdom had some good times of prosperity, and on occasions they were able to expand their territory. But not for long, as other more powerful empires based in Mesopotamia now began a westward expansion. First it was the Assyrians, who in 721 BC attacked and subjugated the northern kingdom of Israel and cowed Judah into submission. Then the Babylonians came along, and in 586 BC they were responsible for the sacking of Jerusalem and the transportation of its leading citizens into exile in Babylon. The Persian empire subsequently replaced the Babylonians as the major regional superpower, and encouraged the exiles from Judah to return to their homeland, though by this time many of them preferred life outside of Palestine and there was never going to be any likelihood that what had been lost might be restored to its former glory. The dream of what might have been – and could still be in the future – never died, and the fervency with which it was occasionally pursued frequently led the later inhabitants of Palestine into conflict with the empires of Greece and Rome. The social and political realities of all these events will form the subject matter of later chapters in this book. But in spite of many upheavals and uncertainties in national life, the everyday existence of ordinary people underwent remarkably few changes over these years.

Village life

For most of the biblical period, a majority of the population lived in relatively compact villages in the hill country to the east of Palestine. This area had always been popular with wandering semi-nomadic peoples. Between about 1000 and 750 BC there was a rapid expansion of villages here, which was probably due to the cities themselves evolving into centres of civic administration, with more public buildings and consequently less space for the dwellings of ordinary people. These villages were not independent entities, but closely identified themselves with the nearest cities. Joshua 17:11 mentions Beth-shean, Dor, En-dor, Taanach and Megiddo as cities with their own dependent villages in the surrounding countryside, but they would not have been the only ones. In some villages, houses would be arranged in a circle around a central shared space, but in others homes and farmsteads were constructed in a more random fashion.

The remains of many houses have been excavated, and it seems that they were mostly constructed with mud that was shaped into bricks when wet and then baked hard in the sun. A typical house had four rooms on the ground floor, but also a second storey and then, beyond that, a living space on the flat roof. The ceiling of the upper storey typically had a hole in the centre of it, to allow light through to the ground floor from above. The dangers posed by having an open shaft between roof and ground floor are highlighted by building regulations that required a parapet to surround the hole so as to prevent people from accidentally falling through the opening.[16] All these features are mentioned in different Bible stories, some of which also give an idea of the scale of a typical home. When Elisha stayed in a home in Shunem, his bedroom on the upper floor had enough space to accommodate "a bed, a table, a chair, and a lamp".[17] Guests might also sleep on the roof itself, as Saul did when he visited Samuel,[18] though more often the roof seems to have been used as workspace. When the Israelite spies arrived at Rahab's home in Jericho, the drying flax that was on the roof served to conceal them, and also offered them a place to sleep for the night.[19]

Entertaining guests was regarded as a duty, and travellers with nowhere to stay would apparently head for whatever common space was at the heart of a community, and wait there for someone to invite them in, along with any animals they might have with them.[20] The arrival of guests was probably one of the few occasions when meat was eaten as part of a regular meal, and the guests would always be given priority when it came to having the best cuts of meat – a pattern that is well illustrated in the account of Saul's visit to Samuel in 1 Samuel 9:22–24. The offering of hospitality was so deeply engrained as an aspect of Hebrew culture that when a stranger was abused the entire community was prepared to take stringent action to ensure it would never happen again.[21]

The household might comprise several generations, and people would typically be identified not only by reference to their own individual circumstances, but through their parents and grandparents. When the writer of 1 Samuel introduces Saul into the narrative, no fewer than five different generations of his family are mentioned.[22] Though they would not all still have been living at the time, those who were might well have been members of the same extended family group, not necessarily all inhabiting the same house but certainly collaborating in their daily work. In agricultural communities, work is generally shared out among the whole family; ancient Israel was no different in that regard and women as well as men could be found working in the fields.[23]

Just as in other parts of the ancient world, so here all the operations of daily life were marked by regular religious devotions. Archaeological investigations have not unearthed any evidence of public religious shrines in the villages, though that does not mean there were none. The account of how Gideon managed to destroy one such place of worship under cover of darkness without anyone hearing suggests that it was probably some distance away from the houses and located in open land outside the village itself.[24] That story describes such a local shrine as being dedicated to Ba'al and Asherah, and there is no shortage of evidence to demonstrate that the worship of Yahweh was often conflated with the sort of ideology and practices that are well documented from Ugarit. The discovery of substantial numbers of female figures holding their large breasts in their hands points in this direction, and the locations in which they have been found suggest that much religious devotion took place in the home rather than in some public space.

Despite its obvious importance, agriculture would not have been the sole concern of villagers, and there is plenty of evidence from the Bible as well as from archaeological discoveries of many different kinds of craft work. The usefulness of pottery as an aid to dating discoveries was noted in an earlier chapter, and wherever there is pottery there will always be a need for potters to make it. Jeremiah used a visit to a potter's workshop as an occasion to deliver a message about the nation and its future, and in doing so he describes the typical process:

I went down to the potter's house, and there he was
working at his wheel. The vessel he was making of clay
was spoiled in the potter's hand, and he reworked it into
another vessel.
Jeremiah 18:3–4

Other items that have been unearthed in large quantities include bits of machinery that must have been used for weaving, particularly spindles and heavy weights with holes through the middle which were used to tension the threads. Metalworking is another trade that must have been widely practised, though in the early period the level of skill was of an insufficiently high standard for native workers to be employed in the construction of the temple, and metalworkers were brought in from elsewhere.[25] The same seems to have been the case with work in wood and stone, for which both David and Solomon commissioned non-Israelites – from Phoenicia in the case of stonemasons,[26] and Tyre for woodworking.[27] By the time the temple needed some repairs, however, it seems that these techniques had been mastered in Israel and there was no longer any need to import experts from outside.[28]

The village gate regularly features as the place where commercial transactions would be carried out[29], and where the elders would meet to discuss village business and also to act as a court of appeal for matters that could not be resolved within the family circle. Whether all this happened literally at the gate that was the entrance to the village, or whether 'the gate' was used as a technical term to indicate the location where such formalities took place, is not altogether certain.

City living

Whereas the earlier city-states of Canaan had in effect been urban sites supported by their own agricultural output, by the time of the earliest Israelite kings the nature of city living was starting to undergo a number of substantial changes. The single most important catalyst for change was the development of a system of taxation that would allow produce from the country to be distributed to city-dwellers who no longer grew their own food, but now worked as full-time officials, administrators, and military officers. It was the rejection or questioning of these bureaucratic functions that led to the division of the kingdom following Solomon's rule, though that hardly prevented their continued rapid development, and the century or so after that saw a massive expansion of the power of the state with cities predominantly becoming centres of government rather than homes for the masses. City populations shrank as a result, and those who moved out generally settled in the villages, where they then worked to produce the goods that would support the rather more leisurely life of city-dwellers.

Safeguarding Jerusalem's water supply

The cities that emerged at this time exhibit many advanced architectural features such as elaborate water systems, as well as more basic structures such as strong fortifications and government offices. Actually, the water systems were themselves integral to the defence of a city. A well-constructed water system could ensure that at a time of siege the inhabitants would maintain a secure supply, though the tunnels and passageways through which water was brought into a city could also provide a clandestine entry point for determined invaders.

Jerusalem itself is a good example. It was built on an enormous rock, which in itself guaranteed a high level of security and made it virtually impregnable except for the fact that the water supply was at the foot of the rock, outside the main fortifications. Even before Jerusalem became the capital of Israel (then later of Judah), its original Jebusite inhabitants had constructed a secret internal water shaft to give them easier access to the springs that would be vital for the city's ability to sustain a long siege. But when David captured the city for himself, he and his troops gained access by climbing up this same water shaft (2 Samuel 5:6–10). At a much later time, Hezekiah (king of Judah 715–687 BC) strengthened Jerusalem's security by blocking up many of the existing water channels and constructing a new access tunnel to bring water into the city (2 Kings 20:20). As long ago as the Middle Ages, pilgrims to Jerusalem had known there was some connection between the Pool of Siloam, at the south-eastern corner of the old city, and the Spring of Gihon, that lies beyond the walls, but the exact location of the tunnel between the two came to light only in 1880. Two young boys were swimming in the Pool of Siloam when one of them found himself in a small passage leading out from the sheer rock face. Further investigation revealed that a narrow tunnel had been cut through the solid limestone, barely large enough for an adult to squeeze through. For some 5 kilometres the passage winds its way upwards, carrying water into the city from the Spring of Gihon to the Pool of Siloam.

But there was more, for just a few yards from the Siloam entrance was an inscription scratched on the tunnel walls, written in Hebrew. This records how the tunnel was constructed in the space of about six to nine months, and graphically describes the excitement of workers digging through from each direction, who could hear the scraping and hammering of those on the other side and eventually broke through to meet in the middle. These words were inscribed by Hezekiah's workers, who must have had considerable stamina, as they were excavating in almost total blackness and with very little air. They were also digging in an S shape and through solid rock, and their achievement was all the more remarkable given that they had no magnetic instruments to point them in the direction that would ensure they met in the middle. The kingdom may have been short of stonemasons, but the ability to carve through solid rock is well attested from the very earliest times, with many large water storage cisterns and even burial chambers being constructed using the same techniques.

While much effort was put into collecting water for the use of city-dwellers, there was no corresponding concern for the disposal of sewage, and more than one Bible passage refers to "the mire of the streets",[30] while Zechariah mentions streets heaped up with dirt[31] that could often become a sea of mud.[32] There is no evidence from the period of the Israelite kingdoms of the widespread use of specially designated toilet facilities, though some remains have been unearthed in what were obviously upper-class residences in Jerusalem. But the spread of infection must have been an ever-present danger. The book of Leviticus includes regulations for the hygienic disposal of human excrement by burial outside the boundaries of the inhabited land,[33] but that would have been easier to do in the villages than in the cities. Burial of the waste was not a universal practice, however, and there are references to it being spread on the ground.[34]

City houses for ordinary people were constructed on a similar pattern to homes in the villages, with four-room houses being the norm. Unlike the villages, cities were generally completely surrounded by fortified walls, which required the space inside them to be better designed than in the villages.

A widely used form of city-wall construction was the casemate, which consisted of two walls, one inside the other, and joined at intervals with other walls running perpendicularly between the inner and outer ones. This created spaces within the walls themselves which might be used as storage facilities, though in some places a further ring of housing was then built alongside the inner wall, with the space between the two city walls being occupied by the back rooms of a house. Rahab's home in Jericho was apparently of this sort of construction,[35] and evidence of the same design in an Israelite city has been unearthed at Beer-sheba.

A major element of the population in the cities would be administrators and judicial officers of one sort or another. Lists of these functionaries in the days of David and Solomon mention a wide diversity of positions,[36] though in addition to these servants of the royal court there would be city elders who operated in much the same way as the village elders. Those who were not employed in the service of the state no doubt followed the same trades as their counterparts in the villages, though city life also offered other opportunities for the growth of service industries. Bakeries could flourish where there was a large enough population base, and Jeremiah mentions an entire street full of them in Jerusalem.[37] Bread was a staple in the diet, and was baked either on a tray over an open fire[38] or in an enclosed oven;[39] the remains of both methods have been unearthed by archaeologists. Isaiah[40] mentions a location called "Fuller's Field", which probably implies that there was also a laundry service in the city. But in spite of such new business opportunities, the expansion of city life inevitably led to social inequalities, and the growing gulf between rich and poor provides the background to the work of many of the biblical prophets. Isaiah[41] and Jeremiah[42] both highlight the extravagant lifestyle of the bureaucrats, while Amos[43] provides plenty of evidence that this sort of exploitation was by no means limited to the southern kingdom of Judah but was just as easy to find in the northern kingdom of Israel.

For the ruling classes, trade was the most important aspect of city life, especially international trade, which had the capacity not only to bring in much-needed revenue but also to enhance the standing of the kings of Israel and Judah in the wider world. The stories of Solomon's reign focus almost exclusively on his international connections: the trade in horses and chariots that he carried on through Egypt,[44] the fleet he kept at the Red Sea port of Ezion-geber,[45] the many wives of different nationalities whom he married,[46] and his growing reputation for wisdom, which brought the queen of Sheba to his door.[47] In view of the level of international trade that it generated, even the building of the temple can be seen as a part of his quest for international recognition.

It is certainly the case that Solomon's fascination with the culture of other nations provokes regular criticism of him in the historical books of the Bible. In particular, his harem of a thousand or more women is regarded as a source of alien spirituality and false religious practices.[48] But he was not the only one. Jeroboam I, king of the northern kingdom of Israel (930–910 BC) is condemned for creating his own centres of worship at Bethel and Dan, where he placed golden calves similar to the Canaanite symbol of Ba'al.[49] Ahab comes in for the same sort of criticism,[50] as do most of the rulers of the northern kingdom. Not that the later kings of Judah were any different, and Ahaz (735–715 BC) and Manasseh (687–642) both installed Assyrian religious icons in the temple in Jerusalem. The regular devotions that formed part of home life in the cities as well as the villages followed a similar syncretistic pattern. Jeremiah complained that "The children gather wood, the fathers kindle fire, and the women knead dough to make cakes for the queen of heaven; and they pour out drink-offerings to other gods".[51]

Culture

Leisure would not have been a meaningful concept to anyone in the ancient world. People were fully occupied with the business of running their lives, working hard enough to sustain themselves and their families. But artistic pursuits still played an important part in the life of the Israelite and Judahite nations.

Music and dance were especially important. In spite of its overwhelmingly cynical tone, the book of Ecclesiastes identifies dance as a regular activity that is as much a part of everyday life as birth and death, love and hate, war and peace.[52] But it was also a regular feature of temple worship in Jerusalem, where its highly developed state can be judged from the surprisingly large number of technical choreographic terms that are used to describe it. The book of Psalms, which in many respects comprises the liturgies for worship at the temple in Jerusalem, has many references to musical terminology, as well as naming various guilds of professional musicians. This is another example of the way in which practices from the culture of Canaan could be adopted, but also intentionally reinterpreted so as to have a different connotation. Virtually all references to dancing that can be found in the Hebrew Bible occur in the context of worship – to such an extent that when worship is mentioned without specific reference to dancing, its presence can almost certainly be taken for granted. The two activities were so closely identified that the same Hebrew word (*gil*) could mean both "rejoice" and "dance".

Significantly, the sort of dance that is described in this context is not performance by experts but a celebratory event that can be shared by the whole community. Examples of such occasions can be found in the dance of Miriam after the slaves from Egypt escaped their pursuers,[53] and in the celebration of Jephthah's victory over the Ammonites[54] or of the achievements of Saul and David.[55] But dance on national occasions was not limited to military successes. David, for instance, was "whirling before Yahweh with all his might" when the ark of the covenant entered Jerusalem.[56] Dance also features in a context of personal and family celebration,[57] as well as being an integral part of the spirituality of the prophets.[58]

But by far the most extensive collection of materials relates to dance as a part of regular temple worship, which as described in the book of Psalms was very much a multimedia experience. Music played a very prominent part,[59] often combined with movement, both individual[60] and corporate,[61] and there are also references to choirs[62] and the playing of a highly diverse collection of musical instruments: tambourines, harps, lyres, trumpets, rattles, horns, flutes, cymbals.[63] Singing itself often appears as a dramatic performance.[64]

There are references to free dance, sometimes connected to specific themes such as forgiveness and thanksgiving,[65] though more often of a general nature.[66] But many more passages provide directions for processional movement of one sort or another,[67] including examples of community dance that used props and took place inside the temple courts around its various altars.[68] Dance could also feature as a form of symbolic re-enactment of key aspects of Israel's beliefs, and a favourite theme in this connection was the celebration of creation.[69] Psalm 68 offers an especially detailed example of this, with elaborate descriptions of a procession with the ark of the covenant, and the celebration of Yahweh's enthronement in the temple. The connection of these themes with Canaanite spirituality has already been noted, and some of these psalms are similar to religious songs and dances found at places like Ugarit, though in the Hebrew Bible they are always contextualized so as to become vehicles for the celebration of Israel's own distinctive faith.

Other passages show historical events being celebrated in the same way (e.g. Passover[70]), and the Feast of Tabernacles came to have a particularly strong association with music and dance. As the annual harvest festival, it is no surprise that the Feast of Tabernacles should have been characterized by great exuberance in worship, and dance was so central to this occasion that it survived in Jewish celebrations well into the Christian era. The rabbis of a much later period describe it in surprisingly animated terms:

> *It was said that the gladness there was above everything.*
> *Pious men danced with torches in their hands and sang*
> *songs of joy and praise, while the Levites played all sorts*
> *of instruments. The dance drew crowds of spectators for*
> *whom grandstands had been erected. It did not end until*
> *the morning at a given sign, when water from the spring*
> *of Shiloh was poured over the altar.*
> **Mishna Sukka IV.9**

Drama also finds a place in Israelite culture, especially in the work of the prophets, who used it to great effect in getting their message over to people who otherwise might not have been inclined to pay much attention to them. Ezekiel is one of the most obvious examples of this, though he generally preferred mime, for the simple reason that he was dumb for much of his ministry.[71] On one occasion he took a clay brick on which he sketched the city of Jerusalem and then, using it as a model, he acted out a military attack on the city, finally covering it with an iron pan or plate to illustrate its remoteness from God.[72] On other occasions he got his message across by laying down on the ground tied up in strong ropes like an escapologist,[73] or shaving himself with a sword instead of a razor, then ostentatiously weighing his hair before burning some of it.[74] Jeremiah orchestrated similar sorts of dramatic performance, using props that could include loincloths,[75] pottery,[76] goblets of wine,[77] stones,[78] and scrolls.[79] The use of drama in worship can also be documented in Psalm 149:6–9, which describes worshippers taking a two-edged sword and symbolically re-enacting God's victories over their enemies. Given the complexity of some of these performances, they must have been carefully choreographed and rehearsed, and some Bible passages provide evidence of that.[80]

Visual arts are less well represented. The first of the Ten Commandments specifically prohibited the making of "graven images",[81] and by the beginning of the Christian era that had become a regular source of contention between Jewish people and the Greeks and Romans, who at that time controlled the Mediterranean area. But there is evidence of statues and elaborate carvings from both archaeological finds and the Hebrew Bible itself. Mention has already been made of the many small figures of what looks like a fertility goddess, holding enlarged breasts out in her hands, and also of the bull statues placed in Bethel and Dan by Jeroboam I of Israel. Small statues of horses have also been unearthed, and the use of these to adorn public buildings is attested in 2 Kings 23:11, when Josiah as part of his reformation of temple practices "removed the horses that the kings of Judah had dedicated to the sun". Some equine statues do indeed show a horse on whose head is a disc that could be taken to represent the sun.

A more common use of modelling skills is reflected in the large amount of carved ivory that has been recovered, dating from the period of the Israelite kings. Here again, there are many mentions of this in the Bible itself. Ahab, king of Israel (874–852 BC), constructed an "ivory house",[82] and at an earlier period Amos complained about "those who lie on beds of ivory",[83] and referred to "houses of ivory",[84] as also does Psalm 45:8. A love of ivory ornamentation was not, however, restricted to the northern kingdom: Solomon himself is said to have constructed for himself "a great ivory throne and overlaid it with the finest gold".[85]

Writing is much harder to find archaeological evidence for in the period of the kingdoms of Judah and Israel, no doubt because some of the materials that were in common use were not very durable. The Bible mentions Solomon having his own official archivists who recorded the events of his reign,[86] and it is widely believed that much of the material now incorporated into the narratives of Samuel, Saul, and David was first written down at this time. The development of highly structured bureaucratic processes for the collection of taxes and the promotion of international trade would also never have taken place had there not been considerable numbers of professional scribes available.

The books of Kings make repeated references to written sources that were consulted in the process of their own composition, and virtually all of the kings of Judah and Israel are referred to as having had their own official archives. The *Book of Jashar* is an earlier source referred to in Joshua 10:13 and 2 Samuel 1:18, along with another one called the *Book of the Wars of Yahweh*.[87] None of these has survived independently of those sections of them which may now be included or quoted from in the Hebrew Bible. But there is evidence to suggest that, while universal literacy is unlikely, reading and writing were not skills that were limited to the upper classes.

One of the earliest known examples of writing in Hebrew is on a piece of limestone that is called the Gezer Calendar, which dates from about 925 BC. This is widely believed to represent an exercise that was copied by someone who was learning to write. From later periods, there are many examples of writing on stones or broken pottery, and the re-use of such material is very much the sort of thing that one can imagine ordinary individuals (as distinct from official record-keepers) doing.

5

The Age of Empires

The story of the kingdom of Israel did not happen in a political vacuum, and the reign of Solomon (970–930 BC) was the only time when any Israelite ruler can be said to have been in full control of the nation and its destiny. Following the division of the nation into two separate political entities, the kings of Israel and Judah were no longer able to retain all the territory that David and Solomon ruled. The province of Aram (based on Damascus) had already broken free during Solomon's reign. It soon became a serious rival to both Israel and Judah, and frequently invaded the Israelite territory to the east of the River Jordan. All but one of the Philistine city-states also regained their freedom from Judah, though by this time they were no longer a military threat. The Ammonites also saw an opportunity to free themselves from Israelite rule, and the Moabites probably did the same. Judah fared slightly better than Israel, and still retained some kind of control over the trade routes through the Gulf of Aqaba in the south. But neither of them by itself was ever going to be strong enough to survive without forming alliances with neighbouring states.

For eighty years under David and Solomon, a united Israel had been the major power-broker in the area, but from now on Israel and Judah were never going to be anything other than pawns in the political games of the superpowers based in Egypt and Mesopotamia. Egypt was the first one to try to re-establish its control of Palestine, and within five years of

Israel's division Shoshenk I (945–924 BC) invaded much of the land. The Hebrew Bible records that Rehoboam, king of Judah, managed to prevent him from attacking Jerusalem only by offering him a considerable amount of treasure.[1] This strategy appears to have worked, for in an inscription in the temple of Amun at Thebes, Shoshenk makes no mention of towns in Judah being captured, though he does claim to have overrun a number of places in Israel. His temple inscription mentions one location called "the Field of Abram", which is the only reference outside the Bible to connect a person of that name with Palestine.

The fact that Israel and Judah were also at war with each other for something like fifty years in a struggle to control the border territory that separated them just north of Jerusalem hardly improved their chances of being able to repel invaders from outside.[2] Israel's rulers had more political awareness than those in Judah, and some of them managed to restore the fortunes of their nation. Omri (880–874 BC) and his son Ahab (874–852 BC) succeeded in making peace not only with Judah but also with the Phoenicians of Tyre. In each case this was accomplished through marriage alliances, with Ahab himself marrying a Phoenician princess named Jezebel,[3] while his daughter Athaliah married Jehoram, king of Judah (851–842 BC). A stele constructed by Mesha, king of Moab, provides some evidence of Omri's expansionist policies, with its note that "Omri, king of Israel, humbled Moab for many years". Such territorial successes did not last long, however, and by the time of Ahab's death the nation was already facing a far more formidable challenge than any seen so far.

Assyria

The story of Assyria's influence in northern Mesopotamia can be traced as far back as the third millennium BC. But it was only in the ninth century BC that it seized the opportunity to expand beyond its homeland westwards into Palestine. It is not hard to understand the attraction of such a move. The area maintained its strategic importance for international trade, but in the tenth century BC it had also experienced a remarkable renaissance of urban life, with the burgeoning of artistic and cultural activities as well as a high degree of economic success. At the same time, the fierce competitiveness of the various local city-states meant that no long-lasting collaboration between them was ever going to be likely, though they could on occasion band together to repel invaders. Eventually, in 853 BC, the Assyrian king, Shalmaneser III marched into Palestine where the battle of Qarqar ensued with a Syrian-led coalition finally quashing the Assyrian assault.

The battle of Qarqar: the Assyrian advance is stopped

The need for Assyria to expand beyond its home into Palestine first arose during the reign of Ahab, when in 853 BC the Assyrian Shalmaneser III (859–824 BC) crossed the Euphrates and marched westward. The king of Damascus brought together an informal alliance to fight the Assyrians, and one of his partners was Ahab himself. The Syrian-led coalition met the Assyrians in battle at Qarqar, just to the north of the city of Hamath, which was one of the allies whose security was most immediately threatened by the advancing armies. Shalmaneser III was repelled, and in his own account of the battle he lists the various nations who were arraigned against him, including Ahab who is described as "the Israelite". Israel's significance at this time can be judged from the fact that Ahab is said to have provided 2,000 chariots, which was more than Damascus and Hamath put together, along with 10,000 troops (the same as Hamath, but only half as many as Damascus supplied). These numbers suggest that while Israel may have had a smaller population than some of its neighbours, it was much richer in material resources.

Israel under siege

However, the coalition of Palestinian states hardly outlived the battle of Qarqar. In no time at all local skirmishes between them were breaking out once more. This was almost an open invitation to Shalmaneser to return, which he did in 841 BC. This time he was able to move systematically through the entire region. Although his earlier incursion had ended in an enormous pitched battle, with something like 50,000 troops on each side, the Assyrians generally tried to avoid such large-scale confrontations. Their preferred strategy was to intimidate others, hoping that the mere sight of their own large army would scare them into voluntary submission. If that failed to work, the unfortified villages would be attacked and their people slaughtered, quite often having their torsos or heads hung up to show what would happen to the cities if they failed to capitulate. Entire settlements would be burned to the ground and their fields filled with salt to render them infertile. If the major city of the region was still resistant, then a siege was the next tactic, though that would typically involve an extended period of verbal appeals to the people to surrender, and breaking down the city walls was always the final resort.

The Assyrian kings all kept meticulous records of their military exploits, and Shalmaneser was no exception. He describes in considerable detail how Damascus was besieged, while Phoenicia and Israel both paid tribute to avoid their own cities being attacked. The account of all this is contained on an obelisk made of black limestone, and it tells how Jehu, who by now was king of Israel (842–815 BC), capitulated before the advancing Assyrian army. The inscription lists the gifts he presented to Shalmaneser:

> *Tribute of Jehu, son of Omri. I received from him: silver, gold, a golden bowl, a golden beaker, golden goblets, pitchers of gold, lead, staves for the hand of the king, javelins.*

The nature of these offerings bears eloquent testimony to the relative wealth of Israel at this time. But the most interesting aspect of Shalmaneser's monument in relation to the Bible is that it has a picture of Jehu bowing low as the gifts are brought out. This line drawing is the only known contemporary depiction of any Israelite person named in the Hebrew Bible. Assyria never made any effort to incorporate these conquered lands into its own territory, and the major motivation for these periodic raids seems to have been economic. Provided that the surrounding states did not threaten Assyria's long-term interests and handed over goods when they were required to do so, they were largely left to their own devices.

After Shalmaneser's death, Assyria had its own brief period of internal political conflicts, which ensured that his immediate successors paid less attention to what was going on in Palestine. This created a space in which the local rivalries could surface once more, and under Jehu's son Jehoahaz (king of Israel 815–801 BC), Israel became virtually a province of Damascus,[4] whose king Hazael also invaded Judah and was dissuaded from attacking Jerusalem only when Joash (king of Judah 837–800 BC) offered to give him part of the temple treasure.[5]

But it was not long before Assyria was back again, and this time with a more carefully developed strategy to expand its own influence through the intentional creation of an empire. Tiglath-Pileser III (745–727 BC) was the mastermind behind all this. He reorganized the internal structure of his kingdom, and established a formidable professional army in which native Assyrians would occupy the elite roles of chariot drivers and horse-riders, while the foot soldiers would largely consist of conscripts brought from the territories that were conquered. Tiglath-Pileser's strategy for expansion was simple. Those local rulers who were prepared to collaborate by volunteering to pay annual tribute to Assyria would be left in place. Those who resisted would in the first instance be deposed and replaced by another local ruler who was regarded as more amenable to Assyrian rule. But if that was not possible, the territory would be taken over in its entirety and turned into an Assyrian province with its own governor. In order to minimize the possibility of further revolution in the future, this final process of incorporating land into the empire often involved the forcible removal of significant numbers of the population and their resettlement in places closer to the Assyrian heartlands in northern Mesopotamia.

All these stages can be traced in the dealings of Assyria with Israel and Judah. The first mention of an Israelite encounter with Assyria is during the reign of Menahem (745–738 BC), who volunteered to pay tribute.[6] His son Pekahiah reigned for only two years before he was assassinated by an anti-Assyrian revolt led by Pekah (king of Israel 737–732 BC). Pekah in turn went on to form a new alliance against the Assyrians with Rezin, king of Syria. They tried to persuade Jotham (king of Judah

742–735 BC) to join them, but he refused, and when a new king came to power in Jerusalem they declared war on Judah. This new king was Ahaz (735–715 BC), who was alarmed by the prospect of an Assyrian attack and sought advice from the prophet Isaiah. Isaiah recommended that Ahaz should exercise a little patience, as the coalition between Syria and Israel could not last for long,[7] but the king ignored that and appealed directly to Assyria for support against Israel and Damascus. In response, the Assyrians attacked Damascus, killed Rezin and deported some of his people.[8] At the same time (734 BC), the most northerly parts of Israel's territory were taken over as Assyrian provinces, as a result of which Pekah was assassinated by his own people and succeeded by Hoshea, who was more inclined to accept Assyrian domination.[9] His subservience lasted only for a very short time before Hoshea decided to revolt and even tried to persuade Egypt to join an anti-Assyrian coalition.[10] By this time Tiglath-Pileser III was dead and his successor Shalmaneser V (727–722 BC) besieged Samaria. He lived just long enough to see it fall into his hands, and he was succeeded by Sargon II, who made Israel into the Assyrian province of Samaria. Following the pattern established under Tiglath-Pileser III, he set about repopulating it with people who would be more amenable to Assyrian rule, and as part of this process he reports that he removed 27,290 Israelite people, who were sent to live in northern parts of Mesopotamia. Once there, all trace of them disappeared from the historical record and they became known as the ten lost tribes of Israel.

Assyria and Judah

This was not the end of Assyrian involvement in Palestine. But Sargon's energies were soon diverted by challenges to his authority closer to home: from Urartu in the north, Babylon in the south, and Elam to the south-east. Once again the Palestinian city-states seized the opportunity to try to reassert their independence, and this time the axis of opposition was an unlikely coalition headed by an alliance between Egypt and four of the five Philistine city-states (Ekron being the odd one out). By now, Ahaz's son Hezekiah was king of Judah (715–687 BC), and he was warned against joining them by Isaiah, who in a dramatic intervention took off all his clothes and walked naked round the streets of Jerusalem in what was declared to be "a sign and a portent against Egypt and Ethiopia":

So shall the king of Assyria lead away the Egyptians as captives and the Ethiopians as exiles, both the young and the old, naked and barefoot, with buttocks uncovered, to the shame of Egypt.
Isaiah 20:3–4

Hezekiah heeded Isaiah's warning, but continued to build up his own country, with the construction of new defences in Jerusalem and elsewhere.[11] He also restructured his army and civil service,[12] and it was at this time that the Siloam Tunnel was built to safeguard Jerusalem's water supply.

In 705 BC Sargon was killed in battle and his body was never recovered, something that dealt a serious blow to Assyrian self-confidence and also provoked the emergence of yet another anti-Assyrian coalition in Palestine. This time Hezekiah was a major player, and even conspired to undermine the position of the Philistine king of Ekron, who still refused to join the revolt. Sargon's successor, Sennacherib, describes all this plotting in his annals: "The officials, the politicians, and the people of Ekron, had thrown Padi, their king, into fetters ... and handed him over to Hezekiah the Jew."

Predictably, it was only a matter of time before Sennacherib took action. Hezekiah's partners capitulated almost immediately, and Shalmaneser moved against Jerusalem using the same tactics to scare and humiliate the people as Tiglath-Pileser III had adopted against the northern kingdom twenty years before. By the time the Assyrians moved in on Jerusalem, Hezekiah was faced with a situation from which there could be no escape. By this time Sennacherib's army had established its front line in the city of Lachish. The siege and capture of this city was obviously important to Sennacherib, as it is depicted on the walls of a room in his palace in Nineveh – a room that was guarded by a whole series of statues of bulls with wings and heads like human persons, a feature that is generally a sign of an especially important part of the building. One section of the inscription provides yet another contemporary image of what ancient Judahites looked like. In line drawings of families leaving the city, the women wear long dresses and an extensive head-covering, while the men have a tunic down to their knees, with a belt round the middle and a headdress wrapped round the head.

Hezekiah realized that there was no chance of his being able to resist Sennacherib's advance, and decided to redeem the situation by paying a huge amount of tribute in the form of large quantities of gold and silver sent to the Assyrians in Lachish. The Assyrian annals – this time preserved on a large clay cylinder – tell the story from Sennacherib's perspective:

> *As to Hezekiah the Jew, he did not submit to my yoke.*
> *I laid siege to forty-six of his strong cities, to walled*
> *forts and to countless small villages in the vicinity and*
> *conquered them by means of well-stamped earth-ramps*
> *and battering-rams brought thus near to the walls.*

*... Himself I made a prisoner in Jerusalem, his royal
residence, like a bird in a cage. I surrounded him with
earthworks in order to molest those who were leaving his
city's gate ... I reduced his country but I still increased
the tribute and the presents due to me as his overlord
which I imposed upon him beyond his former tribute to be
delivered annually.*

All that took place in 701 BC, but Sennacherib's attention soon
had to turn once more to what was happening on his own
doorstep, this time in Babylon. The remaining years of his
reign were spent dealing with one insurgency after another,
with multiple upheavals in Babylon itself as well as attacks from
outside by the Elamites and Chaldeans. He died in Babylon in
681 BC, and was succeeded by his son Esarhaddon, who set
about the reconstruction of Babylon and in an effort to defuse
further opposition tried to present himself as the legitimate
ruler of both northern and southern Mesopotamia. Within
little more than five years, he had restored the semblance
of order to his realm, though his plan to unite Assyria and
Babylon under one monarchy can hardly have succeeded, as
he nominated two of his sons to succeed him as kings of the
two separate kingdoms. But even as an old man, he still had
hopes of regaining the massive empire of Tiglath-Pileser's day.
Egypt remained an attractive prize, not only because of its
obvious wealth but also because of its continuing subversive
influence throughout Palestine.

Esarhaddon died while on the way to Egypt, and the effort
to take it passed to Ashurbanipal, the son who succeeded him
as king of Assyria (669–627 BC). He finally managed to crush
Egypt and captured its capital city Thebes, but his victory was
short lived and his attention was diverted by civil war between

his own new capital, Nineveh, and Babylon, which was now ruled over by his brother Shamash-shum-ukin. Though Ashurbanipal was victorious in that struggle as well, he was not primarily a great warrior. By the end of his reign, the Assyrian empire was finished, the victim of its own success, and brought to an end by internal insecurities. Once Babylon started flexing its muscles, the weakness of the Assyrian policy of deporting large numbers of people from one place to another was exposed, because it ensured that large sections of the population would feel only minimal loyalty to the Assyrian state and had no hesitation about changing their allegiances. The empire collapsed almost overnight when Nineveh was overrun by a coalition of Medes and Babylonians in 612 BC.

Despatches from a beleaguered city

In the Bible the last days of Judah are depicted vividly in the book of Jeremiah, where the prophet's message reflects the disarray and confusion of the people when they could see the Babylonians coming and yet knew they were powerless to do anything about it. The twenty-one letters which were found at Lachish were written on scraps of broken pottery and were found in a location that is believed to have been the guardroom of the city gate in Lachish. Not all of them are now legible, but the majority of those that are were addressed to a man named Ya'osh, who seems to have been the military commander in charge of the city at the time. Many of the messages were written by someone called Hosha'yahu, who was the officer in charge of a military outpost to the north of Lachish. The same name is found in Jeremiah (4:1; 43:2), though there is no way of knowing whether the two sources refer to the same person. The name Jeremiah also occurs in two of the letters, though again it is not possible to make a precise identification of this person with the biblical prophet. There is, though, a clear reference to someone who is called simply "the prophet" in at least two of these letters, and the same term may also be found in a further two. Someone who could be referred to in this way with no further explanation must have been a high-profile public figure, and it is at least possible that this could have been Jeremiah himself.

Whatever the truth about that, the letters do provide a fascinating insight into the same situations as were described by Jeremiah. In Jeremiah 34:1–7, for example, there is a report of a message given by Jeremiah to Zedekiah while Nebuchadnezzar's forces were moving against Jerusalem, and at the time "the army was also attacking Lachish and Azekah, the only other fortified cities left in Judah" (Jeremiah 34:7). Azekah was almost halfway between Lachish and Jerusalem, and in one of the pieces of pottery from Lachish, a man named Hosha'yahu writes that "we are watching for the signals from Lachish ... for we cannot see Azekah". Azekah, perhaps midway between Hosha'yahu's post and Lachish, was being used as a signalling station, which at the time of writing had apparently fallen to the Babylonians.

These letters have been the subject of many fanciful speculations, including the notion that they somehow provide evidence to support an ancient origin for the *Book of Mormon*. But their most obvious value is to be found in the insights they offer into the fear of the people of Judah as they faced the inevitable end of their nation at the hands of the Babylonian army.

Babylon

In the aftermath of the fall of Nineveh, the Assyrians fought desperately to hang on to the fragmented remnants of their once great empire. They made one last desperate attempt to re-establish themselves at Haran, and at this time their old enemies the Egyptians came to their aid. On his accession in 610 BC, the twenty-sixth-dynasty pharaoh Necho II was forced to reassess his foreign policy in light of the upheavals that were taking place throughout Mesopotamia. He realized that his real rival was now no longer the king of Assyria but Nabopolassar, king of Babylon (625–605 BC). For some reason that is never clarified, Josiah (king of Judah 640–609 BC) decided to try to stop the Egyptians as they marched north through Palestine in support of the beleaguered Assyrian army. His effort was unsuccessful, and Josiah died in the ensuing battle at Megiddo. The sense of loss that swept the nation can be judged from the fact that a poem mourning his death was still being repeated centuries later as part of the regular liturgy for worship.[13]

After that, Judah was dominated by Egypt for a while, but nothing was going to halt the advance of the Babylonians. Four years after the collapse of Assyria the Babylonian army met the Egyptians in a fierce battle at Carchemish in north Syria, following which Egyptian influence in Palestine was replaced by that of Babylon. This victory was the work of Nebuchadnezzar, son of Nabopolassar, who died while Nebuchadnezzar was at the battle. He succeeded his father as king that same year, and four years later was back on the borders of Egypt itself to complete the task started at Carchemish. There were large numbers of casualties on both sides. When Jehoiakim (king of Judah 609–598 BC) heard this, he mistakenly imagined that Babylon was finished, and took the opportunity to withhold tribute. When the Egyptians again sent a military force towards Judah, Nebuchadnezzar moved in strength through the whole of Palestine, and besieged Jerusalem with his army, banishing the Egyptians in the process. Jehoiakim died during the course of the siege, and his son Jehoiachin succeeded him and promptly surrendered to Nebuchadnezzar. Following the precedent set by the Assyrians, Nebuchadnezzar took Jehoiachin into exile in Babylon, along with many of the leading citizens and a large quantity of the treasures from both palace and temple.

Nebuchadnezzar in Jerusalem

Zedekiah was appointed ruler of Judah, with the expectation that he would be loyal to Babylon. But he could not resist the temptation to toy once again with the possibility that the Egyptians might successfully repel Nebuchadnezzar's forces. It was inevitable that the Babylonian army would move in once more, and after a siege of eighteen months the city of Jerusalem fell to Nebuchadnezzar in 586 BC. This time the Babylonians made sure there would be no more resistance by systematically destroying all the main buildings in Jerusalem, including the temple. Judah became a Babylonian province, and a bureaucrat by the name of Gedaliah was named as governor.

Glory and decline

Unlike the Assyrians, who produced detailed accounts of everything they did, the Babylonians left only scanty information about their exploits. But it is obvious that Nebuchadnezzar's reign was the heyday of Babylonian power. The grandeur of his city was renowned throughout the ancient world, as evidenced by the hallowed tones in which the fifth-century BC Greek historian Herodotus described it:

*Assyria possesses a vast number of great cities, whereof the
most renowned and strongest at this time was Babylon
… The city stands on a broad plain, and is an exact
square, 120 furlongs in length each way, so that the
entire circuit is 480 furlongs. While such is its size, in
magnificence there is no other city that approaches to it.
It is surrounded, in the first place, by a broad and deep
moat, full of water, behind which rises a wall 50 royal
cubits in width, and 200 in height.*

Herodotus, The History of the Persian Wars 1.178

Nebuchadnezzar was personally responsible for many grand building projects, and his hanging gardens were one of the seven wonders of the ancient world, laid out in about 600 BC as a reminder for his wife Amytis of her homeland in Media. He evidently had a grand design for the city that would portray it as being the centre of the universe, and a location that was the very epitome of order in a world of chaos, thereby creating not only a place of beauty but a spiritual haven whose citizens would have a constant reminder of the key themes of the ancient Mesopotamian creation myths.

Nebuchadnezzar's vision did not outlive him, and when he died in 562 BC he was succeeded by a number of very weak and inept rulers. Only Nabonidus had a reign of any length (556–539 BC), but he made himself very unpopular by attempting to undermine some central aspects of traditional Babylonian culture. His mother Adad-guppi had been a zealous advocate of the moon god Sin, the deity of the city of Haran in northern Palestine, and Nabonidus followed her in this. In 552 BC, he decided to move out of Babylon to live at Teima in the Arabian desert, where he developed a shrine to the moon god, leaving his son Belshazzar to look after things in the capital. This provoked a crisis for the whole Babylonian way of life, which was dominated by the cycle of the seasons and especially the celebration of the annual New Year Festival, the efficacy of which in ensuring the fertility of the land could be guaranteed only by the king's personal involvement. Having abandoned the worship of Marduk, the traditional god of Babylon, it was hard for Nabonidus to avoid the claim that subsequent plagues and famines in the land were his fault. By the time he returned to Babylon after a ten-year absence, it was too late to reverse things, though he still persisted with his policy of converting traditional temples dedicated to Marduk into shrines honouring Sin. When a little-known king named Cyrus from southern Persia presented himself at the gates of Babylon in 539 BC, the Marduk priests conspired to overthrow Nabonidus and Belshazzar, and Cyrus was welcomed as their new ruler.

Persia

Cyrus set about the reinvigoration of Babylonian society. The temples which Nabonidus had neglected were restored to their former glory, and Cyrus himself shared publicly in the worship of the god Marduk. But he had a different outlook from his predecessors, and of all the ancient rulers with whom the Jews had to deal, Cyrus was the most liberal and humane. He did not see politics in terms of armed conflict between various national religions but instead recognized the right of all nations to worship whichever deities they wished. He accepted the diversity of peoples and cultures throughout his empire, which soon expanded to cover a vast area stretching from the north of Greece to the borders of India, and was to last for two centuries beyond his lifetime. As part of this policy Cyrus was prepared to allow citizens the right to live wherever they chose, which was a massive reversal of the policies that had dominated Mesopotamian society for many hundreds of years.

New ways of thinking

Cyrus inherited a population with many ethnic groups who had been uprooted from their own lands and settled in Babylon and other places against their will. Not only did he encourage these displaced people to return to their homelands but he also offered the financial resources that would enable them to do so. The Cyrus Cylinder (a clay cylinder inscribed in cuneiform, from about 539–530 BC) not only describes his rise to power, but also spells out this policy towards conquered people in some considerable detail. Though there is some disagreement regarding his true intentions, his stated approach has been hailed as the earliest known example of the notion of human rights, and in recognition of that there is a replica of the cylinder on permanent display in the United Nations building in New York. The cylinder itself makes no specific mention of the fate of the exiled people of Judah, but it describes the policy itself well enough:

> *I returned the images of the gods, who had resided there [Babylon], to their places and I let them dwell in eternal abodes. I gathered all their inhabitants and returned to them their dwellings.*

In line with this, the book of Ezra[14] preserves the text of an official decree issued by Cyrus with regard to Judah:

> *Concerning the house of God at Jerusalem, let the house be rebuilt, the place where sacrifices and offerings are*

> *brought ... let the cost be paid from the royal treasury.*
> *Moreover, let the gold and silver vessels ... which*
> *Nebuchadnezzar took out of the temple in Jerusalem and*
> *brought to Babylon, be restored and brought back ... each*
> *to its place.*

Interestingly, this decree is recorded in Aramaic – one of very few sections of the Hebrew Bible to use this language, the adopted official language of the Persian empire. The Persians had no long-standing literary conventions of their own, and generally continued the local customs and writing styles of the various places they occupied: cuneiform in Babylon, hieroglyphics in Egypt, and so on. But they chose Aramaic as the administrative language for the empire, to facilitate easy communication between bureaucrats throughout their territories.

These policies were acted upon, and within a year or so of Cyrus's arrival in Babylon, those Jewish exiles who wished to make the journey were on their way back home to Judah. They departed with high hopes, even hailing Cyrus in glowing terms as God's "anointed".[15] But their resettlement was not as straightforward and glorious as they might have hoped. They found their land in a mess and their previously grand buildings in ruins – and other people living there, who had little in common with them. The hardships of this period are well documented in the books of Ezra, Nehemiah, Haggai, and Zechariah. Eventually they rebuilt their temple, in line with the decree from Cyrus, but it was never going to match up to the splendour of the one they had lost when Nebuchadnezzar raided Jerusalem.

Cyrus himself died in 530 BC and was succeeded by Cambyses (530–522 BC), who was probably his son, though the records are not absolutely clear about that. At any event, it was a smooth transition of power, as Cambyses had already been involved in government even before Cyrus was killed in battle. Cambyses continued the expansion of the empire, and in 525 BC decided to move on Egypt. He chose the opportunity carefully, just as Pharaoh Psammeticus III had taken over from his father Amasis II. Cambyses had the support of various Arabian tribes who facilitated his armies in moving westward through the desert, and the Egyptians were hoping that their partnership with Greece might help to defeat the Persians. In the event, this expectation was ill founded, because the Greeks joined forces with the Persians. Just as Cyrus had adopted the Babylonian style of kingship when he conquered Babylon, so Cambyses sought to behave like a pharaoh in Egypt. He took the name Mesutire, meaning a son of the god Re, adopted Egyptian dress, and employed an Egyptian tutor to teach him traditional Egyptian ways. His triumph was, however, short lived, and when he tried to extend his rule east along the coast of North Africa and south into what is now Sudan he suffered heavy defeats. Meanwhile, back in Persia his brother Bardiya seized power and enlisted the support of the people by abolishing taxes. Cambyses was forced to return from Egypt, though it is unclear what happened next. However, within a very short time both Bardiya and Cambyses were dead and power fell into the hands of a military commander by the name of Darius (522–486 BC).

Darius managed to accomplish some of what Cambyses had failed to do, by conquering Libya and moving briefly into some of the countries to the south of Egypt. But he was also forced to deal with trouble elsewhere in the empire, as other cities and states tried to reassert their own independence. In an effort to control this, Darius set about the restructuring of his realm on a more centralized model by creating some twenty provinces, or satrapies, headed by officials who would now enforce his policies in a more uniform manner than had previously been the case. As part of this reorganization, he moved his own capital from Pasargadae, which had been Cyrus's main city, to Persepolis. The reconstruction work that he began there was to go on long after his own reign had ended. But he also set about rebuilding the city of Susa to act as a second capital.

Threats from the West

Darius was increasingly threatened with the break-up of his empire, especially to the west, where Greece was beginning to expand its territories. By 490 BC he had decided to tackle what he regarded as this growing menace, but his forces were defeated at the battle of Marathon. This turned out to be a decisive moment not only for the Persians but for the course that the whole of Western civilization would take for the next thousand years and more. It was the first time that the Greek city-states had been able to repel the Persians in a military conflict, and that in itself gave them a sense of renewed confidence in their own ability, and a conviction of the superiority of their own culture that would inspire future generations to believe that their ideas, as well as their armies, might conquer the world.

Darius was succeeded by his son Xerxes (485–465 BC), who continued the effort to suppress Greece, but abandoned it when it became obvious that he would not be able to succeed. We have little detailed knowledge of the reigns of his various successors, and most of what we do know comes from Greek historians who had the benefit of knowing that Greece had eventually succeeded in banishing the Persians, and naturally wrote their accounts from that perspective. Being convinced of the superiority of Greek ways, they portrayed the final years of the Persian empire and the rise of Greece as a battle between two civilizations: Greece, representing reason and freedom, and Persia as the epitome of oppression and ignorance. Whatever the reality, there can be no doubt that this period was marked by a series of court intrigues, numerous assassinations, and growing instability within the Persian hierarchy. The only possible point of contact between this and the Bible story comes with the reign of Artaxerxes II (404–358 BC), who is believed by some to be the king who is called Ahasuerus in the book of Esther.

Darius III (336–330 BC) was the last of the Persian kings, who came to the throne in the very year that Philip II (king of Macedon 382–336 BC) was commissioned by the League of Corinth to avenge a previous Persian military action that had inflicted damage on some of the Greek temples. As it happened, Philip was assassinated before he had advanced very far, but his son and successor, Alexander the Great, soon confronted the Persians, and though he was almost killed in the process, managed to overcome them at the battle of Granicus (334 BC). The following year, Darius decided to lead his armies in person, but despite having a much larger number of troops he was defeated by Alexander, only to regroup and fight again in 331 BC at the battle of Gaugamela. On this occasion, Darius's chariot was destroyed and his troops presumed him to be dead. This turned out not to be the case, but by now Persian morale was at such a low ebb that one of Darius's own administrators assassinated him. In the meantime, though, Alexander captured the three most important cities – Babylon, Susa, and Persepolis – and it was clear that from now on, the future would belong to Greece.

Greece

Alexander made spectacular progress throughout the whole region. Egypt decided not to resist his advance, and in 331 BC he was able to establish a new city on the Nile Delta, named after himself: the city of Alexandria, which soon became an important centre for Judaism and then later for early Christianity. Alexander's vision was not confined to political power, and the establishment of new cities was a central element in his cultural strategy. His tutor as a child had been the philosopher Aristotle, and possibly as a result of this Alexander was inspired by an almost fanatical fervour to spread the Greek language and worldview. The idea that being "Greek" was something that could be learned and embraced voluntarily had already been expressed by Isocrates (436–338 BC), a near-contemporary of Alexander, who averred that

> *the name Greek suggests no longer a race but an intelligence, and the title "Greek" is applied to those who share our culture rather than to those who share the same blood.*
> **Isocrates, Panegyricus 50**

But Alexander's empire did not survive his death of 323 BC intact. He had no obvious heir, and the years immediately following him saw much feuding among military commanders as they jostled for position to succeed him. The succession was finally resolved only after a major confrontation at Ipsus in 301 BC, following which the empire was split among four protagonists. Cassander was to rule in the homeland of Macedon, and Lysimachus in Thrace (an area to the north-east of modern Greece); Seleucus got Mesopotamia and Persia, and

Ptolemy was confirmed as ruler of Egypt, with various lesser-known characters taking control of the territory in northern India and Syria. Until 1ᶜ8 BC, Judah – or Judea as it was now to be known – came under the control of the Ptolemies (as this new Egyptian dynasty was called). Though there is evidence that Ptolemy I (323–283 BC) forced many Jews to emigrate to the city of Alexandria, which at the time was under-populated, the Ptolemaic policy with regard to conquered peoples was generally similar to that of the Persians before them, and was based on an essentially pragmatic approach that sought to promote anything that would be mutually advantageous to both the rulers and their subjects. Meanwhile, back in Judea itself, the Jewish community was largely left to its own devices and the new Egyptian overlords were quite content to allow the priestly families in Jerusalem to operate as government agents just so long as they collected the taxes and kept good public order.

This was a period of considerable change for Jewish people as they were forced to deal with a way of life that was quite different from anything they had encountered previously. On the whole, it seems that Greek ways of doing things were combined with traditional Hebrew culture on a purely pragmatic basis. While the Greek language was adopted as the essential medium for both commerce and diplomacy, Aramaic continued to be spoken in Judea, though at this period the use of Hebrew as a living language disappeared for good.

At the time of Alexander's death, Ptolemy had not been the only one of his generals to have designs on Judea. Seleucus, who ruled from Antioch in north Syria, was not too happy that Judea and Lebanon should belong to the Ptolemies of Egypt, and throughout the third century their respective successors were constantly at loggerheads over possession of this territory.

For the most part, this manifested itself in diplomatic efforts to out-manoeuvre one another, though there were several military skirmishes as well. The matter was finally decided in 198 BC in favour of the Seleucids, when Antiochus III defeated Scopus, the general of Ptolemy V, at the battle of Paneon.

Alexander's empire

Alexander was remarkably successful in his desire to spread the Greek language and worldview. Although his empire survived for only a short time as a united political entity, the cultural world that he created based on all things Greek (generally referred to as "Hellenism") lasted for nearly a thousand years, and was a key component in the emergence of western European civilization. Hellenistic ideas found a ready audience in places like Egypt because the Greek philosophical interests of the day centred on topics that had long been a source of fascination at the eastern end of the Mediterranean: astronomy, medicine, mathematics, and the workings of the natural world.

After Alexander

Alexander did not live long enough to see his grand intellectual vision fulfilled. By 323 BC he was dead, spending his last days in Nebuchadnezzar's palace in Babylon. The cause of his death is not altogether clear, and all the historical sources say is that he had a fever. The symptoms as described would be consistent with something like malaria or typhoid, though others draw attention to the fact that he was a heavy drinker and speculate that he could have died from alcohol poisoning – or even, since poisonous substances were regularly used as medications, that he may have been killed by substances that were intended to cure him. There can be no denying that he deserved the epithet that the Greeks soon gave him: "Alexander the Great". Within ten years, he had gone from being the son of the ruler of a small city-state in northern Greece to becoming ruler of more or less the whole of the world of which the Greeks had any knowledge, with an empire that stretched from Greece in the west to the borders of India in the east.

Greeks and Jews in Palestine

Antiochus was welcomed by the leaders of the Jewish community in Jerusalem, some of whom (most notably the high priest Simon and members of the Tobiad family) had given him active support in his opposition to the Ptolemies. In return, the Seleucids adopted a tolerant policy towards Jewish scruples, and Antiochus not only reduced the Jews' taxes but also made a generous grant for the restoration of the temple in Jerusalem and formally affirmed their right to live according to their traditional laws and customs. All this ensured the continuation of the generally happy co-existence of Jewish values alongside Hellenistic culture, with mutual advantage to both sides.

Unfortunately, Antiochus did not show the same wisdom in dealing with the rising power of Rome. Having extended his influence from Syria into the territory to the south, he tried to expand his empire westwards, something which the Romans took far more seriously. In 190 BC he was defeated in a land and sea battle at Magnesia, near Ephesus. The peace treaty that he was subsequently forced to sign represented a considerable loss of face, for it required him to abandon completely his territory in Asia Minor. The humiliation of this was bad enough, but it also had financial repercussions; this territory had always been the wealthiest part of the Seleucid empire and its loss pushed him to the brink of bankruptcy. He was soon desperate for money, and just a year after signing the treaty with the Romans, Antiochus himself was killed in Elam while in the act of robbing a temple.

Temples in the ancient world often served as banks where people could leave cash or jewellery in safe keeping, and the temple in Jerusalem was no exception. Antiochus had never sought to gain access to its wealth, and in the early part of the reign of his son and successor Seleucus IV (187–175 BC) nothing changed. However, it was not long before the rise of dissenting factions among the ruling families in Jerusalem necessitated military intervention, in the course of which Seleucus dispatched his chancellor, Heliodorus, to plunder the temple there. His attempt was evidently unsuccessful, but it alerted the Seleucids to the existence of substantial treasures in Jerusalem, while the emergence of internal tensions within the Jewish hierarchy encouraged them to keep a much closer eye on what was going on in this southern part of their domain.

There had been underlying tension in Jewish society long before the Seleucids had first gained control of Judea. Two leading families – the Tobiads and the Oniads – were behind all this, the one representing a more traditional Jewish orthodoxy, and the other being eager not only to accept but also to promote the new Hellenistic culture. The climax of this power struggle happened to coincide with the murder of Seleucus IV and the accession of a new king, Antiochus IV Epiphanes (175–164 BC). A member of the Oniad family called Jason bribed Antiochus to make him high priest in Jerusalem in place of his brother Onias. This suited Antiochus, for Jason was committed to the same policies of thoroughgoing Hellenization as he was himself, and so with Jason's appointment a plan was set in motion that would ensure the radical transformation of Jerusalem into a fully Greek city.

Even the priests in the temple were soon hurrying through their work in order to have time to go to the wrestling arena. The Greeks wore no clothes on such occasions, and to avoid possible embarrassment when they took part, the Jewish men began to undergo surgical procedures to try and disguise the fact that they had been circumcised.

All this was too much for those who wished to remain true to the traditions of their people, and it was not long before Jason was deposed and replaced by Menelaus, a member of the Tobiad family, who was appointed by Antiochus for no other reason than the fact that he had offered a bigger bribe than Jason.

Politics and religion

While all this was going on, Antiochus had set his sights on Egypt. The ruler of Egypt at this time was Ptolemy VI (180–145 BC), who was only a boy, and Antiochus defeated his army without difficulty. Desperate for money, he then went to Jerusalem and robbed the temple before returning home to Syria. But he was soon travelling south again, and in the spring of 168 BC he returned to Egypt. This time, he found that the Romans had already arrived there, and they soon sent him packing. In the meantime, a rumour had spread in Jerusalem that Antiochus was dead, whereupon Jason seized the opportunity to try and get rid of Menelaus. Antiochus was in no mood for compromise. He had already been humiliated by the Romans, and he was determined to keep his grip on Judea. So he moved to Jerusalem again, and took what treasure was left in the temple, assisted this time by Menelaus himself. Antiochus's visit to Jerusalem on this occasion was accompanied by great slaughter and destruction, and some of the inhabitants were forcibly removed and taken into slavery. But things went much further than that, and he also introduced stringent measures to restrict and control traditional expressions of Jewish spirituality. Circumcision, Sabbath-keeping, and the reading of the Law were all banned, and in a very short time Antiochus was insisting that worship of the Greek god Zeus should be incorporated within the rituals of the temple. To add insult to injury, he opened the temple to the whole population of the land, including those who were not fully Jewish. With this, Antiochus embarked on a comprehensive policy of enforced Hellenization, insisting that all elements of the population must be brought together through their acceptance of the Greek way of life, which of course included Greek religious practices.

The reasons for Antiochus's determination to stamp out all things distinctively Jewish are not altogether clear. The nearest comparable effort had been a thousand years earlier when Pharaoh Akhen-aten of Egypt tried to eliminate the worship of every god except Aten and himself. Trying to stamp out an entire religion was not at all typical of ancient empires. People who believed in many deities themselves did not usually think it was either worthwhile or necessary to try to get rid of other people's gods. But Antiochus may have been motivated by an elevated sense of his own importance, perhaps regarding himself as an incarnation of Zeus. The title by which he liked to be known – "Epiphanes" – literally means "a manifestation of God", though even in his own day some writers deliberately corrupted it to "Epimanes", meaning "madman". Both meanings could go some way towards explaining his actions, though he does not seem to have been the sort of person who would have had the capacity for sustaining the grand ideological vision implied by claims to divinity. Far from having any all-embracing strategy, he was an individual who reacted to events spontaneously, motivated more by short-term pragmatism than by any long-term strategy. At this time, he was virtually bankrupt, his kingdom was in a shaky condition, and in addition it may well be that Jewish leaders such as Menelaus and Jason were themselves supporting, if not actually proposing, these policies of extreme Hellenization.

No doubt Antiochus's actions had no one single explanation, but can be traced to all these factors in the social circumstances of the day. In and of itself, the influence of Hellenism had proved to be fairly neutral in relation to traditional Jewish values, and for more than a century the people of Judea had lived happily within this cultural matrix, as indeed their compatriots in other cities around the Mediterranean Sea continued to do. But the way in which Antiochus went about things in Palestine stirred up more opposition than anyone could possibly have bargained for. Jewish resistance to him was fanatical, and was only strengthened when Antiochus insisted that pigs (unclean animals in the Hebrew Bible) should be offered in honour of Zeus. In 167 BC, Antiochus inflicted the greatest indignity imaginable by having the altar of daily sacrifice in the temple replaced by an altar to Zeus, on which pigs were then sacrificed. At the same time, he issued orders that throughout the land people should be forced to offer similar sacrifices in all the villages. Though there was some support for this, a majority of the people were completely unprepared to take part in such ceremonies. The strength of their resolution was matched only by the cruelty of Antiochus's soldiers, who on one occasion skinned and fried alive an entire family who refused to submit to this compulsory Hellenization.

Almost immediately, an organized resistance movement emerged in the village of Modein, when a priest by the name of Mattathias was ordered to offer a sacrifice on a Greek altar. He refused to do so, and when another man stepped forward ready to do it, Mattathias killed both him and the Seleucid officer who had given the order. This action sparked off armed resistance to Antiochus and all that he stood for. Mattathias and his family fled to the hills and began a sustained guerrilla action under the leadership of Judas, one of his five sons, who was nicknamed "the Hammer" (in Hebrew, *ha-Makabi*, from which the whole movement came to be called "the Maccabean revolt"). Most people had little enthusiasm for the armed struggle, even those who otherwise sympathized with its ideological aspirations. Among them was a large ultra-religious group, the Hasideans, who attempted to distance themselves from the conflict by retreating into the Judean desert. The Seleucid army pursued them, and challenged them to battle on the Sabbath day. They refused, for they would not work on the Sabbath, and were ruthlessly killed by Antiochus's soldiers. That convinced many others that indifference or passive resistance was no longer an option, and also that if all Jews continued to observe the Law with that degree of strictness there would soon be none of them left. The Maccabees therefore adopted a more realistic policy by deciding that they would sometimes need to be prepared to break the Law in order to achieve their freedom.

Under the leadership of Judas, the rebels enjoyed some amazing successes, and it was not long before the weary Antiochus was forced to reverse his policies. The Torah was reinstated as the foundation of Jewish society and the temple itself was cleansed and rededicated on 25 Kislev 164 BC, exactly three years to the day from its first desecration. The feast of Hanukkah was inaugurated in celebration of the occasion. People like the Hasideans, who only wanted the freedom to practise their own religion and keep their traditional laws, were now satisfied. But Judas's family (the Hasmoneans), now led by his brother Simon, had tasted power, and it was not long before they had more or less thrown off Seleucid rule and established themselves as a ruling dynasty in Judea. Under their leadership, Judea enjoyed a time of relative political freedom until the Roman general Pompey took the city of Jerusalem in 63 BC.

This period saw a continuation of the many complex internal struggles among different factions within the Jewish leadership, with some Hasmoneans seeming to favour the very things that Judas and his generation had fought so hard to overthrow. As a result, they soon lost the support of the Hasideans, who in turn disappeared as a single identifiable religious grouping. Some of them found the corruption and Hellenizing policies of the Hasmonean kings intolerable, and withdrew into the Judean desert, just as they had done in the days of Antiochus. It was probably a movement of this kind that led to the foundation of the monastic community at Qumrân that produced the Dead Sea Scrolls. Other Hasideans chose not to isolate themselves from the wider culture, but regrouped as a protest movement within mainstream Jewish society, and elements of them might well have been the forerunners of the group known as Pharisees in the New Testament.

Rome

Legend has it that Rome was established in 753 BC by Romulus and Remus, the twin sons of Mars, the god of war. This date is generally supported by archaeological evidence, though there may have been a smaller settlement on the site before that, as it is located at a point where there was a natural ford across the

River Tiber. By the period that we are concerned with here, Rome had undergone several different developments in terms of its political systems. The second and third centuries BC saw a series of wars with Carthage (the Punic Wars), which led to territorial expansion into the western Mediterranean, and by the end of the third century BC its influence was beginning to extend to the east. In 188 BC, the expansionist aspirations of the Seleucid king Antiochus III had been curbed by the growing power of Rome, and twenty years later Rome forced Antiochus IV to withdraw from Egypt. When the Macedonian Wars ended in 148 BC with the incorporation of Macedonia as a Roman province, Rome had effectively taken over the whole of Alexander's empire.

From the late second century to the middle of the first century BC, Rome had its own internal squabbles to contend with, but that hardly affected its tightening grip on the empire. Egypt had never been fully integrated into the Roman system, and continued to be ruled by the Greek Ptolemies, albeit with Roman consent. When Cleopatra VII (69–30 BC) formed a relationship with Julius Caesar, and then following his murder with Mark Antony, it was inevitable that the latter's main rival in Rome, Octavian, would pursue him to Egypt. Antony and Cleopatra were defeated at the battle of Actium in 31 BC, and shortly thereafter the two of them committed suicide, leaving Egypt to become a full part of the Roman empire. Octavian needed to consolidate his own position as emperor and rebuild Rome politically, which he did as the emperor Augustus. The events of his reign take us into the period of the New Testament, and will be discussed in more detail in the following chapters.

6

Romans and Jews in Palestine

The New Testament opens with the four Gospels, Matthew, Mark, Luke, and John, that tell the story of Jesus' life and ministry. Matthew's account locates Jesus' birth "in the town of Bethlehem in Judea, during the time when Herod was king".[1] That one simple statement raises an interesting question for observant Bible readers, because the king in question, known to historians as Herod the Great, is commonly believed to have died in 4 BC, and therefore before the start of the Christian era, which is conventionally regarded as having commenced with the birth of Jesus!

The explanation for this is to be found in the fact that in the early centuries of what we now regard as the Christian era, several different ways of calculating dates were in use. The first person to date events by reference to the birth of Jesus was Victor, bishop of Tunnuna in North Africa, who died around AD 570. But it was the eighth-century English writer the Venerable Bede who introduced the concept of "before Christ" (BC) and "the year of the Lord" (AD), and in due course this system of dating was adopted throughout Europe. Bede was also the one who introduced the convention that there would be no such thing as a year 0 in the Christian calendar, but it would move straight from 1 BC to AD 1. Even this dating left room for ambiguity, as it is unclear whether he calculated these dates by reference to the birth or to the conception of Jesus. But the fact that several parallel dating methods were in use for some considerable time has allowed historians to compare lists of rulers and events from different regions of the ancient world and to establish an agreed understanding of dating. On this set of agreed principles, Herod the Great reigned from 37 BC until his death in 4 BC.

Herod the Great

There is no such ambiguity about the person and character of this Herod. He was the son of Antipater, who according to one source claimed to be a descendant of those Jewish exiles who had returned from exile in Babylon at the time of Ezra and Nehemiah. The more common consensus, however, identifies him as an Idumaean, a native of the place that the Hebrew Bible calls Edom, located between the southern end of the Dead Sea and the Gulf of Aqaba. Edomite ancestry was traditionally traced back to Esau, the twin brother of Jacob, and Jacob was regarded as the ancestor of the Jewish nation. In more recent times, the Hasmoneans had forced the Idumaeans to adopt the Jewish faith, which meant that Herod (like his father before him) could claim to be a true Jewish believer in spite of his tenuous ethnic connections to the Jewish nation. His mother Cypros was a Nabatean; they were a mobile trading people whose sphere of operations extended from Palestine south and east toward the northern part of the Arabian peninsula. It was this ethnic mix that enabled Herod to rise so easily to a position of prominence and power as a ruler of Palestine. He was regarded as sufficiently Jewish to be able to present himself as a genuinely native ruler, while at the same time he was not so thoroughly Jewish as to align himself with those religiously fanatical believers who would continue to press for the re-establishment of an independent Jewish state in opposition to all external rule.

It was the Romans who facilitated Herod's rise to power. For by the time of his birth, probably in 73 BC, they had seized power throughout the Mediterranean lands, and any local ruler who wished to prosper could do so only with their support. Herod's father Antipater had been an influential state official under the Hasmonean kings, who succeeded the Maccabees, and when the Roman general Pompey the Great conquered Judea he promptly aligned himself with Rome. When internal struggles within the Roman hierarchy led to Pompey's defeat at the hands of Julius Caesar, Antipater had no hesitation in switching his loyalties, as a consequence of which he was appointed in 47 BC to be the chief Roman representative in Judea, a position that carried with it the right to raise his own local taxes. Not long after this, Julius Caesar himself was assassinated (in 44 BC), and Antipater showed his political astuteness by transferring his loyalties once more. But by now, those conservative Jews who had never wanted anything to do with the Romans in the first place had lost patience with his policies of appeasement, and within a year of Caesar's death Antipater had followed him, assassinated at the hands of a poisoner.

Despite this apparent setback, Antipater had laid solid foundations for the continuing success of his family by appointing his sons Phasael and Herod to be the governors of Jerusalem and Galilee respectively, and his diplomacy and artful politics paved the way for Herod to rise to power. Following the example of many ancient kings before him, Herod consolidated his position through marriage. In his case, his union with Mariamne, a member of the Hasmonean family, secured support from significant elements of the Jewish population while not alienating the Romans, and it was only a matter of time before he was acknowledged as king of Judea with support from both sides. It is not hard to see why the Romans found him such an attractive proposition. Palestine was on the very fringes of their empire at the time, and it made sense for them to recruit a local ruler rather than commit large numbers of their own troops to a land that had little to offer them. The events of the Maccabean period had shown that there would always be significant resistance to the incursions of people who were regarded as infidels and unbelievers, so what better way to maintain control at minimal cost than by supporting someone like Herod, who was native to the region but also sympathetic to Rome? Because of his mixed ancestry, he could be regarded as a Gentile by the Romans (or certainly not fully Jewish). At the same time, he had married a Jewish wife, and could claim to be a believer himself, which endowed him with a sufficiently strong connection to the Jewish faith and people for everyone except religious extremists to regard him as one of them. It seemed like a perfect solution – and, indeed, it worked well, for his reign of more than thirty years lasted far longer than that of most client kings in similar circumstances.

As a ruler, Herod turned out to combine diplomatic brilliance and personal insanity. Though there is no record of it outside the New Testament, the story of how he murdered the children of Bethlehem after Jesus was born[2] is quite consistent with all that is known of his character and behaviour. Anyone who opposed his policies (or even just incurred his disfavour) could expect violent treatment. As governor of Galilee early in his life, he had suppressed a revolt led by Hezekiah the Galilean in a particularly brutal fashion, and even as he lay on his deathbed he instructed his sister Salome and her husband to gather leaders from every town in Judea and have them killed, so that instead of rejoicing at his own death (as he expected they would), his subjects would be forced to mourn the loss of these others.

He never thought twice about killing even his own family. His wife Mariamne was executed on his orders, even though her death then plunged him into a period of deep depression. He was also implicated in the murder of two of his sons, Alexander and Aristobulus, and only five days before his death in 4 BC he ordered the execution of yet another of his sons, Antipater, the one who had been expected to succeed him. He also orchestrated the violent deaths of countless members of his court and his wider network of family and colleagues, many of whom were subjected to vicious torture in the process. It is little wonder that the Roman emperor Augustus is reported to have said that it was "better to be Herod's pig than his son": since pigs were regarded as religiously unclean beasts in Judaism they were not routinely killed for food.

Herod was clearly an unhappy and unstable man, and it is not difficult to understand why. The mixed ancestry that made him so acceptable to the Romans may well have stunted his personal development, as he struggled with the reality that he was "half-Jewish" and "half-Idumaean/Nabatean". He certainly had an inferiority complex about his personal appearance, and the historian Josephus mentions that his brother-in-law and sons were all taller and better looking than him, something that preyed on his mind repeatedly. He was pathologically suspicious of just about everyone apart from his sister, and was convinced that others were constantly plotting to get rid of him. He also suffered from some severe physical complaints, and Josephus describes his death-throes in excruciating detail:

*fire glowed in him slowly, which did not so much appear
to the touch outwardly, as it augmented his pains
inwardly; for it brought upon him a vehement appetite to
eating, which he could not avoid to supply with one sort of
food or other. His entrails were also ex-ulcerated, and the
chief violence of his pain lay on his colon; an aqueous and
transparent liquor also had settled itself about his feet,
and a like matter afflicted him at the bottom of his belly.
… his privy-member was putrefied, and produced worms;
and when he sat upright, he had a difficulty of breathing,
which was very loathsome, on account of the stench of
his breath, and the quickness of its returns; he had also
convulsions in all parts of his body.*
Josephus, Antiquities 17.6.5

Josephus also provides a graphic and detailed description of
Herod's funeral and burial, which he locates at a site adjacent
to what he calls the Serpent's Pool at the fortress of Herodium,
some five miles to the south-east of Bethlehem in the Judean
desert. This was a location where Herod had always felt safer
than he ever did in Jerusalem, and the complex of palaces and
administrative buildings that he constructed there included
gardens created from specially imported soil and irrigated
by water from Solomon's Pool so that he could have blooms
in the very heart of the desert. On the basis of Josephus's
descriptions, Ehud Netzer, an archaeologist from the Hebrew
University, has discovered Herod's tomb. No remains of the
king himself have been uncovered, though the many pieces
of broken sarcophagus that were found suggest that his grave
was probably ransacked not long after his burial.

In spite of his personal weaknesses, as a politician Herod
deserved to be called "the Great". The peace and order that

he maintained throughout his territory were in stark contrast to the upheavals that marked the centuries immediately preceding his reign. He was also responsible for a massive construction programme that marks him out as one of the greatest builders anywhere in the whole of history. Three of his projects in Jerusalem rank among the largest civil engineering works in the ancient world: the palace known as the Lower Herodium, the plaza of the Temple Mount, and the portico of the Temple Mount itself. In addition to those, he built magnificent palaces in Jericho and Caesarea, along with royal fortresses at Masada, Herodium, and Machaerus – while the harbour of Caesarea was widely regarded as one of the most sophisticated constructions anywhere in the ancient world. As well as the temple in Jerusalem (which was not completed until long after his own death), other religious projects included the reconstruction of the Tomb of the Patriarchs in Hebron, while outside his own realm he financed prestigious projects throughout the eastern part of the Roman world.

After Herod's death

When Herod the Great died in 4 BC, the Romans divided his kingdom among his three remaining sons: Archelaus, Antipas, and their half-brother Philip. At Roman insistence all three of them had been sent to Rome for their education. It would be an exaggeration to say that they were held there as hostages, though there is no doubt that their being in Rome was a move that was expected to have the side-effect of securing their father's continued loyalty. In the light of his pathological tendencies, it is doubtful whether he would have cared about them sufficiently for their absence to affect his policies, though by taking them out of Palestine the Romans also unwittingly guaranteed their survival and ensured that they would be well placed to take over as rulers of Palestine on their father's death.

Archelaus

Archelaus was Herod's own choice to become king in the most significant part of his territory that included Jerusalem. But the Roman emperor Augustus was not prepared to allow Archelaus to enjoy the title "king", which his father held. Instead he was known as "ethnarch" (meaning "national leader") of Samaria, Judea, and Idumea.

Right from the start, Archelaus had difficulties. Taking advantage of Herod the Great's final illness, two religious teachers named Judas and Matthias had orchestrated the removal of the statue of a golden eagle that stood by the entrance to the temple in Jerusalem. Artistic creations of this sort had always been problematic within Judaism due to the prohibition of the making of "graven images" in the Ten Commandments.[3] Those who were responsible for removing the eagle were punished by being burned alive, and as a result Archelaus found himself with a riot on his hands, which led to some 3,000 people being killed during the celebration of the Feast of Passover. Misjudging the mood of the people, Archelaus left the country and travelled to Rome to have his position confirmed by the emperor. But no sooner had he gone than fresh riots broke out, this time influenced by some individuals who were claiming messianic status for themselves. Archelaus's own army was incapable of controlling the crowds, and the Roman governor of Syria, Publius Quinctilius Varus, was forced to intervene in order to restore order. He failed to catch all the ringleaders, but that did not stop him ordering the crucifixion of some 2,000 people.

When Archelaus came back he turned out to be such an inept ruler that the people themselves implored the Romans to remove him. His reign lasted for only ten years, and in AD 6 – and after yet more political unrest, this time organized by Judas the Galilean – Judea became a third-grade province of the Roman empire under an officer of the upper-class equestrian rank, who was himself under the direct command of the Roman governor of Syria. Archelaus was banished to exile in Gaul, and little more is known about the rest of his life. These Roman rulers of Judea were initially known as "prefects", though they were later referred to by the more widely used title of "procurator". The best-known one, certainly in relation to the New Testament story, was Pontius Pilate, who governed Judea from AD 26 to 36.

Antipas

Antipas was another of Herod the Great's sons and in accordance with his father's wishes and with the approval of Augustus he inherited the northern part of Palestine (Galilee and Perea) and ruled as "tetrarch" (a word that literally means "ruler of one quarter", but which could be used more generally to describe a minor ruler under the Romans). This territory lay to the east of the River Jordan, and included the village of Nazareth, where Jesus grew up. Much of Jesus' ministry took place in territory that was under Antipas's jurisdiction.

Antipas was very much like his father, a crafty man who liked living in luxury. To make a name for himself he took great pride in the construction of massive public buildings. Two projects in particular are worthy of notice. One of his major undertakings was the construction of a new regional capital, to be called Tiberias in honour of the Roman emperor Tiberius. It turned out that this new city had desecrated an ancient burial site, and for a considerable period of time no religiously faithful Jewish people would go there – which meant it could develop as a Hellenistic city with a population predominantly consisting of Greeks and Romans. The other significant project was the rebuilding of Sepphoris, a town only 4 miles from Nazareth and which may well have provided some of the background to the ministry of Jesus. Both these cities are discussed in more detail in chapter 7.

Like his father, Antipas projected an image of himself as a faithful Jewish believer and celebrated the key religious festivals in Jerusalem. But the depth of his piety was continually questioned. He features in the New Testament as a slippery customer who could not be trusted. This is the same Herod Antipas who had John the Baptist executed when John questioned whether his multiple sexual relationships were appropriate within a Jewish moral framework.[4] Antipas's first wife was Phasaelis, the daughter of an Arabian ruler named Aretas IV, but he subsequently divorced her and married Herodias, a woman who had previously been the wife of his own half-brother (also called Herod). The relationships of the Herod family were never quite so simple, however. As well as being the former wife of his brother, Herodias was also the daughter of another half-brother (Aristobulus), so she was also Antipas's niece.

The story of how Antipas secured the death of John the Baptist also reveals something of his character: he offered his daughter Salome any gift she wanted as a reward for dancing in public before his guests – and she asked for John's head to be served up on a dinner plate! It was not only the gruesome nature of her request that raised questions, but also the fact that her father had asked her to dance in front of other men, something that no religiously observant parent would ever have done in the cultural context of the day. It is little wonder that Jesus compared him to a "fox" (which was, like a pig, an unclean animal in Jewish thinking). His later involvement in the trial of Jesus himself demonstrates the same traits of deviousness and dishonesty.[5]

As a ruler, Antipas did not have the same flair as his father. He engaged in a fruitless and unpopular war with his former father-in-law Aretas, during which the Arabian ruler enjoyed considerable success – something that, according to Josephus, many people regarded as divine punishment for his marital unfaithfulness. His wife Herodias shared some of the same traits, and when Antipas's half-brother Philip died she plotted to acquire his territory for Antipas, a move that was not approved in Rome and led to Antipas being removed and sent to live in exile in Gaul.

Philip

Philip was the third of Herod the Great's sons to inherit territory on his father's death, becoming "tetrarch of Ituraea and Trachonitis" (territory in the south-west of what is now Syria). The population of this region was quite different from that of other parts of Palestine at this time. Religiously faithful Jews always wanted to live close to the temple in Jerusalem. While Galilee was often dismissed contemptuously as "Galilee of the Gentiles", because its people were regarded as religiously unfaithful, the population in Philip's territory was predominantly ethnically Gentile (non-Jewish). This, together with the relative remoteness of his territory from Jerusalem, ensured that he would never be too closely scrutinized by the religious authorities and gave him considerable latitude to develop his own style. The extent to which he broke with Jewish convention can be seen in the designs on his coins, which typically included not only the head of the Roman emperor but often also a design inspired by that of the pagan temples of the wider empire – both things that could easily have caused a riot in Judea. Many of his people represented the old traditions of semi-nomadic lifestyles that can be traced right back to ancient Mesopotamia, and Philip readily adopted that way of life himself when dealing with the mobile population of the region. His territory also embraced city-dwellers, some of them living in settlements that had been established by Herod the Great, though Philip himself also extended what had originally been smaller villages and these became home to inhabitants of predominantly Greek and Roman origin.

Like his brothers, he depended on the goodwill of his Roman overlords, so he courted the favour of the emperor by renaming the extended village of Paneas (at the foot of Mt Hermon) Caesarea Philippi in honour of the emperor, and renamed Bethsaida Julias after the emperor's daughter Julia.

Of all the sons of Herod the Great, Philip was the only one who proved to be a balanced and humane ruler, and he died peacefully at Julias in AD 34. Even Josephus had nothing but praise for his accomplishments, describing him as

a person of moderation and quietness in the conduct of his life and government; he constantly lived in that country which was subject to him; he used to make his progress with a few chosen friends; his tribunal also, on which he sat in judgment, followed him in his progress; and when any one met him who wanted his assistance, he made no delay, but had his tribunal set down immediately.

Josephus, Antiquities 18.4.6

Philip left no sons who could succeed him, and his territory was incorporated briefly into the Roman province of Syria. But that was a short-lived arrangement. On the death of Tiberius in AD 37 his successor Caligula reorganized it into an independent territory, and Philip's nephew Agrippa was appointed as its ruler, with the royal title of "king". He thus became the first member of the Herod family to be given that distinction since the death of his grandfather Herod the Great some forty years previously.

The later Herods

The story of Herod Agrippa is itself a lesson in the tangled diplomacy of the day, and bears eloquent witness to all the conflicting issues which a ruler of that time needed to be equipped to handle. The father of Agrippa was Aristobulus, a son of Herod the Great who had been executed on the orders of his own father in 7 BC. At that time Agrippa was only three years old and he was sent off to Rome to be educated. While there he made friends with two Romans who would later become emperors: Caligula and Claudius. He felt thoroughly at home in Rome, and it was there that he married Cyprus and where all his five children were born.

As a result of financial mismanagement, though, he made a good number of enemies, and by AD 33 he had found it necessary to leave Rome and ended up living in Idumea. Though he subsequently managed to secure an official appointment in Tiberias, which by now had become the capital city of Galilee, his life was far from secure in Palestine. When he had a disagreement with the governor of the province of Syria he was obliged to move again, this time to Alexandria in Egypt. Life there was no more straightforward either, and eventually he returned to Rome in a move that was made possible when his wife negotiated a resolution to his previous financial problems and guaranteed that his creditors would be repaid. He reconnected with his old school friend Caligula, and in the closing days of Tiberius's reign he plotted to have Caligula installed as emperor. As a result of this he found himself in prison for a couple of years, from which he was released when Tiberius died and was indeed succeeded by Caligula. It was Caligula who reinstated the independence of the territory once ruled by Agrippa's uncle and sent him back there as king. Further machinations followed as Agrippa's uncle Antipas took advantage of the emerging situation to extend his own power, but Caligula realized what was happening and intervened to send Antipas into exile in Gaul. In a final twist, and as a reward for his own friendship, Antipas's territories in Galilee and Perea were added to Agrippa's domains.

By comparison with other Roman emperors relatively little is known about Caligula's short reign (AD 37–41), but one thing that is well attested is his mental instability. Agrippa turned out to be one of the few people whom the emperor trusted, which probably explains why he seems not to have spent too much time in his newly acquired lands but instead supported Caligula in an ill-conceived military excursion into northern Europe.

One episode towards the end of Caligula's reign highlights some of the problems of ruling a distant province like Judea from Rome. Caligula came up with the mad proposal that his own statue should be erected in the temple at Jerusalem, and dispatched Petronius, the governor of Syria, to ensure that it happened. Petronius was only too well aware of the Jewish sensibilities about "graven images", and knew that such a move was certain to provoke massive resistance from the local population. When he warned the emperor of this, Caligula not only insisted on his plan going ahead but also instructed Petronius to commit suicide as a punishment for having dared to question the opinions of his emperor. As a result of climatic conditions at the time, however, the ship carrying this message took three months to make the voyage from Rome to Judea, and while it was on its way Caligula himself was assassinated. Meanwhile, another ship that left Rome much later, bearing the news of his death and the end of his policies, arrived twenty-seven days earlier than the first one! In circumstances where it could take months for a decree signed by the emperor in Rome to be delivered to the outposts of the empire, it was doubly important that the authorities in Rome could trust their local representatives to be loyal while also exercising their own discretion in relation to regional conflicts of interest. This requirement was to be sorely tested in the next thirty years.

Caligula himself died in AD 41, stabbed to death by Roman officials who had had enough of his hostile behaviour towards them and the traditional institutions of state. Claudius was his successor – and was another old school friend of Agrippa, who played a key role in ensuring his appointment. In return for this, Claudius concluded the period of rule by Roman governors, and added the territories of Judea and Samaria to those already held by Agrippa. This meant that he was now in control of a vast Palestinian empire that was virtually the same as that of his grandfather Herod the Great – and with the same title of "king". No doubt modelling himself on his illustrious predecessor, he reinstated Jerusalem as the capital city of the whole of Palestine, and in celebration rebuilt the ancient city walls. Following Herod the Great's example, he promoted himself as a friend of both Romans and Jews, cementing both relationships through impressive building projects in Jerusalem and in the city of Beyrouth (modern Beirut), which by now was a thoroughly Hellenistic city at the heart of the Roman province of Syria. Here, Agrippa sponsored the construction of Roman baths, along with an amphitheatre and other buildings.

Josephus and the New Testament both bear witness to the fact that Agrippa was no friend of the Christians. More than that, they both testify to his own aspirations to divinity, and both connect this to his untimely death in AD 44. The New Testament book of Acts offers this brief description of the event:

> *[King Herod] went down from Judea to Caesarea and stayed there ... In an appointed day Herod put on his royal robes, took his seat on the platform, and delivered a public address to them. The people kept shouting, "The voice of a God, and not of a mortal!" And immediately, because he had not given God the glory, an angel of the Lord struck him down, and he was eaten by worms and died.*
>
> **Acts 12:19–23**

Josephus's account mentions that Agrippa was in Caesarea to celebrate games that he had instituted in honour of the emperor Claudius, and identifies his distinctive clothing as a gown made entirely of silver threads, which was illuminated by the bright morning sun as he entered the arena, in such a way that the crowd began to believe that he must be more than merely human. As in the New Testament account, it is Agrippa's evident acceptance of this ascription of deity that leads to his downfall. Josephus recalls how, when he had been briefly imprisoned under Tiberius just before Caligula came to power, Agrippa had seen a vision of an owl, which at the time was interpreted as a good omen, indicating that he would soon be released (and he was). However, this vision was accompanied by the warning that if he ever saw the same thing again it would be a harbinger of doom and he would die within five days of that happening.

This is Josephus's account of what happened next:

As he presently afterward looked up, he saw an owl sitting on a certain rope over his head, and immediately understood that this bird was the messenger of ill tidings, as it had once been the messenger of good tidings to him; and he fell into the deepest sorrow. A severe pain also arose in his belly, and began in a most violent manner. He therefore looked upon his friends, and said, "I, whom you call a god, am commanded presently to depart this life; while Providence thus reproves the lying words you just now said to me; and I, who was by you called immortal, am immediately to be hurried away by death. But I am bound to accept of what Providence allots, as it pleases God; for we have by no means lived ill, but in a splendid and happy manner.'

After he said this, his pain was become violent. Accordingly he was carried into the palace, and the rumour went abroad that he would certainly die in a little time. But the multitude presently sat in sackcloth, with their wives and children, after the law of their country, and besought God for the king's recovery. All places were also full of mourning and lamentation. Now the king rested in a high chamber, and as he saw them below lying prostrate on the ground, he could not himself

> *forbear weeping. And when he had been quite worn out*
> *by the pain in his belly for five days, he departed this*
> *life, being in the fifty-fourth year of his age, and in the*
> *seventh year of his reign.*
>
> Josephus, Antiquities 19.343–350

The New Testament attributes the death of Agrippa in this manner not only to his refusal to deny the divine status given him by the crowd, but more directly to God's judgment for the way he was persecuting the Christians. Foremost among his victims was James the son of Zebedee, one of the original disciples of Jesus, who was beheaded on Agrippa's orders. But he was not the only one to suffer, and Peter had also been thrown into prison during his reign.

Herod Agrippa had a son, Julius Marcus Agrippa, who was probably a teenager when his father died. In the immediate aftermath of the elder Agrippa's death, the Romans briefly imposed direct rule on his territories; but it was not long before the son's rights of inheritance were recognized, and by the mid 50s he was himself ruler of much of the territory once governed by his father, though not including Judea, which again came under the control of Roman governors. He is usually called Herod Agrippa II to distinguish him from his father, Herod Agrippa I. As with previous members of the Herod dynasty, his time was mostly divided between the cities of Caesarea and Jerusalem, giving him the opportunity to enjoy a thoroughly Hellenistic lifestyle at the same time as he was projecting himself as a faithful adherent of the Jewish faith – something that was especially important in his case, as the Romans gave him the right to appoint the high priest at the temple in Jerusalem and generally to oversee its operations. Since the Roman governors also had residences in these two cities, it facilitated close contact between the two jurisdictions. This was the Agrippa whom Paul met in Caesarea in the year AD 58, and who declared himself to be almost persuaded to become a Christian.[6]

The latter years of Agrippa II's reign were to be characterized by growing civil unrest and political tensions, partly sparked off by the eventual completion in AD 63 of the massive rebuilding of the Jerusalem temple that had been initiated by Herod the Great. National pride at this achievement was tempered by concern at the numbers of workers who found themselves unemployed as a consequence, and when that uncertainty was combined with high levels of taxation and shortages of basic foodstuffs, political instability was inevitable. While Agrippa was on a visit to Alexandria in Egypt two or three years later, the Roman governor stepped in to try to stem the growing tide of unrest. This only made matters worse, and led to an escalation of violence that spun rapidly out of Agrippa's control. Elements within the population who had always resented the Roman occupation seized the moment, and within a short time the entire country had descended into what was effectively a civil war.

Agrippa took the side of the Romans, seeing them as his best chance for personal survival, and one of the bloodiest episodes in all ancient Jewish history unfolded as the Roman commander Vespasian set about trying to pacify the country. There was a brief hiatus in AD 68 when the emperor Nero was assassinated and Agrippa – along with his queen Berenice and Vespasian's son Titus – left for Rome to pay homage to Galba, who was Nero's designated successor. Galba himself was short lived, though, and in less than a year he also was dead. Agrippa stayed behind in Rome, no doubt hoping to find favour with whoever might turn out to be the new emperor. In the meantime Titus had returned to Jerusalem to succeed his father as commander of the troops there, while Vespasian himself decided to take the initiative in restoring order to a Rome that was being torn apart by civil war as one leader after another vied to become the next emperor. By the time Agrippa got back to Judea early in AD 70 he was just in time to witness the final demise of his kingdom. In the effort to restore order, Titus found himself with no option but to storm Jerusalem itself, and in the process he destroyed not only the city and its infrastructure but the temple which had taken so long to rebuild.

After this debacle, Agrippa was soon back in Rome again, but it was not long before Vespasian rewarded him with new territories that were mostly located in Syria, where he appears to have lived in relative tranquillity until almost the end of the first century. After his death, though, the Herod family no longer featured in the affairs of Palestinian politics.

Roman rulers in Palestine

The story of Rome's dealings with Palestine began in 63 BC with an invasion orchestrated by Pompey, but Herod the Great was such a successful local ruler on their behalf that the Romans hardly needed to engage at all with the land and its people until his death in 4 BC. Even then, they were reluctant to become too involved in the day-to-day affairs of Jewish life, but the various failures of Herod's successors forced them to pay more attention than they might have wished to this eastern outpost of their empire. It was only its strategic position that attracted the Romans there at all, for they found the religious foibles of its people both incomprehensible and problematic. Yet the story of their dealings with this land and its people created the cultural matrix within which the ministry of Jesus was placed and to some extent established the terms of reference of other episodes in the life of the earliest Christian churches.

When Pompey entered Jerusalem and went into its temple he was amazed to find that what was regarded as the high place of the entire structure (the Holy of Holies) was empty. His surprise at this discovery was just the first evidence that Romans would find the Jews very hard to understand. Of course Pompey was just following the custom of the day by surveying the territory he had just acquired. But he may well have been driven by natural curiosity as well, eager to understand this nation that had been such an enigma to so many others before his time. In the process of doing so, however, he immediately identified himself to zealous Jewish believers as an infidel and unbeliever. Not only was he a Gentile, whose access to the temple would in any case have been severely restricted under the religious protocol of the day, but the Holy of Holies itself was a space to which access was strictly limited even among the accredited priesthood. Imposing Roman rule on these people would never be a simple matter, as neither side really understood the other and every encounter was a potential source of tension, if not of outright conflict. This is why Herod the Great turned out to be such an attractive proposition for the Romans: he was acceptable to the vast majority of Jews yet was also prepared to be loyal to Rome. Given the unstable nature of Roman politics during this period (which also turned out to be the final years of the Roman Republic), allowing Herod considerable leeway was the best option for both sides.

By the time of Herod's death, circumstances had changed in Rome as well as in Palestine. Faced with the ineptitude of

Herod's son and successor Archelaus, the emperor Augustus was forced to step in to ensure the future stability of Judea, which, with Jerusalem at its heart, was always central to this part of his dominions. Shortly after Archelaus was deposed and sent off into exile, Quirinius, the imperial legate of Syria, was dispatched to take a census of the taxable property of Judea, as the first stage in its organization as a regular Roman province. Following this, Judea was given a Roman governor of equestrian rank by the name of Coponius, who ruled for three years (AD 6–9). We know very little about how these individuals were allowed to govern their provinces. There has even been some doubt as to what their official title was. Tacitus described one of them, Pontius Pilate, as a "procurator", though that title did not have formal sanction until after AD 44, and inscriptions indicate that prior to that they were known as "prefects".

The major function of such governors was to ensure the smooth running of their province in accordance with the precepts of Roman law. This was always a sensitive matter in Palestine, though, as Jewish law based on religious values was in some ways at odds with notions of Roman jurisprudence – not to mention the fact that, precisely because of its being embedded in religious ideas, anything that looked like interference on the part of a Roman could easily become a cause for resistance if not outright revolt. Josephus makes it very clear that Coponius "was entrusted by Augustus with full powers and authority to inflict the death penalty" (*Antiquities* 2.8.1) – a statement which seems to imply that the governor had the equivalent of the *imperium* exercised by the proconsuls in other parts of the empire. While there is no clear-cut definition of what this *imperium* amounted to, it apparently conferred supreme power in administration, defence, the dispensation of justice, and the maintenance of public order within a given territory.

The maintenance of public order was always a major concern throughout the Roman empire, but was especially important in a province such as Judea, which not only had an unpredictable and volatile population but also occupied a strategic position along the eastern boundary of the whole empire. Though the Roman governor would have had absolute authority in matters of life and death within his province, in practice very few cases would actually come to his court. Most minor affairs would be settled through a network of local courts that were to be found throughout Judea, which was divided into eleven toparchies, or districts, for the purpose. Each village within a toparchy had its own council, presided over by a village clerk, which would deal with civil cases and certain less important criminal ones. Even if ultimate power was vested in the Romans, this was often a theoretical concession that in practice gave the people the opportunity to use their own traditional processes of government, though any real independence of action was always going to be strictly limited. The tax-collectors who feature so prominently in the New Testament stories of the life of Jesus were a part of this local administrative structure.

The Sanhedrin in Jerusalem served as a kind of higher-level religious court where the religious law could be interpreted and applied along traditional lines. This council consisted of seventy men drawn from the two major religious groupings, Pharisees and Sadducees, and was presided over by the high priest – who, of course, was a political appointee approved by the Romans. Whereas Herod the Great had appointed high priests in order to keep the system under his own control, the Roman governors were more inclined to sell the office to the highest bidder. The person who held the office the longest was Joseph Caiaphas (AD 18–36), the high priest who features in the stories of the arrest, trial, and crucifixion of Jesus. In exchange for their loyalty the Romans were prepared to honour Jewish scruples by (for example) exempting Jews from official duties on a Sabbath or other holy day, and by issuing coins bearing no artistic devices that might be understood as "graven images".

Most of the time, Romans and Jews managed to live in this kind of mutually suspicious truce. There was always going to be a strong Roman military presence in Jerusalem, but the governors generally stayed out of the city except for special occasions and preferred to live in their official residence in Caesarea, a city with a distinctively Hellenistic flavour and therefore more to their liking.

Most of the Roman governors were fairly inconsequential characters of whom little is known apart from their names, though presumably they were trusted by the central authorities in Rome itself. They would need to be, as communications between Rome and such far-flung parts of the empire were far from straightforward in the first century. Pontius Pilate is the only one who features at all prominently in the New Testament, though little is known about him before he became the fifth Roman prefect of Judea in AD 26. As governor of Judea his normal residence would have been in Caesarea, and his name has been found there on an inscription, which confirms that he was known by the title of "prefect". He was also accompanied by his wife,[7] which was a relatively recent innovation introduced by the Roman senate only five years before his appointment. There are stories connecting his childhood to locations in Scotland, Spain, and Germany, and there are also many legendary accounts of his later life after he left Judea in AD 36. None of them can be substantiated, and all reflect the curiosity of later generations, who wanted to understand the sort of person who played such a prominent part in the trial and crucifixion of Jesus. This involvement is Pilate's only claim to any sort of fame. Tacitus (*Annals* 15.44) mentions him only in this connection, though the Jewish writers Josephus and Philo both supply more information about his general disposition. They had a low opinion of him, and describe him as a brutal and callous man who cared little either for Jewish religious scruples or for common human values.

One story recounts how, not long after becoming prefect, he had Roman standards bearing the image of the emperor taken into the city of Jerusalem under cover of darkness. Predictably, the people were offended by this and pleaded with him to remove them, some of them even lying down in protest outside his residence for five days. When they refused either to move or to accept the presence of such "graven images", Pilate threatened them with death. He was so amazed when they all expressed a willingness to be killed rather than betray their religious scruples that he backed down and withdrew the offending standards. Something similar happened at a later time when he brought some decorated shields into Herod's palace at Jerusalem, inscribed with the name of the emperor Tiberius along with his own name. On this occasion, the Jews took their complaint direct to Tiberius himself, who proved to be more sensitive to their demands than Pilate had been and had the offending artefacts removed and placed in the temple of Augustus at Caesarea (which was a Roman city). Pilate was not always so amenable to Jewish concerns, though, and when he helped himself to temple funds to finance the construction of an aqueduct to bring water into Jerusalem, he had the protesters beaten to death with clubs while he himself sat and watched the gory spectacle (Josephus, *The Jewish War* 2.10.4). This is widely believed to be the occasion alluded to in Luke 13:1, when Pilate ordered the death of some Galileans and then "mingled their own blood with their sacrifices". Episodes like this may well be the reason why Antipas never had much time for Pilate[8], and it might have been sensitivity to this particular situation that led Pilate to send Jesus to him for trial.

He never learned his lesson, though, and it was a similar episode – this time involving Samaritans – that led to Vitellius, the governor of Syria, eventually discharging him from office and sending him to Rome to give an account of his behaviour to the imperial officials there. What happened after that is unknown. Some traditions claim that he and his wife later became Christians, and the Coptic Church honours them both as saints and martyrs. But Eusebius reports more plausibly that he eventually committed suicide during the reign of Gaius (AD 37–41). His rule was the second longest of all the Roman governors, which suggests that he may well have been an efficient administrator. But the Gospels present him as a weak man and an opportunist who condemned Jesus to death, not out of any respect for the Jews, but only as a means of preserving his own reputation with the authorities back in Rome, who had already had to endure enough problems during his rule in Judea.

There was a hiatus in direct Roman rule for the brief period when Agrippa I was ruler of the entire territory (AD 41–44). On his death, however, the procurators once more took over the running of Judea. All historical sources are unanimous in declaring them to have been an inept and corrupt group of men. The only two to feature in the New Testament are

Felix and Festus, with both of whom Paul had dealings in the course of the trials that took place towards the end of his life. Marcus Antonius Felix (AD 52–58) had taken as one of his wives Drusilla, the daughter of Agrippa I and sister of Agrippa II. By all accounts, he shared some of the traits of the Herod family, and the Roman historian Tacitus described him in derogatory terms: "Practising every kind of cruelty and lust, he exercised royal power with the instincts of a slave" (Tacitus, *Histories* 5.9).

It was Florus who sparked off the events that led to the revolt of AD 66–70, which culminated in the destruction of the temple by Titus. The event that started it was, predictably, connected to matters of religion. Florus ransacked the temple treasury for seventeen talents and in doing so ignited the smouldering unrest that had never been far from bursting into flames. Jewish revolutionaries managed to repel an attempt to quell the rebellion by the imperial legate of Syria, and this only added to their determination to drive the Romans from their homeland. But when Nero appointed Vespasian to subdue the territory, it was only a matter of time before the Romans would gain the upper hand. Josephus has left very detailed accounts of this period, because he himself was involved in these conflicts. As a commander in Galilee, he gave Vespasian the support he needed, even predicting that he would become emperor – a prediction that was indeed fulfilled within a very short time. Pockets of resistance remained elsewhere in the territories for several years, and the final fortress to fall to the Romans was Masada (probably in AD 74), whose garrison committed suicide rather than surrender to what they regarded as infidels. From this point on, Judea became a full province of the Roman empire, and the local organizational structures were dismantled – including the Sanhedrin. The religious leaders realized that if Judaism was to survive in any coherent form they would need to reorganize their affairs. It was at this time that Rabbi Johanan ben Zakkai emerged as a key figure, and the religious school that he established at Jamnia was eventually recognized by the Romans as the official authoritative centre of the Jewish faith. The rabbis who congregated there became the *de facto* successors of the Sanhedrin, and their discussions were to play a pivotal role in transforming the nature of Judaism from a faith with different manifestations centred on the temple in Jerusalem to a unified religious community. Its main focus would now be the synagogues, which were not limited to just one locality but could be established wherever a sufficient body of Jewish believers was to be found.

The history of the time

This period of Palestinian history is well documented from a variety of sources. Latin authors were generally uninterested in what went on at the eastern end of the empire, regarding its people and their politics as beyond comprehension, though there are occasional mentions of Palestine and its rulers in the context of references to the spread of Christianity into the major cities of the Mediterranean world. This means that the New Testament itself is a significant source of information, but even more substantial than that are the writings of Josephus, which have already been referred to throughout this chapter.

Josephus was a Jewish writer, born after the time of Jesus (in AD 37 or 38), who lived through into the early decades of the second century. (His death is harder to date, but occurred sometime between AD 110 and 120.) His father was a priest and his mother a member of the Hasmonean dynasty, which gave him a claim to be both priestly and royal and therefore a trusted member of an upper-class Jewish family. When the Jewish revolt broke out in AD 66 he was appointed commander of the Jewish opposition forces in Galilee, though their chances of military success were always going to be minimal.

After seeing thousands of his troops and fellow citizens humiliated and slaughtered by the Roman armies, Josephus and forty of his comrades made a suicide pact to ensure that they would die by their own choice and not at the hands of the Romans. They decided they would draw lots to determine the order in which they would commit suicide, and Josephus ended up as one of the two final survivors. This fortuitous coincidence allowed him to persuade his fellow survivor that, instead of following through on their agreement to die, it might be more sensible for the two of them to surrender to the Romans. They were taken prisoner by forces commanded by Vespasian and his son Titus, and Josephus offered Vespasian a prophetic word to the effect that he would in due course become emperor. When that turned out to be the case, Josephus was released from imprisonment and subsequently made his way to Rome as a member of Titus's victorious army. There he was rewarded by being made a Roman citizen and given a financial settlement that secured his future. It was at this time that he adopted the name Flavius, as a mark of gratitude to his sponsor Vespasian, founder of the Flavian dynasty.

Once settled in Rome, Josephus set himself to the task of redeeming the reputation of the Jewish people. He wrote several works in which he sought to rehabilitate their religion and culture in ways that would appeal to educated Romans. He was at particular pains to retell the story of his nation in a way that would commend its values and demonstrate that the anti-Roman sentiments that had provoked such a vicious backlash from the imperial legions did not accurately reflect the mainstream of Jewish opinion, but were the work of a small handful of extremists who represented a minority interpretation of the Hebrew scriptures.

Four major works by Josephus survive today. *The Jewish War* tells in seven books the story of Jewish history from the time of the Maccabees (167 BC) to the start of the final revolt against the Romans in AD 66. When he first settled in Rome, Josephus had little confidence in his ability to write the sort of Greek that would be acceptable in educated circles, so this work was originally written in Aramaic, though it was soon translated into Greek with the help of friends who had enjoyed the benefit of a classical education. For much of the story, Josephus was able to give his own first-hand testimony, since he had himself played a role in the latter part of it. The earlier sections were inspired by books like 1 Maccabees, while the official records compiled by Nicholas of Damascus (Herod the Great's archivist) were also used extensively, as were the annals of Vespasian and Titus. If there is an overriding theme, it is one of praise for the Romans, emphasizing their tact and patience in the face of intransigence and bigotry on the part of Jewish insurgents.

Josephus's *Antiquities of the Jewish People* was even more ambitious in its scope, and was deliberately intended to commend all things Jewish to a sophisticated Roman readership. In twenty books Josephus told the story of his people, this time starting with creation and once more going right through to AD 66. This work was completed in the mid 90s, some fifteen to twenty years after *The Jewish War*. In the meantime Josephus had obviously immersed himself in the traditions of classical historians, most obviously the work of Dionysius of Hallicarnassus, a Greek historian who taught in Rome just before the start of the Christian era and whose work *The Antiquities of the Romans* provided the model for Josephus's account of his own national heritage. The major source in this case was obviously going to be the Hebrew Bible, while the sections dealing with the more recent periods of Jewish history offer a fuller and more reflective account than the one he had offered in his *Jewish Wars*.

Two shorter works complete the known writings of Josephus: *A Life*, which is what its title implies, with a special emphasis on the part he played in the defence of Galilee against the invading Romans; and *Against Apion*, a two-volume work refuting the views of Hellenistic philosophers who were inclined to dismiss Judaism as unsophisticated and primitive and therefore unworthy of consideration by intelligent individuals. Apion was a philosophical devotee living in Alexandria in Egypt, which had a significant Jewish population and where such questions were the subject of widespread debate. In order to rebuff his dismissal of Jewish values, Josephus set out to prove that in many respects (especially with regard to family life and personal ethics) the best of Judaism ran parallel to the best of the teachings of the philosophers.

Though Josephus had his own agenda in all his writing, he still offers fascinating insights into the world of the Bible, especially for the New Testament period. In three places he mentions characters who also feature in the New Testament: John the Baptist, Jesus, and James the brother of Jesus and leader of the early church in Jerusalem. The accepted text of the passage about Jesus contains the statement that he was

a wise man, if indeed one might call him a man. For he was one who accomplished surprising feats and was a teacher of such people as accept the truth with pleasure ...

> *He was the Messiah ... Pilate ... condemned him to the*
> *cross ... On the third day he appeared to [his followers]*
> *restored to life, for the holy prophets had foretold this and*
> *myriads of other marvels concerning him.*
> Josephus, Antiquities 18.3.3

This is universally regarded as a passage that was inserted into the text long after Josephus's death so as to include detailed theological statements about Jesus. All the earliest Christian sources make it clear that he was neither a Christian nor a Christian sympathizer, and there is no reason to suppose that he would have been interested in Jesus, or known very much about him. If Josephus did know anything substantial about Jesus, his writings show little sign of it. In common with many of the Roman and Greek classics, his writings are known mostly through editions published in the early Middle Ages, which left plenty of scope for editorial additions and alterations. Nevertheless, his accounts of the Romans and their dealings with Palestine and the Jews in the first century AD are still widely accepted as authentic narratives of the events they describe.

7

Daily Life in the Time of Jesus

History always records the stories of those who were rich and famous. Politicians, business people, empire-builders of all kinds – these are the sorts of people from the past whose names are most likely to be familiar to us. But of course it was ordinary people who actually made society work and whose lives supported the structures that their kings and governors relied upon. While rulers lived in palaces and had the equivalents of ancient spin doctors to record their exploits for posterity, the lives of less influential people often remained undocumented and are correspondingly more difficult to reconstruct.

Home and family

In very many fundamental respects life for ordinary people in the villages of Palestine at the time of Jesus was virtually unchanged from what it had been for centuries. Due to its strategic position, the country had been fought over more intensely than just about any other similar parcel of land anywhere in the world, and its people had been systematically exposed to different lifestyles and traditions. But rather than creating an open and inclusive culture, in the centuries immediately preceding the Christian era the exact opposite had been the case, and learning from others had come to be regarded not merely as a betrayal of traditional values but also as disobedience to divinely revealed law.

Men and women

In practice, though, some aspects of family life had changed since more ancient times. Though relational structures were still firmly patriarchal, with men holding all the reins of power and decision-making, their absolute power was being questioned in some quarters. The Hebrew Bible might have given men absolute power over their wives, but discussions were taking place among the rabbis about the meaning of some of its stipulations.

One of the issues on which Jesus was invited to offer an opinion was the matter of divorce and remarriage, and the way in which the question was put to him shows a clear connection with debates between two leading thinkers of the day, the rabbis Hillel and Shammai. Hillel believed that traditional interpretations could still be sustained and a man ought to be free to divorce his wife for any trivial reason that he cared to think of – like burning his dinner. But Shammai proposed that the right of a man to divorce his wife should always have a moral dimension and sexual infidelity was the only appropriate ground on which this could be justified. Given the culture of the day, in which if a man raped a woman she was then labelled an adulterer, this could hardly be described as a feminist agenda – but by any reckoning it was more progressive than earlier practices. Jesus raised the discussion of such matters to another level altogether, not only by refusing to collaborate with the imposition of the death penalty on a woman apparently caught in the act of adultery[1], but also by including women among his regular companions and discussing theology with them. This was such a striking and surprising aspect of Jesus' lifestyle that the Gospel writers continue the theme, even depicting women as the key witnesses to the resurrection and the first Christian preachers – something that went well beyond the inherited social attitudes of the day.

In spite of the fact that such debates could take place between religious teachers, actual family life had changed little. By this time, it was less usual for a man to have several wives, though arranged marriages were still the norm and everyone was expected to marry, usually in their early teens for girls and at the age of eighteen for men. Though it was not entirely unknown, it would have been very unusual for a man not to marry at all; and a proverb quoted by many rabbis said that "He who has no wife lives without joy, blessing, or good." The fact that such matters were extensively discussed by the rabbis serves to emphasize that marriage was regarded very much as a religious affair rather than a civil matter, though of course in a Jewish context it was always difficult to separate life into distinctive spheres like this because religious values and attitudes were all-pervasive and affected just about anything that anyone might think of doing.

Many aspects of marriage in this context were similar to practices in the wider Hellenistic world, especially the actual traditions that both preceded and followed the formal ceremony. Marriage was not just a matter for the individuals concerned but was in essence a contract between two families. The actual process started with a betrothal, which itself had the same legal standing as marriage and involved various commitments on behalf of the parties. This was the state of Mary and Joseph's relationship when she became pregnant, and it explains why there would have been legal procedures to go through had Joseph decided to abandon her at that time.[2] While it was not unknown for a man to move into the bride's family home without any further ceremony, this was not generally approved of by the religious authorities. More usually there would be a formal ceremony at which the bride would be escorted from her own family home to the bridegroom's home, where promises would be made under a canopy specially constructed for the purpose (the *huppah*). After this there would be celebration and feasting that lasted over a period of a whole week.

Children and schooling

Having children was regarded as an essential part of life, and women who turned out to be infertile could expect to find themselves cast aside as a matter of course. Jesus met a woman by a well in Samaria, who is reported to have had five husbands and was at the time living with another man to whom she was not married.[3] Modern readers easily understand that as an example of serial promiscuity on her part, but the more likely reality is that she had been discarded by her successive husbands because of her infertility, and quite possibly the person she was then living with would have been a eunuch who was not eligible to marry. The chances of a woman who was a serial adulterer escaping death in the cultural circumstance of the time would have been so remote that we can be sure some other explanation is required.

Sons were especially valued as they were the ones who would continue the family name. They were also the only ones who could expect to be offered some level of education, though among the population of Palestine there was no agreed opinion on what that education should be. When Antiochus IV instituted his programme of Hellenization in 167 BC he established a Greek educational facility in Jerusalem that was intended to mirror the educational institutions of the wider world, in which boys regularly began formal education at the age of seven and then in their later teens progressed to the "gymnasium" with its syllabus of philosophy, poetry, music, drama, and rhetoric – along with athletics and other sporting activities. What angered religious traditionalists at the time was not just the emphasis on Greek literature and learning, but the inclusion of physical activities that required scanty clothing or, in some cases, no clothes at all. As a result, this was a short-lived experiment that did not survive for long, and traditional models prevailed to ensure that education would continue to be mostly of a religious nature.

There is little evidence of organized education for young children until the second century AD, at least outside of Jerusalem. Children were deemed old enough to learn to read the scriptures by the age of five, and would do so either in the home or in the synagogue, where the teacher would be a scribe or maybe even the attendant who kept the place in good order. Memorization of scripture played a large part in this education, and familiarity with aspects of the synagogue liturgy would also be included. Most Jewish boys would continue in the environment of this "house of reading" (the *beth sepher*) until about the age of thirteen, when the more gifted ones might proceed to the *beth midrash* ("house of instruction"). Having learned the basic contents of the Torah (the "Five Books of Moses", Genesis to Deuteronomy), this next level offered the opportunity to explore the commentaries on the Law that had been developed by the rabbis over the centuries. It was probably also based in the local synagogues. Only at the end of that would those who were destined to be rabbis themselves move on to more advanced study under the tutelage of a leading rabbi in Jerusalem. Over and above all this, however, every Jewish boy, regardless of his social circumstances or educational accomplishment, was required to learn a craft.

This system is reflected in the New Testament. Paul is known to have had his early education in his home city of Tarsus, but was sent to Jerusalem to study with the rabbi Gamaliel[4] – yet at the same time, he also had a trade, tentmaking. Paul's evident erudition meant that the religious authorities could not afford to ignore him. When some other apostles, who had not been entitled to the same opportunities, demonstrated their familiarity with the interpretation of scripture before the Sanhedrin, they amazed that highly educated body because "they were uneducated and ordinary men".[5] Jesus had evoked a similar mixture of admiration and resentment when, after reading the scriptures in his home synagogue (something that would have been open to a person with his level of education), he then proceeded to offer an interpretation of it (something that was the preserve of those who had received a higher level of education[6]). Of course, he may well have belonged to a family with close ties to the Pharisees, which could help to explain the ease with which he engaged with their concerns, even from an early age.[7] The vitriolic exchanges he later had with them would certainly be characteristic of someone who had been raised in a tradition but then questioned it. His brother James was described both in the book of Acts and by Josephus as being an active Pharisee.

Work and home

It has been estimated that the population of Jerusalem in the time of Jesus was as many as 50,000 regular residents, though that figure was increased on a regular basis as pilgrims travelled from Jewish communities around the world to celebrate the major religious festivals such as Passover or Pentecost. As in most cities, a majority of the people living in first-century Jerusalem were relatively poor and depended for their livelihood on the business ventures of those who were better off. The houses of the poor were simple and closely crowded in narrow streets, though there is no evidence of the sort of multi-storey tenements that housed working populations in cities such as Rome. Alongside these small houses, though, were large houses built to Roman designs, with under-floor heating and piped water supplies. Little now remains of the streets themselves from this period, but there is evidence of some paved roads that were flanked by stone holders for torches that, when lit, would serve as street lights. Given the amount of building work that was initiated by Herod the Great, we can be sure that Jerusalem must have been a pleasant city with some grand buildings, both public and private.

But the majority of the population lived in much smaller communities focused around the two occupations that are most frequently mentioned in the stories of Jesus: fishing and farming. Both of them could create significant wealth for business owners, though rich country people are generally less ostentatious than their urban counterparts. In New Testament times there was a flourishing fishing industry based around the inland Sea of Galilee, and it was among these people that Jesus found his first followers. It is easy to construct a romantic image of these disciples as hard-working but poverty-stricken individuals, though the reality was probably quite different. The brothers Peter and Andrew, and James and John, clearly had their own businesses and would have been quite well off. Not only did they own rather substantial homes, but they were also able to take time out of their work to travel with Jesus, knowing that others would carry on in their absence. The same can be said of those whom he attracted in the farming community – for why else would he tell a story about farmers who were so successful that they built bigger barns, if he were not speaking to exactly the sort of person for whom that might be a real possibility?[8]

Food laws and religious observance

Little is known about the sort of food that formed the daily diet, though it is unlikely to have been anything like as rich as can be imagined from reading the various food laws that were intrinsic to the faithful practice of the Jewish religion. The sheer variety of different meats and the scriptural instructions about how food was to be prepared, cooked, and eaten can create the impression that there was a huge choice available. In reality, meat was a treat for special occasions, not only in the villages but also among ordinary people in the cities. The sacrifice of animals continued to play a central part in temple worship and in that context their meat was cooked and eaten in the nearest thing that ancient Jerusalem had to a restaurant. But going to the temple for a meal with one's friends and family was not an everyday occurrence. For many, it must have been a once-in-a-lifetime experience. But wherever it was consumed, food was always governed by strict religious regulations, as indeed was the whole of life.

Food laws dictated how food should be prepared, and in New Testament times this involved many rituals of washing. In earlier times, the high priest had been required to wash his hands before engaging in any ritual practices (Exodus 30:19; 40:13) but by the time of Jesus many devout people were doing this as part of their normal routine and would regularly wash their hands first thing in the morning and then again before meals. Such practices had nothing to do with hygiene but were intended to ensure an individual's ritual purity. Since none of this had actually been required by the traditional laws, that offered plenty of scope for later rule-makers, who had even developed regulations prescribing exactly which parts of the hands should be washed and the order in which it ought to be done. When all this was combined with the already complex dietary rules of the Hebrew Bible, even a simple thing like eating food had the potential to spark off lengthy religious debate. When Jesus was challenged about his own failure to keep all these regulations, he did not enter into discussion on the issue. He simply stated (quoting Isaiah) that as far as he was concerned, rules of this sort were unnecessary additions to the scripture: "You abandon the commandment of God and hold to human tradition" (Mark 7:8). As if to reinforce his indifference to such matters, he went on to talk about the things that, in his opinion, really could make a person unclean: "avarice, wickedness, deceit, licentiousness, envy, slander, pride, folly" (Mark 7:22). If some members of Jesus' own family were Pharisees, that may easily explain how he came to be so well acquainted with this kind of behaviour, even though it was not, so far as is known, official Pharisaic policy.

Rites of passage

Marriage, already discussed, has traditionally been one of the major rites of passage in all societies, and in the ancient world it was generally the precursor to the birth of a child. Indeed, a woman was regarded as not having fulfilled her true purpose in life until she gave birth, preferably to a male child. The safe arrival of a child was always a time for much joyful celebration, and the stories of the births of John the Baptist and Jesus both mention this.[9] Children were named at birth, and the name that was chosen generally had a meaning that expressed some aspiration for the person the baby might become, or the qualities that he or she would display in later life. In the case of Jesus, his name was known long before his birth, being revealed in angelic encounters not only with his father Joseph, which convention might have expected,[10] but also with his mother Mary, which was quite unexpected.[11]

For a male child, circumcision was a regular part of the celebrations of the birth, and occurred on the eighth day after birth in the context of a religious ceremony.[12] The practice of circumcision was by no means an exclusively Jewish phenomenon, but in that context it was regarded as an initiation rite signifying membership of the community and faithfulness to its traditions.

Since male circumcision was essential for full membership of the Jewish religious community, and since Jesus and his disciples were all Jewish and his message was, from one perspective, a form of revised Judaism, it was inevitable that the issue of circumcision should become especially contentious once non-Jews were attracted into the Christian faith. There was much controversy over the question of whether it might be necessary for a person to become a Jew first, in order to be a proper Christian. The argument raged not just in Jerusalem[13] but also among converts with no previous connection to Judaism (Galatians). Christians who had no background in Judaism were soon in the majority, so it disappeared as a practical question, though it continued to be discussed on a theological level for centuries to come – for if the church was in some sense a successor to the divine community of the Hebrew scriptures, in which the sign of membership was circumcision, how and why was it no longer a valid religious practice?

Coming of age is the next significant point in life, though our knowledge of the way in which this was marked in New Testament times is somewhat fragmented. In the Jewish community today, a boy's coming of age is marked by a Bar Mitzvah ceremony at the age of thirteen, with a similar Bat Mitzvah ceremony marking a girl's coming of age. But the Bar Mitzvah first appears in the Talmud (a collection of rabbinic discussions of and commentaries on the oral law), while the idea of a ceremony for a girl is a much more recent innovation. However, since thirteen was the age at which a child might progress from the *beth sepher* to the *beth midrash*, it is a reasonable supposition that this was probably also the age at which a boy was deemed to have become a man. An indirect confirmation of this may be found in Luke's story of Jesus being in the temple at only twelve years old and already engaging with the teachers of the law as an equal – suggesting that, even before he was old enough to receive formal training in such matters, he had an innate understanding of the traditions of his people.[14]

The final rite of passage was, of course, death, and in all societies this would be marked by elaborate rituals of one sort or another. Because of the climate – not to mention religious considerations that regarded a dead body as ritually unclean – the funeral generally marked the beginning of the rites surrounding death, rather than their conclusion as often happens in Western society today. A body would be prepared for burial by being washed and then wrapped in a shroud, all of which might be accompanied by the ministrations of professional mourners, who knew how to weep in an appropriately demonstrative way. But the burial itself would have to take place speedily, preferably on the very day of the death. All these features can be found in New Testament passages that refer to death.[15]

Death plays such a large part in the New Testament story, because of the nature of Jesus' own death through crucifixion. Though there is plenty of documentary evidence to show that the Romans regularly used this punishment for criminals throughout their empire, surprisingly little is known about the way it was carried out. This is largely because those who were crucified were generally never buried; rather, their bodies were simply left hanging to be eaten by animals or to rot in the sun. Only one set of remains of a man crucified in Palestine has been discovered, consisting of bones from an ossuary, which were preserved because the individual concerned (whose name, inscribed on the ossuary, is given as Yehohanan son of Hagakol) had friends who cared enough to give him a decent burial. These bones are the only indication we have of how crucifixion might have been carried out, and in his case show that his feet were probably nailed one either side of his cross rather than both feet on the front as artists have conventionally depicted it. Fragments of wood still adhering to the nails show that his cross was made of olive wood, or indeed that he might just have been nailed to an olive tree. His legs were also broken, offering an obvious comparison with the crucifixion of Jesus himself.[16] If this crucifixion was typical, it would also help to explain other features of the death of Jesus, including the easy access that others had to offer him drink,[17] for olive trees are low bushes, and anyone crucified on one would probably be at eye level to the bystanders – something that not only would heighten their awareness of the gruesome nature of this death, but would facilitate the sort of personal conversation that took place between Jesus, his mother and the beloved disciple.[18]

Bodies and bones

Disposal of a body in Palestine was invariably by burial, though it was also common for the remains to be exhumed after a year, when the bones could be gathered together and placed in a receptacle known as an ossuary, which would occupy a smaller space. This is probably the context in which Jesus recommended one of his followers to "let the dead bury their own dead" (Matthew 8:21–22), where the reference would be not to the initial funeral that took place at the death of the questioner's father, but to this subsequent ceremony held to gather up the bones of the dead and marking the final conclusion of the time of mourning. So when Joseph of Arimathea offered his own grave for the burial of Jesus (Mark 15:42–47), he would have assumed that it was only a temporary arrangement, as the bones would not rest there for ever. In the event, of course, they were there for a much shorter period than even he could ever have foreseen. The sort of grave described in that story (Mark 16:3–4) and also in the account of Lazarus's burial (John 11:38) – a cave whose opening could be closed with a large stone – was typical of Palestinian customs of the time, but was not the only pattern. A grave might also be below ground, where its presence would be marked by a brightly painted plaque, not to celebrate the life of the deceased, as in a modern cemetery, but to warn the unwary of their presence so they could avoid the accidental ritual contamination of walking over them – something that Jesus used to devastating effect in describing his religious antagonists (Matthew 23:27).

Religion

By New Testament times, religion played a key function in relation to the national identity of the Jewish people. It had always been important to their Hebrew ancestors, but now, faced with a world that embraced quite different values, maintaining the religious traditions was even more important than ever. For faithful religious believers there was no aspect of life that was not directed and controlled – and noted and celebrated – by religious procedures. To ask about life for ordinary people always involves an enquiry about their faith. The faith that inspired people in the time of Jesus could trace its own origins way back into the dim mists of ancient history. But thanks to the emergence of world empires whose grasp was even more wide-ranging than that of previous generations had been, many things were changing, and the requirements of living and believing within a multicultural world all raised new questions for the Jewish people. New circumstances created a need for new institutions, but the old traditions called for faithfulness and courage. Establishing an appropriate balance between the old and the new was always a tough challenge, not least because the Herod family were presenting themselves as preservers of the old and heralds of the new – a claim that, not surprisingly, attracted a degree of derision from many within the population, to whom it seemed that anything the Herods did was solely for their own benefit.

The festivals

Judaism was a religion of observance, whose contours were marked out by the regular celebration of religious festivals. They ranged from the Sabbath, which was a weekly celebration, to particularly holy days that occurred just once a year, such as the Day of Atonement. Not all the historic festivals feature in the New Testament stories, but some are of considerable significance for understanding the life of the earliest churches.

The Sabbath is one of them, and the procedures for observing it became a matter of some controversy in relation to Jesus' teaching and lifestyle. The question of Sabbath observance surfaces within the first two or three pages of Mark's Gospel, and is never far from the centre of the action thereafter. Jesus was roundly condemned by religious leaders when he insisted on healing people on the Sabbath or allowed his disciples to pick ears of grain as they walked through a cornfield.[19] This was more than an argument about social convention. Observance of the Sabbath as a day of rest was enshrined in the Ten Commandments, which in turn claimed that it went back to creation itself. According to the Old Testament, the people were to rest on the seventh day because "I the Lord made the earth, the sky, the sea, and everything in them, but on the seventh day I rested".[20] In Jesus' day, defining the Sabbath rest had become a major preoccupation of some religious experts. What does it mean to rest – or, for that matter, for it to be the Sabbath? Since in the Jewish reckoning a day ran not from midnight to midnight but from sunset to sunset, who could tell precisely when any given Sabbath would begin and end? In order to ensure that faithful believers would never risk breaking the Sabbath, other subsidiary regulations had been developed to protect the law itself, though it was well known that those in the know often managed to stretch the rules beyond breaking-point by adopting practices that might appear to keep the letter of the law while denying the spirit of it. The notion of a Sabbath day's journey was typical. There was a secondary regulation that defined the distance of an allowable journey as 2,000 cubits, but it was possible to travel further without actually breaking the law by designating a point 2,000 cubits from one's normal residence as "home" for the Sabbath day, maybe by storing some food there in advance – which would then give a legal entitlement to travel at least 4,000 cubits, if not more! In the light of this sort of casuistry, Jesus had good reason to ask why it was considered wrong to heal someone on the Sabbath.[21] His insistence that "the Sabbath was made for humankind, and not humankind for the Sabbath",[22] became one of the main bones of contention between him and his opponents.

Passover was less contentious for the early Christians, not least because it was the occasion of Jesus' crucifixion, which meant that it would never remain simply a Jewish festival but was endowed with its own particular Christian meaning. Like the Sabbath, it was celebrated in the home, though because of its significance it was one of the major pilgrim festivals for which Jewish believers would travel to Jerusalem from all over the world. Its origins are to be found in the events surrounding the exodus; on this night family groups would tell the story of how their ancestors had been delivered from slavery in Egypt and in the process of doing so would re-enact key elements of the narrative. Jesus' family were in the habit of making a regular annual trip to Jerusalem for this celebration,[23] where they would be joined by tens of thousands of others who came from all over the Roman empire. Some aspects of the celebrations took place in the temple itself, notably the killing of the lambs that constituted the main dish of the Passover meal. But even those who had travelled to Jerusalem from a distance then met in their family groups to share the meal and tell the traditional story. The actual boundaries of Jerusalem were extended to accommodate this influx of people, with homes that were normally not considered part of the city itself being temporarily designated as such so that everyone could celebrate the event in a location that, at least for that night, was within the city. The story of Jesus' last meal with his disciples reflects this tradition, as they too were visitors to the city and needed to hire a room from a local householder for the purpose.[24] Though there is no mention of a lamb being consumed by the disciples, all the other aspects of their meal reflect rituals connected with Passover observance.

Pentecost is the other major festival that features in the New Testament. It takes its name from the Greek word for "fiftieth", because it took place on the fiftieth day after Passover and the start of the harvest. It was originally known as the Feast of Weeks (fifty days = seven weeks plus one day), and was the main harvest festival, though by New Testament times it was also an occasion to mark the giving of the Torah to the Israelites at Mt Sinai. Like Passover, it was another festival that attracted considerable numbers of pilgrims from all around the empire. For the early church it came to have an entirely different significance, for this day marked the occasion on which a dispirited band of disciples gained new confidence through the gift of the Holy Spirit, when Peter saw 3,000 people accept his message about Jesus.[25] The fact that they were visitors drawn from all over the empire then played an important part in the rapid spread of the church well beyond the boundaries of Palestine, when they returned to their home cities and reported what they had heard.

Fasts and new moons also played a regular part in Jewish devotion and, like the more significant festivals, had their origins in the Hebrew scriptures. They would be part and parcel of the life of all faithful families, and along with Sabbath-keeping and food regulations they were the source of much debate – and not a little controversy – in some of the churches in the wider empire. Colossians provides evidence that some Christians were using these traditions as a way of disciplining their bodily functions in the hope of making themselves more spiritually attuned, a practice that Paul rejected as being not only unnecessary but also in conflict with some fundamental aspects of Christian belief.[26]

Place of Worship

Synagogues first sprang up to sustain the devotion of the dispersion (or Diaspora) of Jewish people that followed the destruction of Jerusalem by the Babylonian king, Nebuchadnezzar, and wherever Jewish people went throughout the world they built synagogues that would serve as cultural community centres as well as places of prayer. The new forms of worship that developed became so successful that in due course they were established in local communities throughout Palestine itself – for even here, not everyone was in a position to visit the Jerusalem temple on a regular basis. When he was twelve years old, Jesus' parents famously lost him in the temple at Jerusalem in the course of what is described as their annual pilgrimage. Despite the relatively short distance between Nazareth and Jerusalem, this was not a trip that even the most committed would make on a weekly basis. But they would join in the worship of the local synagogue on the Sabbath day.

The synagogues

The centre of Jewish worship had always been the temple in Jerusalem, where animal and other sacrifices played a central part in the ritual. For as long as the temple flourished, other forms of worship were either marginalized as being illegitimate or were confined to the home – as the traditional celebrations of Passover and the Sabbath always had been. But things changed once sizeable populations of Jewish people started to spring up in places so far removed from Jerusalem that regular travel to worship there was no longer a practical possibility.

There was a strong conviction that animal sacrifices could legitimately be offered in only one place, and that was in the temple at Jerusalem. That rule was not always kept as strictly as the religious traditionalists would have liked, though the Jewish temple at Elephantine in Egypt, described in chapter 3, does seem to have been the only temple outside Jerusalem. There was generally no widespread appetite for flouting convention, which meant that in synagogue worship the central place of sacrifice had to be replaced by something else. So a form of worship had developed that allowed no place for sacrifice but instead placed a new emphasis on those traditional observances that could be carried out anywhere: prayer, the reading of the Torah, keeping the Sabbath day, circumcision, and the observance of the ancient regulations concerning the preparation and consumption of food.

Not all synagogues were exactly the same. Unlike the worship of the temple, for which there was a specific mandate in the Hebrew Bible, the synagogue had no scriptural foundation – which meant that local synagogues had much greater freedom to develop their own ways of thinking. This was a natural outcome of their origins in the wider world beyond Palestinian culture, for the challenges facing Jewish people in Babylon were quite different from the challenges facing Jews in Rome – and the Egyptian city of Alexandria was different again. In each local centre people had to work out for themselves how best to adapt their ancestral faith to the demands and opportunities of their new environments. Even within the same locality different synagogues might reach different conclusions. In Rome, for example, some Jews were quite happy to go along with many aspects of pagan society, even giving their children Latin or Greek names and eagerly embracing the art-forms of Roman civilization, while others in the same city deplored what they saw as a dilution and betrayal of their ancestral faith and stuck rigidly to a more traditional understanding of the laws of the Hebrew Bible. It seems that the same distinctions were reflected in the religious life of synagogues in Palestine, and even in Jerusalem there were more conservative synagogues alongside more liberal ones. The clashes between their respective ideologies had quite an influence on the development of the earliest Christian churches, with the outlook of individuals like Stephen, who was at the liberal end of the Jewish spectrum,[27] contrasting sharply with the likes of James, who was much more at home in a deeply conservative environment.[28]

Religious loyalties

The Jewish historian Josephus reports that three main opinions were common among the Jews in Palestine:

> *Jewish philosophy takes three forms. The followers of the first school are called Pharisees, of the second Sadducees, and the third sect, which has a reputation for being more disciplined, is the Essenes.*
> **Josephus, The Jewish War 2.8.2**

He also mentions a fourth group, the Zealots, but since he does not always include these among what he calls philosophical sects it seems likely that he regarded them as forming a much looser kind of association (*The Jewish War* 4.3.9). In reality, Judaism in the first century was even more complex than Josephus suggests, with other groups in addition to these, while there were also subdivisions within some of these groups themselves.

Pharisees

Numbers are notoriously difficult to estimate for a period so far in the past, but a consensus has it that there may have been around 6,000 Pharisees at the time of Jesus, which would make them as influential as the New Testament seems to suggest they were. Their origins are shrouded in the mists of time, but are certainly to be found in the days following the Maccabean revolt and the establishment of the Hasmonean dynasty. The word "Pharisee" is often said to be derived from the Hebrew word *parush*, which can mean "to separate" and also "to interpret". Whether these two meanings were connected in the Pharisaic mind is impossible to say – and in any case, "Pharisee" seems to be the name given to them by other people, as their self-declared successors in the later rabbinic schools only ever referred to them as "the sages". By the New Testament period they had no political power, but functioned as a group concerned to preserve the religious traditions in such a way that they could be observed in everyday life, especially in relation to matters of ritual purity.

Many of them were professional students of the scriptures, but others had ordinary jobs. They were a national organization with a large number of local groups found in most villages throughout Palestine, each with their own officials and rules. They were probably the most influential religious group during Jesus' lifetime. The New Testament regularly distinguishes them from the Sadducees, and there were real differences between the two. The Sadducees' chief complaint against the Pharisees was that they had collected many rules and regulations to explain what they regarded as the real meaning of the Law. Though the Pharisees treated the Torah as their supreme rule of life and belief, they also realized that it no longer had any direct application to the kind of society they lived in, and to remain relevant it would need to be explained in new ways. One of the writings influenced by them, the *Pirke Aboth*, opens with the advice to "make a fence for the Law", which was understood to be a way of protecting the Law from infringement by surrounding it with cautionary rules that could act as an advance warning to stop people before they got within breaking distance of the actual God-given commandments themselves. This intention was praiseworthy enough, but there can be no doubt that eventually it led to the multiplication of petty rules to such an extent that keeping the Law easily became an onerous burden rather than the joyful celebration of God's goodness that it was intended to be.

In spite of the ease with which such legalism can be parodied, there can be no doubt that many Pharisees did actually keep these rules, and Josephus comments that "the people of the cities hold them in the highest esteem, because they both preach and practise the very highest moral ideas" (*Antiquities* 18.1.3). Jesus had a great deal in common with the Pharisees and agreed with them on many issues – not surprisingly, if we are right to speculate that some members of his own family might have been among the Pharisee faithful. But he disagreed with them strongly on some key issues. To

Pharisees (as to many religious people of all types), being faithful involved keeping apart from others who did not share their understandings of ritual purity or personal morality – whereas to Jesus, it was possible to distinguish between a person and his or her behaviour, to be involved with "sinners" in order to journey with them, and in the process challenge them to think differently. As part of this, Jesus questioned any understanding that made rules and regulations (even those that might claim to be of divine origin) more important than people. He also challenged the supremacy of the traditional scriptures, for example on the matter of divorce, by going further back than the Law to the principles enshrined in belief in God as creator.[29] And he was not averse to highlighting the sort of self-righteous hypocrisy that characterizes many religious people, not only Pharisees – as when he invited those who were "perfect" themselves to be the first to carry out the stoning of a woman caught in adultery.[30]

Jesus' challenge to the Pharisees may also have had a socioeconomic motivation, for it seems that a person's ability to keep the Law had to some extent become a form of social stratification – something that Jesus repeatedly questioned with his insistence that God had a special love for the outcasts and marginalized members of society, and a corresponding disdain for those who were conventionally religious.

Sadducees

Though the Sadducees are often mentioned along with the Pharisees, the two groups were not intrinsically related but were quite separate and actually held opposite opinions on almost everything. Whereas we have information about the Pharisees from some of their admirers (Josephus and the later rabbis), in the case of the Sadducees everything that we know comes from their opponents (Josephus and Christians). Our certain knowledge of them is therefore rather limited and is more concerned with what they did not believe (but which others did) than with any positive statement of their fundamental orientation. So, for example, we know that they played down the importance of the Prophets and the Wisdom literature in the Hebrew Bible by allowing ultimate authority only to the Law given by Moses in its first five books (the Pentateuch, or Torah). They consequently clashed with others who derived their beliefs from the rest of the scriptures, because they were unable to accept ideas that were not explicitly contained in the Torah. This meant that, unlike the Pharisees, they did not generally believe that God had a purpose behind the events of history, or in such things as life after death, resurrection or a final judgment.

The name "Sadducee" seems to mean "son of Zadok", although the Sadducees were certainly not direct descendants of the priest Zadok mentioned in 2 Samuel 15:24–29. Other meanings for the name are also possible: either from the Hebrew word *sadiq*, meaning "moral integrity" or "righteousness", or from the Greek word *syndikoi*, which could mean "members of the council". It is certainly true that the Jewish council of seventy (the Sanhedrin) had many Sadducees among its members, though since the remaining members were Pharisees it is doubtful if this would be the origin of their distinctive name. Many priests were Sadducees, though not all of them, so it is not possible to make a straightforward identification of Sadducees and priests. But the leading priests in the temple at Jerusalem were Sadducees, together with the most well-to-do classes of Jewish society. While projecting themselves as extreme conservatives in religious terms, they adopted a pragmatic attitude toward the Romans, which meant that they had more access to the levers of political power than almost any other group of Jewish people. Because the temple was their power base, and its life was rigorously regulated by reference to religious rules that they alone could operate, they were able to maintain a strong position until its destruction in AD 70. There is no evidence that they enjoyed a Hellenized lifestyle, though their separation of the sacred (what went on in the temple) and the secular (how they regarded Roman power) would easily have tended in that direction. The fact that after the temple's disappearance they were not regarded as the guardians of the religious heritage rather suggests that they were more compliant with Roman rule than were the Pharisees, who soon emerged as the natural interpreters of the nation's scriptures.

Essenes

The Essenes are mentioned by several ancient writers. Philo of Alexandria, the Latin author Pliny, and Josephus all mention them, though they are not explicitly named by any of the New Testament writers.

Though there is a good deal of debate surrounding the matter, it is widely supposed that one section of the Essenes wrote the Dead Sea Scrolls. This group had their headquarters at Qumrân near the north-west corner of the Dead Sea. The people of Qumrân probably had their origins among the religious supporters of the Maccabees, but became disenchanted with the corruption of their successors, the Hasmoneans, and chose to withdraw from mainstream society to live in an isolated community in the desert, where they could more easily preserve the traditions of religious and moral purity they believed they could find in the Hebrew Bible. Not all Essenes lived in this way, however, for Josephus says that they "occupy no one city, but settle in large numbers in every town". He also writes of others who, unlike the monastic groups, were married, though he emphasizes that for them this was regarded only as a means of continuing the human race (*The Jewish War* 2.8.2–13). There is also written evidence that another group lived in the desert near Damascus, whose organization was slightly different from the group at Qumrân.

There is no clear account of the relationship between these different groups, nor any certain knowledge of how they might have been related to the Essenes who were apparently scattered throughout the towns and villages of Palestine. Indeed, it might be that the term "Essene" was a generic one applied to several groups with similar ideas but not necessarily directly connected to one another. The community at Qumrân is certainly the best known, because of the discovery of their writings, and at most points these documents are in harmony with the statements made by Josephus. The Dead Sea Scrolls reveal that the people of this community regarded themselves as the minority in Israel who stayed faithful to their religion. So far as they were concerned, the rest of the nation, including especially the priests and other leaders in Jerusalem, had wilfully jettisoned the true faith; only their own leader ("the Teacher of Righteousness") and his faithful followers had preserved knowledge of the true meaning of the ancient scriptures.

Like some of the other religious groupings, the Essenes looked forward to a day of crisis in history when God's sovereignty over all things would be reaffirmed, and in the process all heretics would be banished, along with foreign enemies such as the Romans. The members of the group, rather than the whole Jewish nation, would be recognized as God's chosen people and would take over and purify the temple in Jerusalem. They expected three leaders to appear in connection with these events: the coming prophet who had been predicted by Moses;[31] a royal Messiah, who would be a descendant of King David; and a priestly Messiah, who would be the most important. In order to keep themselves in a constant state of readiness for these events, the Essenes of Qumrân went through many ritual washings. Everything they did had some religious significance. Even their daily meals anticipated the heavenly banquet, which they believed would take place at the end of the age.

There are many points of connection between the beliefs found at Qumrân and ideas circulating among the earliest Christians. John the Baptist's ministry took place in the Judean desert and involved cleansing through water as well as reflecting the same sort of ascetic lifestyle that is commended in the Scrolls. Scepticism about the temple can also be found in the preaching of Stephen,[32] while the sort of fascination with the little-known priest-king Melchizedek that is found in Hebrews[33] was also foundational at Qumrân. Then there is the importance of meals, not to mention the self-consciousness of being part of a distinctive community, and the common use of certain terminologies to describe life in and out of the community ("light and darkness", "flesh and spirit" and so on). But in all these cases, the Christian belief in Jesus gave a distinctive understanding, and the most that can be said is that Essenism offers a glimpse of sectarian Judaism that illustrates some of the ways in which the earliest Christians sought to contextualize their message within the wider cultural situation of the day.

Zealots

These people were probably not a unified or co-ordinated movement, but the term is still a useful way to refer to those individuals and groups who became most involved in direct action against the Romans. Josephus reports that

> *these men agree in everything with the opinions of the Pharisees, but they have an insatiable passion for liberty; and they are convinced that God alone is to be their only master and Lord... no fear can compel them to give this title to anyone else.*
>
> **(Antiquities 18.1.6)**

He identified their founder as Judas, a Galilean who led a revolt in AD 6, about the same time as Archelaus was removed from office by the Romans (*The Jewish War* 2.8.1), though there is some doubt over how widely the term "Zealot" might have been used before the time of the final Jewish War of AD 66–70. At least one of Jesus' disciples, a man called Simon, is identified as a Zealot,[34] though Matthew[35] and Mark[36] describe him as a "Cananaean", which seems to be a parallel word. It is also often thought that Judas Iscariot was a Zealot because one branch of these revolutionaries was known as the *sicarii*, or "knife-men", a word that sounds a bit like "Iscariot".[37] But more typical Zealots seem to have been people like Barabbas, whom the crowd chose to liberate in preference to Jesus,[38] or the unnamed rabble-rouser with whom Paul was once confused.[39]

Samaritans

Like many other aspects of the religious life of the time, the origins and identity of those people who appear in the New

Testament as "Samaritans" are not very clear. For a long time it was supposed that they must have been the descendants of the original inhabitants of Samaria, the city that, in the period of the kingdoms of Israel and Judah, had been the capital of the north and which was destroyed by the Assyrians in 721 BC. On this understanding the Samaritans would have been the remnant of the population of Israel that escaped exile in Assyria and who were later viewed with suspicion as religious renegades by Ezra and Nehemiah. But nothing that is reported of those people corresponds with what is known of the Samaritans of the New Testament period. Far from being open to influences from other religious traditions (as Ezra and Nehemiah found), these people appear to have been very conservative, sharing with traditional Judaism a strong commitment to belief in only one God, along with Sabbath observance, circumcision, and rigid adherence to the food laws. They regarded only the first five books of the scriptures as authoritative (and had their own version of them). And they also had their own expectation of a messianic-type figure, the *ta'eb* or "one who returns" to restore all things. The one thing that distinguished them is highlighted in Jesus' exchange with a Samaritan woman: the question whether God might be worshipped on Mt Gerizim (in Samaritan territory) as well as in Jerusalem, and whether their priesthood or the Jerusalem one was the more authentic.

It is impossible to say where the Samaritans of New Testament times came from, but they were certainly a religious sect rather than an ethnic grouping. Probably they emerged, along with many others, in the turbulent times following the Maccabean revolt. Their distinctive beliefs can certainly all be found within groups that would be regarded as somehow in the mainstream of Judaism of the time: like the Sadducees, they paid special attention to the Torah, like the Pharisees they expected a Messiah figure, and like the Essenes of Qumrân they questioned the legitimacy of Jerusalem and its temple.

Hellenistic influences

In spite of its distinctive Jewish culture, Palestine was still part of the Hellenistic world, as it had been ever since Alexander the Great extended his empire into the eastern Mediterranean. But it is not easy to get an accurate picture of the extent to which Greek and Roman attitudes and values had been embraced within the culture, as many of our written sources come either from those who were opposed to external interference in the affairs of Palestine or from others (such as Josephus) who wanted to commend themselves to the Romans and so tended to paint a rosy picture of their achievements in the land. Yet in Jerusalem itself, there were synagogues that could be distinguished from one another by reference to the degree to which they identified with a Hellenistic outlook,[40] and many of the tensions in the early church arose out of the fact that even among the first followers of Jesus some were more reluctant to compromise with the culture of the empire than others.

One thing that all the sources are agreed on is that Galilee, the place where Jesus grew up, was more open to Hellenistic influences than most other parts of the country. The strictest religious people generally regarded the inhabitants of Galilee as being too relaxed in their dealings with non-Jewish culture and spoke of the area in disparaging terms as "Galilee of the Gentiles". Making an accurate assessment of the size of ancient populations is fraught with difficulty, but it is generally reckoned that Galilee had more non-Jewish than Jewish residents. It was certainly a great contrast to the southern province of Judea, whose people could more easily isolate their lifestyle from external influences – something that would have been much more difficult in Galilee, if only because of its physical location. For it was criss-crossed by major trading routes going between east and west that ensured it could never be completely isolated from the wider life of the empire. Growing up here in Nazareth, Jesus would never have been far away from people who were not Jewish, and it is quite likely that he (and no doubt many of his first disciples) would have been familiar with, if not fluent in, the Greek language, which was the international language of commerce and government used everywhere throughout the Roman empire. Peter certainly must have been, as he spent much of the rest of his life travelling and preaching in the wider empire, where the language most used at home in Palestine (Aramaic) would have been quite unknown.[41] This impression of Galilee as a place that was more open to Hellenistic culture is also supported by the fact that it became the location for two of the most prestigious building projects to be completed in the first century, both of them cities constructed along Greek and Roman lines: Sepphoris and Tiberias. They, along with the Roman garrison city of Caesarea, are worth a closer look.

Sepphoris

Sepphoris is of particular interest in relation to the world of the Bible because it was located only a very short distance from Nazareth itself – maybe 4 miles to the north, and therefore just a little more than an hour's walk from Jesus' home. By the first century AD it was already a place with some history, but it had fallen into disrepair during the reign of Herod the Great. It was also a centre of Roman rule at that period, and Gabinius, proconsul in Syria, favoured it as the location for a Roman judicial council in 55 BC. In the upheavals that accompanied the death of Herod the Great, some inhabitants of the city saw an opportunity to challenge Roman rule. This led the governor of Syria at the time, Varus, to send in a military force that brought about the near destruction of the place. Once stability had been restored to the region, it was included in the territory allocated to Herod Antipas, and he decided to rebuild it as a model Hellenistic city. Much of this rebuilding was taking place during Jesus' childhood, and since Joseph's trade (and, by implication, that of Jesus himself) is described as that of a *tekton* (meaning a general builder, rather than a narrowly specialized "carpenter"[42]), and since Sepphoris was so close to Nazareth, it has been conjectured that Jesus himself might have been involved in this work of reconstruction. A traditional story identifies Sepphoris as the home of Joachim and Anna, the parents of Jesus' mother, Mary, which in turn has provoked speculation that Joseph could have met Mary while he was working on a construction site in Sepphoris.

Even if Jesus was never a member of the workforce in Sepphoris, it is highly likely that he was familiar with the place. Josephus described it as "the ornament of all Galilee", and excavations carried out there show why he was so impressed by it. Its streets were designed in a grid, paved with limestone and lined by impressive public buildings as well as ample homes for both rich and poor. One of the most striking structures was an amphitheatre seating something of the order of 4,000 people, with a huge stage to match. Then there was a royal palace, a marketplace, banks and archives. Several of the buildings featured artistic frescoes of a kind that would have been frowned upon in more conservative parts of the country. One of the most characteristically Roman features of the city was a public bath house, served (like the rest of the buildings) by an extensive water system running through a series of aqueducts that in turn connected to an underground reservoir, thus ensuring a reliable supply even in times of drought. There has been much debate as to whether Sepphoris was an exclusively Hellenistic city or whether it included a sizeable Jewish population as well. There can be no doubt that most of its inhabitants would have been working for the Romans, though the discovery that many of the houses had their own large baths, with steps going down into them after the pattern of Jewish ritual baths, may indicate religiously faithful observance. The discovery of synagogue remains would confirm this, and some Jewish writings do mention more than one synagogue in the city, though those that have been found so far belong to a period much later than the first century.

One thing we can say for certain is that those Jews who did live in Sepphoris certainly adopted a more benevolent attitude toward the Romans than their fellow citizens in Judea did. Josephus reports that at the time of the final Jewish revolt of AD 66–70, its people refused to join in the war against the Romans and in fact met with the Roman general Vespasian to solicit his assistance in protecting themselves against their own neighbouring settlements in Galilee, which were opposed to what they regarded as traitorous collaboration with their enemies. Their strategy paid off, and Vespasian stationed a sizeable contingent of troops there (1,000 cavalry and 6,000 infantry soldiers), which ensured the city's safety as well as offering the Romans a useful base of operations.

Though there is no specific story that explicitly documents Jesus' presence in Sepphoris, there is every reason to suppose that he was familiar with its culture and almost certainly will have walked its streets. When Josephus called it "the ornament of Galilee", he was referring not only to its beauty but also to its location, set on the top of a significant hill. It is not straining credibility to suggest that when Jesus encouraged his disciples to be "the light of the world" because "a city built on a hill cannot be hidden",[43] he may well have been alluding to the city of Sepphoris, whose lighted streets must have created quite a glow in the night sky of the region. It is equally feasible that his condemnation of "hypocrites" was motivated by the way in which play-actors in the Roman theatre were described (the Greek word *hypokrites* meaning someone who plays a part, often wearing a mask); the idea that play-acting was something that went on in the synagogues as well as the theatres, and that received only a short-term reward in the form of applause at the end of the performance, will have stung his hearers.[44] To suggest that there could be any connection between something as traditional as the synagogue and as dissolute as the theatre must have sounded quite heretical to strictly religious people of the day.

Tiberias

Though Antipas had good reason to be proud of his accomplishments in the reconstruction of Sepphoris, it is not hard to see why he soon relocated his own residence and many government offices to the city of Tiberias, on the western shore of the Sea of Galilee. Built over seventeen underground hot mineral springs, it is the only city from the biblical period to have survived as a tourist venue into modern times. Tiberias is located right in the centre of the area where much of Jesus' ministry took place and was only a couple of miles to the north of Bethsaida, the home base of several of his earliest disciples. There were already some small settlements in this area, which are now part of the modern city of Tiberias; but for his new city Antipas selected an already derelict site on which the village of Rakkat had previously stood, and which in effect gave him a blank space in which he could use a thoroughly Hellenistic design and then name the place in honour of the Roman emperor Tiberius. Antipas seems to have moved his own headquarters there in the mid 20s of the first century AD, and the city soon attracted an eclectic group of inhabitants.

Rumour had it that in the course of the building works, human bones came to light, perhaps implying that the site of the city had previously been a cemetery. This fact alone would have been enough to make religiously committed people reluctant to settle there, as any sort of contact with the dead was believed to render a person ritually unclean. In spite of this, it is likely that most of the population were Jewish, though there is evidence that Antipas instigated a programme of enforced settlement by moving people from other parts of Galilee into the area and also openly welcoming those who might elsewhere be regarded as outcasts. It is all the more surprising therefore that after the fall of Jerusalem and the destruction of its temple in AD 70, the Sanhedrin moved to Tiberias, and some of the most important rabbinic schools flourished there. What is less unexpected is the fact that during the revolt of AD 66–70, the city surrendered to the Roman army without a fight, thereby ensuring that some of its most important buildings would survive more or less unscathed. Like Sepphoris, Tiberias was distinguished by its magnificent buildings, including Antipas's royal palace, which was decorated with elaborate frescoes and murals, along with a synagogue, a public hall of administration and a stadium.

Tiberias had one obvious advantage over Sepphoris, for it was placed more centrally in Galilee, which made it easier for Antipas to connect with all his territory; and it was also at a point where several trade routes converged, especially those between Egypt and Damascus. When Antipas was packed off into exile in France in AD 39, Tiberias passed to Agrippa I, who held it until he died in AD 44, after which it came under direct rule by the Romans before being included in the territories of Agrippa II in AD 61. There is only one specific mention of the city itself in the New Testament,[45] though its influence was sufficiently widespread that the Sea of Galilee could also be known as the Sea of Tiberias.[46] It is often concluded from this paucity of references that Jesus never visited the city, or even that he deliberately avoided it because of its overtly Hellenistic style. But this is an argument from silence, and in any case the Gospel-writers make it clear that the incidents they record were carefully selected to serve the different purposes for which they were writing.[47] On many occasions Jesus was castigated for associating with "gluttons, drunkards, tax gatherers and sinners",[48] who are exactly the sort of people it would be far easier to meet in a place like Tiberias than on the streets of a more traditionally religious place.

Caesarea

The name of the city of Caesarea tells its own story. Herod the Great established it on the site of an older Phoenician port and renamed it in honour of the emperor Augustus Caesar. Because of its convenient location right on the Mediterranean coast, it was always going to be attractive to the Romans, allowing them easy access by sea to Palestine. This was enhanced by the construction of city walls that incorporated massive breakwaters so as to create what was eventually the largest harbour at the eastern end of the Mediterranean. Constructed in a Hellenistic style, the city had many impressive public buildings. These included a royal palace in classical style, with a centrally located pool surrounded by porticoes, and also an elaborate temple dedicated in honour of Augustus and containing large statues depicting him in various heroic activities. A wide stairway led straight from the harbour up to the temple, ensuring that the temple would be the first thing encountered by visiting dignitaries. As in other Roman cities, entertainment facilities were included in the city's design. At the southernmost end of the city was a theatre, probably the first such structure to be built anywhere in Palestine, complete with staging and an elaborately decorated space for musicians. It must have been a wonderful auditorium in which to gather, with its thousands of seats not only angled towards the stage but also overlooking the Mediterranean Sea. There was also another huge outdoor arena that originally accommodated around 8,000 people, but was later enlarged to hold nearer 15,000. Its shape and size suggest that it was designed for chariot-racing, and inscriptions discovered on the site name some charioteers of the New Testament period. Unlike similar structures elsewhere in the empire, it would not have been used for mime and drama, but was what in Italy would have been called a circus, and what in the eastern Mediterranean was traditionally known as a hippodrome – though it was remodelled in the second century to become a more conventional theatrical space with staging and changing-rooms for actors. As in other cities built by the Romans, the infrastructure was supplied with water through an elaborate system of aqueducts and pipe work, much of which can still be seen today, including the viaducts which were one of the major technological innovations to be developed by Roman engineering ingenuity.

In AD 6, the Roman procurators of Judea settled in Caesarea, and both documentary evidence and inscriptions indicate that it also became the headquarters of the Second and Tenth Legions of the imperial army. This was the regular home of Pontius Pilate during his time as prefect of Judea, and an inscription bearing his name has been unearthed in the remains of the theatre. Having the main Roman garrison stationed here was convenient for everyone. For religiously observant Jews, it meant that they could get on with their own traditional practices without too much interference from the Romans – always provided, of course, that they did not step too much out of line. For the Romans, life in Caesarea replicated what they would have enjoyed elsewhere in the empire, while being sufficiently close to Jerusalem that it was possible to move troops there speedily whenever the need might arise – and with the added bonus that one could take a ship direct from Caesarea to Rome itself. Though the New Testament story locates Pilate in Jerusalem at the time of Jesus' crucifixion, he would have been based there only for short periods of the year; Passover was one of them, when the influx of pilgrims not only from the rest of Palestine but from other parts of the world required that a closer eye than usual be kept on what was going on there. It would have been more usual for cases falling under imperial jurisdiction to be sent to Caesarea for trial, as happened in the case of Paul. This is where he stood before Felix,[49] and later before Festus and Agrippa, and it was from Caesarea that he boarded a ship on his final journey to Rome.[50]

Of course, the population of Caesarea cannot have been entirely non-Jewish, and most likely there were a small number of Jewish inhabitants who worked within the civil service of the day, liaising with the Roman authorities. Synagogue remains have been discovered, dating to a later period than the New Testament, but the story of Cornelius bears witness to the existence of some sort of Jewish religious community in the first century AD. Cornelius was a centurion within the Roman army, nominally in charge of 100 soldiers, though if "the Italian cohort" that he commanded[51] was comparable with other units that were given the same designation, it could have included nearer 1,000. He occupies an important niche in the story of the early church because he is the first truly non-Jewish convert to be mentioned.

8

Life with the Romans

Rome was not the first great empire to impinge on the Bible story, but it was undoubtedly the most successful, and lasted far longer than any of its predecessors. Like the Greek empire of Alexander the Great, Rome started off as a city-state, but had certain distinctive characteristics that contributed to its long-term survival. There was always a conviction that what happened in Rome was the best way of doing things, not just for pragmatic reasons but because it was grounded in some higher eternal order. But unlike almost all its predecessors (with the possible exception of the Persians), the Roman way embodied a flexibility that allowed it to be hospitable to the peculiarities of the cultures and peoples whom it conquered. Regardless of an individual's origin, it was always potentially open to anyone to become a Roman citizen – and native-born Romans for their part welcomed learning from other cultures and ways of life. Though the traditional deities of Rome both guaranteed and underpinned the structure of the empire, the gods of other nations could easily be incorporated in ways that took their claims seriously. In the ceremony of *evocatio*, a regular part of military strategy, the Roman armies invited the gods of other cities to change their allegiances, promising that the Romans would be even more committed to them than their original devotees had ever been.

Politicians and rulers

It is a tribute to the genius of Roman pragmatism that this acceptance of diversity never threatened the empire's essential internal unity. For underwriting everything was the Roman understanding of law, which in turn was reflected in the structures of government. Writing in the second century BC, the Greek historian Polybius observed that Roman civic life combined the best of all possible political systems, acknowledging the role of supreme rulers (the consuls) alongside powerful aristocratic interest groups (the Senate), in partnership with democratic engagement by the people (local assemblies) – all of them founded on commitment to the traditional deities, expressed through the performance of regular rituals.

By the time of the New Testament, Rome already had a long history. For centuries it had been a small and struggling city-state, one among several in Italy. Its expansion had started in the fourth century BC, and by 275 BC Rome controlled the whole of Italy. But it was not until it inherited Alexander's Greek empire that its influence spread to the eastern Mediterranean. Alexander had a philosophical vision for creating a single unified world, but it was Roman technology that brought the vision to fruition as roads and shipping lanes opened up countries that had previously been isolated from one another and from the great cultures of Greece and Italy. In its western expansion, Rome had spread the influence of Latin language and lifestyles. In the east, the Greek culture of Alexander continued to flourish, and eventually spread westwards to Italy itself, so that by the second century BC any educated person there would have been fluent in at least two languages, Latin and Greek.

Augustus (31 BC–AD 14)

The two centuries immediately preceding the Christian era were turbulent ones for Roman society, but by 31 BC Octavian (subsequently known as Augustus) had succeeded in establishing himself as emperor in all but name. In fact, he played a very clever political game: recognizing that the old guard in Rome would be resistant to handing over absolute power, he allowed himself initially to be elected as consul on an annual basis. Within less than ten years, though, he had managed to put a new constitution in place that gave the appearance of accountability while in reality endowing him with supreme power – a constitutional shift that is often referred to as the movement from republic to principate (*princeps* being the term most often applied to him, meaning literally "the chief citizen"). Whatever might be said about the way in which he accomplished all this, his style was undoubtedly what was needed at that time. It was under his rule that peace was established throughout the empire (the *pax romana*), and safe travel ensured the expansion of trade and commerce, which in turn fuelled economic expansion. He also set about reconstructing the city of Rome itself and was responsible for many new buildings of both a religious and a civic nature. In documenting his accomplishments the historian Suetonius was full of praise for his public works:

> *Since the city was not adorned as the dignity of the empire demanded, and was exposed to flood and fire, he so beautified it that he could justly boast that he had found it built of brick and left it in marble. He made it safe too for the future, so far as human foresight could provide for this.*
>
> **Suetonius, Life of Augustus 28.3**

The renewal orchestrated by Augustus went far beyond bricks or marble, and the entire culture underwent a significant transformation as a result of his endeavours to bring stability and self-confidence to the somewhat disjointed empire that he had inherited. During his rule, artistic creativity was heightened, and it has rightly been called the Golden Age of Latin literature. Virgil (70–19 BC), Horace (65–8 BC), Livy (59 BC–AD 17), and Ovid (43 BC–AD 18) all flourished in this period and helped to promote the idea that through Augustus the world was on the cusp of some new adventure that would radically transform the lives of all its people. In his Fourth Eclogue, Virgil depicted this time as a messianic age to be ushered in by the birth of a child who would release people from their guilt, and "release the earth from its continual dread … have the gift of divine life … see heroes mingle with gods … and shall sway a world to which his father's virtues have brought peace" – an expectation so similar to the Christian hope that some have understood it to be a prophecy about Jesus, albeit from a "pagan" writer. In reality, the child of whom Virgil wrote was almost certainly the offspring of the consul Pollio, who is also mentioned in the poem – but the images all this evokes certainly sum up the optimistic spirit of the age, in which anything at all seemed possible.

It was the foundations laid by Augustus that facilitated the amazing expansion of the Christian church and allowed it to spread from the edge of the empire to all its major cities in less than a single generation. The development of regular safe modes of transportation by both sea and land, along with the fact that a single language (Greek) could be spoken and understood everywhere, coupled with the sense that this was a world in the process of being re-imagined – all these things contributed very positively to the spread of the Christian message.

Tiberius (AD 14–37)

Tiberius was Augustus's stepson, son of his second wife Livia, but also his son-in-law, since he had married Augustus's daughter Julia. By the time he became emperor at the age of fifty-five, he already had a distinguished military career behind him. His accession was the occasion for considerable uncertainty, as the role he was about to fulfil had been created by Augustus and there was no clear process regarding succession. When Tiberius appeared before the Senate to be confirmed in his new position, he declared himself to be too old for the job and asked if he could be given some lesser form of responsibility in government. Perhaps he was just intending to be modest and needed some reassurance that he really was the right person, but his attitude failed to impress the senators, who concluded that he was just being awkward – though they themselves had no clear idea of what the correct procedure might be. The deadlock was broken when Quintus Haterius asked him, "How long, Caesar, will you suffer the state to be without a head?" According to Tacitus, Tiberius was not pleased by this, but finally gave in:

> *Wearied at last by the assembly's clamorous importunity and the urgent demands of individual Senators, he gave way by degrees, not admitting that he undertook empire, but yet ceasing to refuse it and to be entreated.*
> **Tacitus, Annals 1.13**

It was not the end of the matter for Haterius, though, and he was fortunate to get out of the situation with his life.

While Augustus had revelled in his interactions with the Roman Senate, Tiberius kept himself at a distance throughout his reign. Historians are undecided as to whether this behaviour was intended as a deliberate ploy to gain respect, which somehow backfired, or whether it should be seen as a sign of some kind of mental illness. Either way, Tiberius ended up on the margins of his own political machine, and for the last ten years of his reign lived on the island of Capri, where he did not need to engage with the political life of Rome itself. He handed over the day-to-day governance to Sejanus, who was prefect of the praetorian guard (the emperor's bodyguard), and Sejanus's deeply anti-Semitic attitudes probably influenced Roman policy in Palestine. Tacitus reports how he persuaded the Senate to expel the Jewish population from Italy and send 4,000 of its young people to Sardinia to fight on behalf of Rome. Though it is unclear to what extent this succeeded, the language in which his resolution before the Senate was expressed shows nothing but contempt for what he regarded as alien opinions:

> *A resolution of the Senate was passed that four thousand of the freedmen class who were infected with those superstitions [Judaism] and were of military age should be transported to the island of Sardinia, to quell the brigandage of the place, a cheap sacrifice should they die from the pestilential climate. The rest were to quit Italy, unless before a certain day they repudiated their impious rites.*
> Tacitus, Annals 2.85

Sejanus was the one who appointed Pontius Pilate as prefect of Judea, and his ambivalent attitude towards the Jewish people no doubt reflected what was going on in Rome at the time. Eventually Sejanus fell out of favour with Tiberius, and was executed on his orders in AD 31.

It is hard to get a comprehensive picture of Tiberius's character and personality, partly because he was obviously something of a recluse, but also because what we know of him has been filtered through what was reported back in Rome by Sejanus, in whose interest it was to portray the emperor as a distant and somewhat depressive individual. Our main source of information about him is Tacitus, who also had his own agenda in reporting Tiberius's life. In relation to the Bible story, Tiberius is the emperor during whose rule Jesus' public ministry took place, and the emergence of John the Baptist is dated in Luke 3:1 by reference to his name. He must also be the emperor who is often referred to in the Gospels simply as "Caesar", and it must have been his face that was on the coin that Jesus famously identified as one of the "things that are the emperor's", when asked a question about taxation[1].

Caligula (AD 37–41)

Caligula's real name was Gaius, and "Caligula" was a nickname (meaning "little boots") that he was given as a child while his family lived in Germany, where his father Germanicus was a military commander. At one time, it had seemed as if Germanicus himself might have been the successor to Augustus, who was his great-uncle and with whom he enjoyed considerable favour. According to Tacitus, Augustus instead forced Tiberius to adopt Germanicus and designate him as his own successor (*Annals* 4.57). Germanicus achieved considerable fame and popularity in Rome for his military exploits, but never lived long enough to become emperor and died in suspicious circumstances that appear to have been orchestrated by Sejanus. It is little wonder, then, that Caligula found it hard to know whom to trust, in spite of the fact that the Senate welcomed his appointment. Once he became emperor his paranoia soon showed itself, and he declared himself to be divine. This conviction caused considerable tension with

Jewish communities in various parts of the empire, as well as
with the political establishment in Rome itself, and his short
reign was brought to an end with his assassination by his own
bodyguards, acting in collusion with senators who hankered
for the restoration of a republic along the lines of what had
existed before Augustus started reorganizing the Roman state.

Claudius (AD 41–54)

The plan for a restoration of the republic never got off the
ground, since the praetorian guards who had killed Caligula
adopted Claudius on the very same day as their favoured
candidate to be his successor. After some delicate negotiations
between the praetorian guard and the Senate – conducted by
Herod Agrippa I – Claudius became emperor, and Agrippa
was rewarded with the gift of extended territories in Palestine.

Claudius was aged fifty when he became *princeps*, and
by all accounts was not a pretty sight to look at, with a
pronounced limp and a reputation for slavering all the time.
But he was much brighter than his appearance might have
implied, and seems to have been quite a scholar. He certainly
took his responsibilities as emperor far more seriously than
his immediate predecessors. He needed to, for one of the
ongoing sources of potential conflict concerned the status of
Jewish people whose sensitivities had been outraged not only
in Palestine but also by the actions of Sejanus and Caligula.
Anti-Jewish riots had taken place in Alexandria just a few years
previously, and when the Jews of that city sent a delegation
to Rome seeking some redress, they were not well received.
One of the first things Claudius did on his accession in AD
41 was to send a letter to all the inhabitants of Alexandria,
instructing the civic authorities to be even-handed in dealing
with different sections of the population and telling the Jews

to expect no more privileges than they already enjoyed. A papyrus copy of this letter survives and is worth quoting at length, if only because it demonstrates that the Jewish communities of the Diaspora were not quite the innocent victims of Hellenistic imperialism that they sometimes liked to imagine. Not only were they quite capable of artificially boosting their own numbers (and therefore influence) by encouraging immigration from elsewhere; they were also not averse to actually trying to disrupt the sorts of practices that they disapproved of, in particular the Greco-Roman passion for athletic games and other artistic pastimes. Claudius's letter reads:

> *I explicitly order the Jews not to agitate for more privileges than they formerly possessed, and not in the future to send out a separate embassy as if they lived in a separate city, a thing unprecedented, and not to force their way into gymnasiarchic or cosmetic games, while enjoying their own privileges and sharing a great abundance of advantages in a city not their own, and not to bring in or admit Jews who come down the river from Syria or Egypt, a proceeding which will compel me to conceive serious suspicions; otherwise I will by all means take vengeance on them as fomenters of what is a general plague infecting the whole world.*

When this document first came to public attention early in the twentieth century, it evoked a good deal of speculation over the nature of the "general plague infecting the whole world", in particular whether it might be a veiled reference to the spread of Christianity. Christians certainly were active in Alexandria by this date, evidently led by a man called Apollos, whose concern for the integration of the Hebrew scriptures with the ideas of Greek philosophical speculation suggests some obvious comparisons with Philo, a Jewish scholar who specialized in precisely the same things.[2] While it is doubtful whether this is specifically what Claudius was referring to in this context, there is more plausible evidence suggesting that the tensions between Jews and Christians in Rome itself were having an impact on civic order not long after this. The historian Suetonius reports on a series of riots that took place in Rome during AD 49, and attributes them to someone he calls "Chrestus" (Suetonius, *Life of Claudius* 25.4). While it is possible that this refers to an individual of that name, there is good reason to think that the events he describes were fomented by arguments about the new beliefs of those Roman Jews who had become Christians and were hailing Jesus as their expected Messiah. ("Messiah" is a Hebrew term whose equivalent in Latin was *Christus*, or in Greek *Christos*, and which could well have been reported as "Chrestus" by someone not entirely familiar with the details of the conversation.) As a consequence, the Jews became very unpopular and Claudius "ordered all Jews to leave Rome"[3] – though it is unclear how such a policy could be universally enforced, or indeed how the city could have continued to function smoothly without a major section of its commercial infrastructure.

Beyond these matters, Claudius's reign was marked by significant gains in territory (Britain became a part of the Roman empire during this period) and also in governmental reforms within Rome itself, through the establishment of new rules for the acquisition of Roman citizenship and the rationalization of many administrative functions under the control of the imperial court.

Nero (AD 54–68)

Nero is probably better known to the general public than any of his predecessors, and whenever his name is mentioned the madness of his later years is usually the first thing many people think of. But his reign actually began auspiciously. He was only sixteen years old at his accession and recognized the importance of being advised by older and wiser people; in his case, they were the philosopher Seneca, and Burrus, the head of the praetorian guard at the time. They were in charge for the first five years of Nero's reign, and almost certainly their competent handling of the affairs of state was one of the major reasons why Paul felt confidence in encouraging Christians (specifically his readers in Rome) to trust the empire as an honourable institution that would safeguard the rights of ordinary people and uphold the law of God.[4] Paul had also encountered the even-handedness of Roman justice at first hand, when he appeared a few years previously before the tribunal of Gallio, proconsul of Achaia, who was himself the brother of Seneca.[5] It is debatable whether he would have placed quite so much faith in Roman justice had he been writing the book of Romans just a few years later, for within a relatively short time both Burrus and Seneca had died (in AD 62 and 65 respectively, Seneca being ordered to commit suicide), and Nero turned into a monster. His wife Octavia was killed on his orders so he could marry a woman named Poppaea. Christianity was already despised in educated circles as being superstitious nonsense (in Latin, *superstitio*) that served only to encourage disdain for the traditional practices of civic religion (in Latin, *religio*), and Seneca himself had written that "*religio* honours the gods, *superstitio* dishonours them" (*On Mercy* 2.5.1). Given the respect for law that was at the heart of the Roman constitution, and the close identification between traditional religion and the state, it was only a matter of time before Christianity came to be seen as a threat.

In AD 64 a huge fire in Rome gave Nero just the right opportunity to move against the Christians. It apparently started at the eastern end of the Circus Maximus, which was near to a Jewish ghetto adjacent to the Capena Gate. Nero could have blamed the Jews, but he was the one who had allowed them back into the city after their exclusion under Claudius, and he probably had no stomach for stirring up further controversy with that section of the population. Of course, at the time many Roman Christians were Jews (as can be seen from the concerns addressed by Paul in his letter to them), and quite probably lived in the same quarter of the city. At any rate, it was the Christians who were singled out for blame, and the punishments heaped upon them were gruesome in the extreme. The Roman people were well enough accustomed to cruelty, but even they were shocked by the barbarous treatment of the Christians. The historian Tacitus had no time for what he knew of Christian beliefs, regarding them as superstitious and shameful; but he began his account by noting the vindictive nature of the allegations made against them, and for which the fire was but an excuse:

> *An immense multitude was convicted, not so much*
> *of the crime of arson, as of hatred of the human race.*
> *Mockery of every sort was added to their deaths. Covered*
> *with the skins of beasts, they were torn by dogs and*
> *perished, or were nailed to crosses, or were doomed to*
> *the flames. These served to illuminate the night when*
> *daylight failed. Nero had thrown open his gardens for*

the spectacle, and was exhibiting a show in the circus, while he mingled with the people in the dress of a charioteer ... Hence, even for criminals who deserved extreme and exemplary punishment, there arose a feeling of compassion; for it was not, as it seemed, for the public good, but to glut one man's cruelty, that they were being destroyed.

Tacitus, Annals 15.44

This is almost certainly the situation referred to in the New Testament in 1 Peter, whose original readers found that their faith was being "tested by fire",[6] and whose enemy could be described as "a roaring lion, looking for someone to devour".[7] It is certainly the circumstance in which two of the leading lights in the Christian church met their deaths: Peter by being crucified upside down, in a gross caricature of the death of Jesus, and Paul being beheaded, in a bizarre display of protocol to honour his status as a Roman citizen.

By the time Nero committed suicide in AD 69 at the age of thirty, his realm was in a mess. It was not only the Christians whom he had alienated: by this point, the praetorian guard was in revolt, as were several of the imperial legions in the western empire, while in the east the Jewish revolt that concluded with the fall of Jerusalem in AD 70 was already moving into its final stages. There was no obvious successor to Nero, and within the space of a single year four different claimants came to power: Galba (the governor of Spain), Otho (one-time governor of Lusitania), Vitellius (army commander in Germany), and finally Vespasian (who had been engaged in fighting Jewish insurgents in Palestine, but returned to Rome to seize power for himself).

Vespasian (AD 69–79)

Up to this point, all the emperors had been related in one way or another (what is often referred to as the Julio-Claudian dynasty). With Vespasian (and his successors, who came to be known as the Flavian dynasty) there was a clean break with the past. He belonged to a different stratum of Italian society, whose power base was not in Rome but in the Italian hinterland, and it was from these people that he appointed new members to the Senate, something that had the effect of integrating local and national government in Italy as well as giving him an opportunity to adopt the sort of new ideas that were required if stability was to be restored after the turbulence of the aftermath of Nero's demise.

More is known of Vespasian's career before he became emperor than of what he actually did once he took over that position. He made his name in the first instance as a military commander and had been involved in the invasion of Britain during the reign of Claudius. But then from AD 51 to 63 he went into retirement, only to be recalled to be governor of North Africa, where he served briefly before joining Nero's royal court. But he was dismissed from that position for being insufficiently attentive during one of Nero's musical recitals. He came back to prominence only in AD 66, when he was appointed to spearhead the Roman attack on Jewish insurgents in Palestine. He stayed with that operation until he became emperor in AD 69, leaving his son Titus to complete it, which he did successfully in AD 70. What we do know of him as emperor suggests that he was very down to earth and that he invested his energies in stabilizing the financial and organizational base of the empire and its capital in Rome.

Titus (AD 79–81)

Titus succeeded his father Vespasian, but reigned for only a very short time before dying of natural causes. The two key events of his reign were the eruption of Vesuvius in AD 79, which destroyed the cities of Pompeii and Herculaneum, and the official opening of the still unfinished Colosseum (it was eventually completed under his brother Domitian, who succeeded him). By all accounts he was held in high regard by the general population, not least for his untiring efforts to provide relief for those who were displaced by the eruption.

Domitian (AD 81–96)

Domitian is the last emperor whose reign impinged on the events recorded in the Bible. He was the younger brother of Titus, and for much of his life lived in his shadow. Titus was the one who made a name for himself as a valiant soldier, most notably through his involvement in the Jewish Wars of AD 66–70. Some ancient historians have implied that Domitian had a hand in Titus's death, killing him by default by choosing not to offer him appropriate care when he was struck down by a fever. These accounts may well reflect the resentment that he stirred up among the traditional families whose members had been influential in the Senate for generations, but equally there is no evidence that the two brothers had much affection for each other. Domitian certainly had a high opinion of himself, insisting on being called "lord and god" (*dominus et deus*); and the coins of his reign depict him enthroned as the "father of the gods", characteristics which led many of his contemporaries to regard him as a self-opinionated tyrant, if not another insane emperor who bore comparison with the likes of Caligula and Nero.

The New Testament book of Revelation was written during Domitian's reign, and is often thought to reflect the way in which his perception of himself as divine was worked out through the persecution of anyone who could not accept this designation. There is no hard evidence for any widespread and officially orchestrated persecution at this time, though sporadic violence against Christians was a common enough occurrence, and would not be inconsistent with what is otherwise known of Domitian's character, for he was certainly inflicted with the same insecurities and paranoia as Nero before him and had no hesitation in arranging the execution of anyone of whom he developed a suspicion. Like many of his predecessors, he was assassinated in a conspiracy supported by his own praetorian guard and other establishment figures. Suetonius depicts him as a fearful man, obsessed with astrological predictions, among which was one that said that, whenever he died, it would be at the fifth hour of the day (noon). He evidently had an intuition about what day that would be, and when he asked a servant for the time (which was the fifth hour), was told that it was in fact an hour later. Suetonius continues:

> *Filled with joy at this, and believing all danger now past, he was hastening to the bath, when his chamberlain Parthenius changed his purpose by announcing that someone had called about a matter of great moment and would not be put off. Then he dismissed all his attendants and went to his bedroom, where he was slain.*
> **Life of Domitian 16**

Everyday living

While Christianity started in rural Galilee, its rapid expansion began only once it had moved beyond Palestine itself and into the major cities of the Roman empire. The growth of the early church is inextricably linked to the story of Roman cities. Here, in a vast melting-pot of cultures, races, and classes, this new faith could take root and find resonances with the aspirations of many different sorts of people. From the retirement complexes of Philippi, largely populated by ex-military people and former bureaucrats, to the seedy city of Corinth, with its reputation for immorality and syncretism, the Christian message struck a chord with the ambitions of people who otherwise might have had little in common with one another. Different social contexts enabled the emergence of many different styles of Christian community, and there was never any guarantee that the church in one place would be the same as the church in a different setting. Indeed, this ability to contextualize itself within such diverse cultures is perhaps the one thing that, above all others, explains the attraction of the Christian gospel. Nor did the apostles insist on imposing a rigid uniformity, as we can see from the various letters that were written to the different churches. On the contrary, they addressed themselves to the issues of the moment that mattered in a particular location, to such an extent that subsequent readers of the New Testament have often struggled to find any consistent themes in their writings. Paul is a good example. At one and the same time he can seem to be deeply engrossed in wrestling with questions that only Jewish believers would have come up with (as in Romans and Galatians), and dealing with the more esoteric speculations that were commonplace in the so-called mystery religions that were flooding the Roman cities in the first century (1 and 2 Corinthians and Colossians). If we are to understand the life of the early church, we cannot ignore the realities of Roman culture.

Society and its structures

Roman society was very carefully regulated along lines of social class. While it was not impossible to move from one class to another, it was not something that happened every day, and most people simply accepted the social circumstance into which they had been born. Though it was possible for people to better themselves through education and successful military service, ownership of land was the real key to civic influence. This is what determined who could belong to the two major aristocratic groupings in Rome, the senators and the knights (or equestrians).

The major qualification for membership of the Senate was ownership of property worth at least a quarter of a million denarii, though in order to be an actual member it was necessary to be appointed to a formal position in the city of Rome itself. A typical member of a senatorial family might finish his education around the age of twenty, then be given some junior bureaucratic position, which might be followed by a period of military service (often in a managerial rather than a combative position). After that, a good candidate could expect to become a *quaestor* (finance officer), which carried with it a Senate seat, and then a *praetor* (a legal position). The most talented might then be appointed as consuls or provincial governors. By and large, Christians tended not to come into direct contact with this level of Roman governance, though there are some exceptions. When Paul and Barnabas visited the island of Cyprus, they were invited into the court of the proconsul Sergius Paulus,[8] and Paul also met with

Gallio, proconsul of Achaia, in the more formal setting of his legal tribunal.[9]

Paul later came face to face in a judicial setting with Felix and Festus, procurators of Judea, who belonged to a different class altogether. Little is known of Festus, though it is reasonable to assume that he was a member of the equestrian order (the knights), the qualification for which was ownership of property worth only 100,000 denarii. There was a certain fluidity between this group and the senatorial order, and it was also possible for someone not born into it to become recognized as a knight. They were the bureaucrats and civil servants of the empire, and serving as a procurator in some far-flung territory would be part of a typical career path. Though Felix was also a procurator, he was not an equestrian but a "freedman", a term that means what it says: he was from a family of slaves who had been granted their freedom. He owed his rise to prominence to the influence wielded by his brother Pallas in the court of the emperor Claudius, though the Roman aristocracy could still regard him with disdain, and Tacitus summed up his career with the statement that "he exercised the power of a king with the mind of a slave" (*Histories* 5.9).

Another common procedure that could lead to a change in a person's status was the practice of adoption, something that could happen at any age and which generally marked the start of a new life for the one adopted. This practice is one of the complexities we face in understanding the imperial succession in Rome, which could involve emperors adopting either their own stepchildren or even complete outsiders. Adoption represented a far more thoroughgoing reorientation of lifestyle and future prospects than would be the case today. To be adopted meant the cancellation of all one's debts and a total reversal of an individual's previous fortunes; the adopted person not only took on the name of his or her new family but was entitled to all the privileges of that family, including full rights of inheritance. In return, of course, the adoptee came under the control of the new family's head (invariably the father), who determined the future course of his or her life while offering safety, security, and family solidarity in exchange. In other words, an adopted person enjoyed exactly the same status as a person born into the family – something that Paul used as an appropriate metaphor for the gift of God's grace experienced through faith in Christ.[10]

One further category worth noting is that of citizenship. In the earliest days, of course, citizenship was a localized concern: you were a citizen of whatever city or province you happened to be born into. More or less from the start, Roman citizenship had extended slightly beyond Rome itself, as provincial alliances with different areas of Italy were forged. But it was Augustus who extended the notion so that citizenship became a mark of distinction rather than a narrowly defined geographical designation. Paul is the most prominent New Testament example of a person who was a Roman citizen, and he exemplifies this non-geographical principle very well, for he could quite easily be regarded as a citizen of two cities: of Tarsus, his birthplace,[11] and of Rome[12] (even though, at that stage, it is unclear whether he had ever been to the city). This is another theme that Paul used to illustrate his understanding of Christian faith, insisting that there was no intrinsic incompatibility between being a good citizen of Rome as well and owing loyalty to a "citizenship … in heaven",[13] which involved being "no longer strangers and aliens, but … citizens with the saints and also members of the household of God".[14]

An individual could become a citizen by various routes: by being born to parents who were already citizens, as a reward for some special service on behalf of the empire (either commercial or military), or even as part of a package of privileges granted to freed slaves. Though in theory no distinction was drawn between these various pathways to citizenship, Paul used the fact that he was "born a citizen" to his advantage when dealing with Claudius Lysias, who had arrested him in Jerusalem but who had secured his own citizenship only on payment of "a large sum of money".[15] It was usual for someone gaining citizenship under these circumstances to adopt the name of his or her sponsor, which suggests that the tribune had only recently gained citizenship – in the time of Claudius, during whose reign it was evidently quite easy to purchase citizenship. By New Testament times, citizenship involved very few formal duties other than loyalty to the empire, though it bestowed important privileges, including exemption from degrading punishments such as flogging and crucifixion, and the right to appeal to the courts in Rome over the head of the local judiciary – both of which feature in the stories of Paul.

Slaves and Freedmen in Roman Society

Slavery was commonplace, and according to some estimates as much as a fifth of the entire population of Rome consisted of slaves. Warfare provided a significant supply of slaves in the form of defeated soldiers, but there was also a ready supply in the form of children who were abandoned or sold by their parents, or indeed of individuals who sold themselves into slavery. Slaves had no legal rights and were regarded as less than human. Even an enlightened philosopher such as Aristotle had written that "the slave is a living tool, and the tool a lifeless slave" (*Nicomachean Ethics* 8.11), though the way any slave was treated eventually depended on the attitude of his or her owner. In theory slaves were not allowed to marry, though there are many examples of slaves forming intimate long-term relationships, having children and living in something resembling a family. This was most often the case with household slaves, who might be afforded safety and security by their masters in exchange for loyalty and obedience. Slaves in these circumstances could be entrusted with important positions in civic and domestic life, and certainly had it a lot easier than those who were incarcerated in industrial situations such as working in mines or on seagoing ships.

Slaves appear frequently on the pages of the New Testament, a fact which no doubt reflects the stratum of society in which the early churches most easily took root, namely the extended household of the equestrian classes with their villas that would be large enough to provide housing for a substantial community. In socioeconomic terms, these people occupied the same sort of niche as regular employees in today's society. They even earned "wages" in the form of money that was still legally owned by their masters though available for the slaves to spend. Many of them saved this up in order to buy their freedom. A common way of doing this was a ceremony in a religious context (which could include the synagogues). Since a slave was not entitled to enter into a legal contract, the idea was that the deity would do that on the slave's behalf, with the price of freedom being paid into the temple coffers. A fraternal club could also serve the same purpose, and at a later date churches operated in this capacity. This is the context in which Paul encouraged Philemon to grant freedom to his slave Onesimus. It is often thought that this process of paying a ransom to a third party is the background against which Paul's language describing the freedom of faith in Christ is best understood (see, for instance, 1 Corinthians 6:19; 7:22–23; Galatians 3:13; 4:5).

Marriage, families, and children

Marriage was the foundation for society in all the social contexts encompassed by the biblical literature. While there were variations in the details of how a marriage contract might be drawn up, in ancient Greece and Rome the basic principle on which a marriage could be recognized was the consent of the two parties to live together, and a central purpose of marriage was to have children. Though love was by no means excluded, the underlying rationale for marriage was of an essentially economic nature, and this is acknowledged and expressed in the practices and conventions with which it was celebrated. Religious rites were always important, with the deities that connected with the traditions of hearth and home being invoked at such times. The home had always been a centre of spiritual devotion, with participation in simple rituals and sacred meals a regular aspect of daily life. Many of the trappings of Western weddings even today derive from antecedents in Roman culture. A typical ceremony would begin with the bride, having bathed and put on special clothing, being escorted to the house of the bridegroom, most often in a torchlight procession. There, the couple would join hands, make promises, and sign a formal contract. This would be followed by a blessing and a celebratory meal, after which the bride and groom (both now adorned with wreaths on their heads) would retreat to their new home, where the bride would be carried over the threshold. All these elements are extensively illustrated on both Greek and Roman inscriptions and vases, though characteristically the Greeks tended to depict the theatrical elements of all this, while Roman art more often highlighted the legal aspects. They also occasionally appear in the New Testament as metaphors for various aspects of Christian belief.[16]

Prior to the time of Augustus, marriage was largely an inter-family concern, but he introduced a legal framework that brought it under the purview of the state. His intention in doing this was to encourage people to marry and so to increase the size of the population. As part of this, unmarried men's inheritance rights were restricted, penalties were imposed on those who had no children, and bonuses were given to those with three or more. Adultery and divorce were also brought into the legal system at this time, and strict timetables were laid down within which divorced or widowed women ought to remarry. All this was within a framework of monogamy, though sex was hardly contained within marriage and prostitution was common. So was divorce, which was easy to obtain – partly because (unlike in the Jewish situation, where marriage was a contract between two families) marriage was based on consent between the partners, and therefore if consent was withdrawn there was no longer any legal basis for its continuation. For similar reasons, this right could be exercised by women as well as by men, and although children would go with the father in the event of divorce (for they were his possessions), the woman had a right to have the original dowry returned to her.

While it would be anachronistic to compare the opportunities open to Roman women with those enjoyed in Western culture today, they certainly had more freedom than either their Greek or Jewish counterparts. There is evidence of women holding positions in local government and working in medicine and manufacturing as well as taking part in the athletic games and other educational and artistic pursuits. Some, by virtue of being born into families of high status, were able to exercise influence that went well beyond the male-dominated social theories of the time. All this is reflected in the New Testament, with Lydia, apparently the first convert in Philippi, exemplifying the first-century businesswoman.

Much of the debate over precisely how much (or how little) active participation by women was encouraged in the life of the early church focuses on the different expectations within different ethnic communities. In traditional Greek culture, women had been largely confined to their own spaces within the household – where, however, they ruled supreme. Macedonian women had always enjoyed greater freedoms, something that by the first century had gradually spread to most of Greece and Asia Minor. Jewish women might not have been closely confined to their own quarters, but their households operated in much the same way as traditional Greek ones, with domestic duties being their main concern along with maintaining an attractive appearance for their husbands and being readily available for sex. From a religious point of view there was a certain tension in this, because many of the most important festivals (Sabbath and Passover, for example) were home-based and so came under the control of women, but at the same time women were regarded as incapable of fulfilling all the requirements of the Torah, mostly for reasons of ritual impurity connected with their female bodily functions.

This is the picture of women's lives that is reflected in New Testament passages such as the pastoral letters (1 and 2 Timothy and Titus), where women are exhorted to keep their families in order and avoid shaming their husbands,[17] and also in the various sets of instructions on how different individuals should relate within the family.[18] It is also the background against which the conflicts in Corinth need to be understood. Corinth was predominantly a cosmopolitan city, largely because of its geographical location as a convenient stopping-place for travel between the eastern and western ends of the Mediterranean. In this context, it would have been taken for granted that women should be free to play a significant part in the life of the church, just as they did in many other religious contexts of the day. In a community that also included culturally conservative Jewish converts to Christianity, however, that was bound to create conflict, for not only were women banned from speaking in the synagogues, they were not even allowed to occupy the same space as the men.

Given all this, Paul's much-debated instructions to the women of Corinth can be seen as an attempt at forging a compromise that would keep them all happy, for he affirmed the right of women to play a public part in worship while proposing that in order to pacify the more conservative members they should do so only with covered heads.[19] Actually, in Roman religious shrines, men as well as women would cover their heads when offering sacrifices. This was not with the sort of veil found in Islamic culture, but more like the corner of a dress or toga pulled over the head, and its purpose was to restrict one's peripheral vision so that undivided attention could be paid to the religious task in hand. Jewish men had not at this time adopted the custom of covering their heads while praying or reading the scriptures, so Paul's advice on this reflects an attempt to bring together Jewish and Roman customs.

The theme of freedom for women continued later when he found himself advising a couple of women who were causing trouble in Philippi: he never even thought of suggesting that they should withdraw from church leadership, but gave exactly the same sort of advice as he would have given to men, urging them to settle their differences because he actually valued them as co-workers.[20] While it would be unreasonable to judge Paul, or any other first-century person, by reference to the expectations of the twenty-first century, he certainly turns out to be much more supportive of women in ministry than his detractors often suppose. In Romans 16 he explicitly affirms his appreciation of the work being done by Phoebe and Prisca, Tryphaena and Tryphosa, and several other unnamed women, as well as Junia, whom he describes as "prominent among the apostles".[21]

It is natural for us to move on from here to think briefly of the lives of children in these ancient cultures, but that is a way of speaking that would have been alien to the people of the day. For the notion of childhood is a more recent construct. To the Romans, children were simply adults in waiting, and childhood was nothing more than a time of preparation for the time when an individual would become fully rational and adult, something that typically occurred on marriage for a girl and at the age of seventeen for a boy, which was when it was possible to be registered as a citizen. To live as long as that was itself quite an achievement, for there was a high rate of infant mortality, some of it through natural causes, though there was also a high level of infanticide. Abortion was a regular practice that was eventually banned by a later emperor, Septimius Severus (AD 193–211), but selling children into slavery or just abandoning and leaving them to die was more common still. A child was not regarded as part of the family until the father accepted him or her in a religious ceremony, which meant that infanticide was regarded not as murder but as the only possible consequence for a child that had no legal status as part of the community.

Jews (followed by the Christians) took a dim view of all this, regarding human life as of value right from conception. By suggesting that even adult disciples had something to learn from children, Jesus himself placed value on the state of childhood,[22] and there are hints that this was taken seriously in the life of some of the early Christian communities. When Paul paid his final visit to the church in Troas, the entire group stayed up all night, during which one of them fell from a window.[23] While this episode is often interpreted to imply that Paul spoke for so long that Eutychus (usually identified as a young adult) fell asleep out of boredom, a close reading of the text suggests a different scenario. Not only did Paul not preach a monologue (a literal translation would have him engaged in dialogue, followed by informal conversation) but when Eutychus fell from the window he is described by a word (*pais*) that very often means "a child" – not to mention the fact that Paul is said to have picked him up and cradled him in his arms. It is at least plausible to think that Eutychus was actually no more than a toddler who was placed on the windowsill to sleep because of his age, and unfortunately rolled over and out of his makeshift cot. The idea that children might be excluded from gatherings of the church on account of their age can also be questioned on the grounds that most church meetings took place in homes, and it is reasonable to suppose that if children were part of the household they would also be reckoned to be part of the church.

Education

The Latin word for education was *humanitas*, which also meant "humanity" or "human nature", as well as "kindness". In other words, it encapsulated all that it means to be fully human and fully mature – and that was the perceived purpose of education: to nurture the development of a fully rounded human being. In spite of this high-sounding ideal, teachers were not always well regarded. Insofar as there were schools, they tended mostly to be run by single teachers who charged their own fees, though in some big cities wealthy patrons provided schools as a public service. The European education systems of today still follow a pattern laid down by the Romans, with a school year starting in the autumn and running through to early summer of the following year. Even the structure of education is largely unchanged, with children normally starting at around the age of seven, and learning basic skills such as reading, writing and arithmetic. By the age of about eleven, children of aristocratic households had the opportunity to proceed to a more advanced educational regime in the liberal arts, with a curriculum based on the fundamental seven subjects that were adopted as basic reference points well into the Middle Ages and beyond: grammar, rhetoric, dialectic, geometry, arithmetic, astronomy, and music. By the age of eighteen students might spend a further year at a finishing-school, which would educate them in civic rights and duties and equip them with the sort of skills that could guarantee acceptance in the wider marketplace. This was the context in which the skills of rhetoric would be acquired, and by the end of this period students might embark on a career in the army or civil service. Rhetoric was concerned with the appropriate delivery of speeches and other forms of public speaking, enabling an individual to develop an argument and participate in debate.

While education was not universal, and was also voluntary, all the evidence suggests that a high proportion of Roman children, girls as well as boys, went at least to elementary school. The profession of scribe was widespread, which itself suggests a significant level of literacy, not only among the scribes themselves but on the part of those who employed them, who presumably lived their lives in a context where written documents were important. It was not uncommon for individuals who could write themselves to use scribes (most of the New Testament letters were written this way), but the vast quantities of personal letters that have been recovered also imply a high level of literacy among people as diverse as soldiers sent to the battlefield (who wrote home to report on their experiences), children in school writing to their parents, and ordinary people writing letters to their bankers and employers, not to mention love letters and other personal communications. Literally hundreds of thousands of such letters, written on papyrus, have been preserved from this period, especially in Egypt, where the dry sand and high temperatures provided perfect conditions for their survival.

Signs of all these educational attainments can be found in the New Testament. In recent years there has been a good deal of interest in tracing the patterns of traditional rhetoric in certain letters. Paul regularly conjures up imaginary opponents with whom to have a discussion, pitting different sides of an argument against each other in order to adduce some conclusion.[24] But so does James,[25] a book that appears to be deeply rooted not in the Hellenistic world but in the less sophisticated environment of rural Palestine – while Hebrews (another book with a decidedly Jewish orientation) demonstrates many of the characteristic traits of Hellenistic oratory and casuistry. Paul also easily uses analogies drawn from the actual practice of education. For example, he compares the role of the Torah in the life of the Jewish nation with the "pedagogue" who would accompany children to and from school (and often beat them up in the process) – and uses this to suggest that while such treatment can serve to set children on the pathway to good behaviour, it is always a temporary role and never a sufficient motivation for them to continue that way as adults, which is exactly what he wanted to claim for the Old Testament Torah.[26]

But it is in the frequent use of letters that the New Testament bears eloquent testimony to the influence of the Roman educational system. All ancient writings followed carefully circumscribed patterns, and simply by looking at the style of a given piece it is possible to know the sort of context in which it was written. The letters of the New Testament were written in a style that would be used for relatively informal communications, the sort that might be sent between members of the same family or to close friends. This type of letter had a more or less fixed structure, and Paul in particular always used this pattern when he wrote to the churches.

Galatians is a good illustration of how closely Paul kept to this pattern even when he was writing what must have been a very hurried letter. He began by giving his own name, "Paul an apostle", and he also associated with his letter "all the members of God's family who are with me", before naming the recipients, in this case a group of churches: "the churches of Galatia". Then comes the greeting, "Grace… and peace", expanded into a brief sentence of praise to God.[27] There is no thanksgiving in Galatians (though other letters have quite extensive ones[28]), for in this case Paul is too angry with them even to begin to think of paying them compliments. Instead, he launches straight into the main body of the letter, with a doctrinal and theoretical section[29] followed by practical advice for Christian living.[30] No personal news and greetings finish this letter, perhaps because of the haste with which Paul was writing or because he had no time for such pleasantries with people with whom he was so angry (but for a typical list of such greetings, see Romans 16). He did, though, include a final appeal in his own handwriting, which provides the interesting information that his own writing was much larger than that of the scribe who wrote most of the letter.[31] Paul then drew his letter to a conclusion with a blessing that was also a prayer for his readers.[32]

Ancient letters

- Unlike a modern letter, an ancient one would always begin with the name of the writer, and only then would it name the person to whom it was sent. Paul follows this quite closely.
- Then followed the greeting, usually a single word, the most common being *chairein* (meaning "hail" or "greetings"). Paul regularly replaced this with a distinctively Christian greeting (*charis*, "grace" – which in Greek both looked and sounded very similar to the conventional everyday greeting), together with the traditional Hebrew greeting (*shalom*, "peace").
- The third part of a letter was a polite expression of thanks for the good health of the person addressed. This was usually expanded by Paul into a general thanksgiving to God for all that was praiseworthy in his readers.
- Next followed the main body of the letter. In Paul's letters this was often divided into two parts: doctrinal teaching (quite often in response to questions raised by his readers) followed by advice on aspects of the Christian lifestyle.
- Personal news and greetings came next. In Paul's case this was more often news of the churches and prominent individuals in them, though occasionally there might be more intimate news about Paul himself.
- In Paul's letters there was often also a note of exhortation or blessing in his own handwriting, as a kind of guarantee of the genuine and personal nature of the letter.

- Finally, ancient letters regularly ended with a single word of farewell, a feature which Paul almost always expanded into a comprehensive expression of blessing and prayer for his readers.

Letter-writing was by no means the only literary form with which people in the Roman world would have been familiar. There was also a long tradition of philosophers, poets and historians (who were often the same people) writing down their ideas, and indeed their works formed the basis of regular Roman education. But one other particular type of literature also found its way into the New Testament, and that is the biography. A modern biography tends to trace the story of its subject from birth to death, focusing on his or her psychological and moral development. An ancient biography would never have been like that, because it was conventionally assumed that an individual's personality was fixed and unchangeable right from the start rather than being the product of circumstances or experiences. Some of these biographies amounted to little more than propaganda, written to extol the bravery or intellectual brilliance of their subjects. In his early campaigns, Alexander the Great took with him one such writer, named Callisthenes, who was charged with writing flattering accounts of Alexander's exploits, often drawing parallels with the stories of the gods and their deeds in traditional Greek mythology. But when he started to raise critical questions about some of Alexander's actions in the context of war, he found himself dismissed and thrown into jail. The most important Roman biographers tended to be less fanciful, and used the stories of their heroes as moral examples to instil virtue in the lives of their readers or to commend a particular philosophical outlook – though there was still a market for romanticized fictional stories.

There is an ongoing debate about whether the Gospels of the New Testament should be thought of as biographies in the Greek and Roman sense or whether they represent a different form of literature altogether. There is no similar literary genre to be found anywhere in Jewish literature, and this naturally suggests that we should look in the direction of Hellenistic biographies to find comparable models. But the way in which Jesus is portrayed in the Gospels does not quite follow the moralistic conventions of other biographical works. They have some traits in common with the rabbinic stories of Judaism, though these stories never paid much attention to the rabbis' own personalities and preferred to use episodes in their lives as examples to teach a religious or ethical lesson. Nor do the Gospels closely follow the pattern of a typical Roman biography, especially in their stated intention of inviting their readers to faith in Jesus.[33] Similar questions arise in relation to the book of Acts, which was written by Luke as a follow-up volume to his Gospel. This book also bears some of the marks of ancient biography (though it concerns the stories of many individuals, not just one), but would more obviously fit the genre of history-writing. It is often imagined that ancient historians, by definition, must have been less sophisticated than their twenty-first-century counterparts, but there is a lot of evidence to show that they worked long and hard to ensure the accuracy of their stories, checking eye-witness accounts, visiting the scenes themselves, cross-referencing their narratives with other documentation, and where appropriate including quotations from diaries and other first-hand evidence. Luke very obviously worked within that tradition, and in the introduction to his entire two-volume work (the opening paragraph of the Gospel) he describes how he compared materials from different sources, both written and oral, in the course of producing his own narrative.

The opening of both of Luke's books also makes it clear that he was writing for the general public and not just for his friends. One question that often puzzles people today is understanding what it might mean for a book to be "published" in an age when every copy had to be written out by hand. The answer again is to be found in style. As we saw with the letters, there was a very rigid structure to literature of every kind. In that example, the style itself of Paul's letters demonstrated that they were not intended for distribution beyond the communities to which they were originally sent. Luke's formal dedication of his books to "Theophilus", and the language in which this is expressed, fits into a wider pattern of literary style that shows he was not only intending his work to be read quite widely, but also that he expected that audience to be educated to a high standard and therefore that they quite probably belonged to the aristocratic upper classes of Roman society. Organizing public readings was another way in which a book could be "published", and among the upper classes large numbers would gather to hear some new work read out and then to engage with its concerns. In the narrative of how Paul was invited to give an account of himself before the learned citizens of Athens, Luke observes that "all the Athenians ... would spend their time in nothing but telling or hearing something new",[34] and one of the ways they would do this would be through listening to the public reading of the latest literature. The same practice of reading out loud was followed in the churches when Paul's letters were received,[35] which raises some interesting questions for today's readers of the New Testament, for a text is received differently when it is heard in public rather than read privately by an individual. It also raises the interesting question of whether Paul ever intended or expected people to find significance in every last detail of his words (as some modern Christians tend to do), rather than having a more general and fluid sense of what he wanted to say.

Travel and trade routes of the Roman empire

Of all the many achievements of the Romans, the establishment of roads and sea lanes throughout the ancient world is probably the most outstanding. They created an international infrastructure stretching from Scotland to the Persian Gulf, creating an estimated 53,000 miles of roads in the process. While the initial motivation for that had been to ensure ease of access for the imperial legions, it became a vast trading network that created a huge market in both goods and ideas and facilitated cross-cultural communications in a way that was hardly superseded until the late nineteenth century. It played a major part in the rapid spread of the Christian message. In his account of the Day of Pentecost, Luke gives a list of the many nationalities that heard Peter's message: "Parthians, Medes, Elamites, and residents of Mesopotamia, Judea and Cappadocia, Pontus and Asia, Phrygia and Pamphylia, Egypt ... parts of Libya ... visitors from Rome ... Cretans and Arabs" (Acts 2:9–11). Their presence in Jerusalem had been made possible only by the efficient Roman transportation links, and when 3,000 of them became Christians they returned home by the same routes, to share their new faith with people back home.

Once a letter had been written, an extensive distribution network was available. It was not a postal service in the modern sense, but was restricted to the transportation of official communications by diplomats, civil servants and military commanders. Everyone else had to make their own arrangements, which meant they often asked friends to take their letters to distant parts, while those who were rich enough would have slaves to do it for them. One of the advantages of using a personal friend was that he or she could be given an informal commentary on the content of the letter and authorized to explain anything that might not be clear. For communications among the churches, this could be a distinct advantage, especially in circumstances where the Christians might be suspected of some seditious activities. It also gave the recipients of the letters an opportunity to quiz the messenger over anything that might not be entirely clear. When 2 Peter complains that some parts of Paul's letters are "hard to understand",[36] it might well reflect the fact that Paul expected those who delivered his letters to offer more extensive verbal explanations of his argument.

Paul himself was no stranger to travel, of course. He was even more intentional in utilizing this network of road and sea routes to help spread the message. His travels were never haphazard, and every city he visited was easy to access along a major route. As a strategic thinker, he knew that he could either spend months, even years, making his way laboriously across country paths to reach remote places – or he could restrict his own endeavours to building up Christian communities in key cities of the empire, from where his own converts could take the message into the more remote and sparsely populated areas. At least one of the churches to which Paul later wrote a letter – Colossae – was founded in exactly this way, when Epaphras (a convert in Ephesus) went into the hinterland of the Lycus Valley and made his own converts there. Such travel was not always easy, in spite of the excellent facilities provided by the Roman roads, and an overnight stay was likely to be especially challenging. There were of course many inns, but outside Italy they were of very dubious quality, and even the better ones had a reputation for muggings and robberies, while some were nothing more than brothels. Aristocratic travellers would tend to stay with their own friends or relatives, and some synagogues incorporated basic guest rooms for Jews who might need accommodation. The new Christian communities raised such hospitality to a different level altogether, and both the New Testament and later Christian literature attest to the fact that welcoming fellow believers into one's home and family came to be regarded as an intrinsic part of Christian devotion.[37]

The way in which travel impacted the nature of Christian community differed in detail from one city to another, and there is no space here to consider all the places that feature in the New Testament story. But one city and its travellers exemplifies many of the tensions – as well as the opportunities – presented by the Roman trade routes. This is the city of Corinth, which was not only a major centre of communication between the eastern and western Mediterranean but also home to one of the largest (and, by all accounts, most problematic) of Paul's churches. Corinth was an ancient Greek city that had been rebuilt as a Roman colony in 46 BC, but by the time of the New Testament its major significance was as a transit point for travel between other major ports, including Antioch (in Palestine), Alexandria (in Egypt), Ephesus (in Asia Minor), and Puteoli (in Italy). Though navigational methods were well advanced, ancient sailors still preferred to stick close to the coastline whenever they could, and Corinth took advantage of their fear of the sea to establish itself as one of the foremost centres of trade and transportation. The city was located at the narrowest point in the mainland of Greece, and therefore had easy access to the Aegean Sea on the east and the Adriatic Sea on the west. Though even in New Testament times there were plans to build a canal from the Aegean Sea to the Adriatic, it was many centuries later before the project was carried through. At the time when Paul visited the city, it had two separate harbours on each of its coasts – Lechaeum and Cenchreae – and between the two was an intricate construction like a conveyor belt, along which vast numbers of slaves would haul ships from one harbour to the other. Corinth was therefore an important transit point at which ships could pass from the Aegean to the Adriatic without navigating the dangerous waters off the southern tip of Greece. Because of its strategic position roughly midway between the eastern end of the Mediterranean and Italy, there was a constant stream of traffic passing through.

The progress of Paul's mission to Corinth highlights some aspects of city life that were to be found throughout the empire. He began his work by visiting the synagogue, something that for him was a natural starting-point, for not only did he himself feel at home in this Jewish context, but it also gave ready access to the sort of Roman city-dweller who was most likely to be open to what he had to say. While the prime purpose of synagogues was to serve as a worship and cultural centre for the Jewish Diaspora, they also attracted significant numbers of non-Jewish people. Some of them were fascinated by the alien nature of Judaism when compared with the traditional observances of Roman and Greek spirituality, while many more found that the strict rules governing everything from food to sexual behaviour offered an attractive framework within which to live a disciplined life. Some became full converts to the Jewish faith ("proselytes") and took on themselves the entire duties and responsibilities of the Torah, while others embraced the religious beliefs without the accompanying lifestyle (a lesser form of commitment in which they were known as "God-fearers"). Whether born into Jewish families or converts, these were people who were familiar with the Hebrew Bible and would potentially be open to the added belief brought by Christian missionaries, with the conviction that Jesus was indeed the Messiah promised in the ancient texts. In Corinth one of the synagogue leaders became a Christian (Crispus[38]) along with Titius Justus – a "God-fearer" and perhaps also a city official. It was hardly surprising that Paul found a ready hearing among people like this, who were at the centre of civic life, for he himself belonged to the same stratum of Roman society. They were also the sort of people who owned property and land and were able to provide an accessible meeting-place for the newly formed Christian communities.

But they were not the only element in the population of a city like Corinth. As a staging-post for sailors and merchants travelling far from home, it could also boast one of the largest number of prostitutes anywhere in the empire, and in other popular writing of the day the term "Corinthian" became a byword for sexual perversion. In addition to that, the city was a melting-pot for the many different cultures of the empire, and the Christians were by no means the only ones offering a religious message to its inhabitants. Advocates of the mystery religions with their roots in traditional Egyptian spirituality rubbed shoulders with more philosophically inclined teachers from places like Athens or Alexandria, while yet others were bringing together the ingredients of what in later generations would emerge as the new-fangled ideas of Gnosticism. All these are reflected in Paul's dealings with the church in Corinth, and their influence can be traced in the letters he wrote to them over something like a two-year period between about AD 53 and 55.

The pivotal place occupied by the home as the central meeting-point for Christians provoked some heated debates and disagreements within the church. Among the sort of people rich enough to own their own property, dinner parties were commonplace and would be a natural context in which the likes of Titius Justus might expect to entertain the Christian community. At a regular banquet, of course, there would be a strict demarcation between the various strata of society and there would always be one person who presided over things. The precise form of such presidency varied, with the Greek preference being for a president to be chosen for the occasion by the guests, while the Roman custom decreed that the pecking order should be determined by reference to an individual's rank in civic life. The Greek pattern would have been closer to Paul's emphasis on the egalitarian nature of the Christian community. The important people, whether Greeks or Romans, would always be served by the slaves. Since slaves were also included among his converts, this inevitably raised a particular challenge. So also did the conventional entertainment that would be enjoyed on such an occasion, with party games, dancing and circus acts, often accompanied by much drunkenness and the attentions of female companions (*hetairai*), who provided the men with entertainment and also often with sexual favours. Tensions created within this environment are all well documented in 1 Corinthians in particular. Paul highlights the way in which social segregation was creating separate groupings, as the rich enjoyed their food while those less welloff were left to provide for themselves.[39] Other passages deal with the question of what sort of food was appropriate for Christians to eat anyway,[40] not to mention matters related to sexual behaviour,[41] general complaints about conflicting cultural attitudes and beliefs,[42] and concern over the sort of free-for-all that could happen even in worship in the typical party atmosphere of the Roman villa.[43] The likelihood that Paul's advice was being given against this background is further supported by the way in which he uses imagery that alludes to the sort of pompous speeches that might be made on such occasions,[44] even down to a reference to the musical instruments that would most typically be played as entertainment ("the flute or the harp ... the bugle"[45]).

There is less mention in the New Testament of some of the other places where Greeks and Romans would go for entertainment, namely the theatre and the athletic games. The only places where the theatre is mentioned both depict it as a place of bad news – in one case when an enraged mob congregated in the theatre at Ephesus,[46] and in the other as the place where Herod Agrippa met an agonizing death.[47] This is one point at which Jewish sensibilities apparently prevailed over the lifestyles of Greece and Rome. At the same time, the athletic games (another facet of Hellenistic life that was never fully embraced by religiously scrupulous Jews) provided a ready source of imagery with which New Testament writers could describe the Christian life.[48]

Bureaucrats, magistrates, and kings

This chapter has focused exclusively on life in the cities of the Roman empire, for one simple reason: that is where most people lived. Rome was probably the first truly urban empire, and though its upper-class citizens often had country estates they could not stay away from city life for long. City life has always tended to create social divisions, and the life of the average Roman city was no different. The documentary and monumental evidence always depicts the relatively secure lifestyle of the ruling classes, but a majority of city-dwellers must have had a hard time. This was a major challenge for the early Christian communities, for by definition they needed those who were relatively rich to open their homes to their gatherings, though at the same time their underlying message was one of equality for all. Advice about how to deal appropriately with economic and social diversity while remaining true to the Christian message features significantly in almost every New Testament letter.

Pollution was also a major issue in many cities of the empire, even in Rome itself, where the streets were so polluted by the ancient equivalent of burger stalls that in the middle of the first century AD Seneca reported positive health benefits whenever he left it:

> *As soon as I escaped from the oppressive atmosphere of the*
> *city and that dreadful aroma of reeking cooked-meat*
> *stalls, which when trundled about belch forth a mixture*
> *of soot and all the offensive smells they have accumulated,*
> *I immediately felt an improvement in*
> *my health.*
>
> Seneca, Epistulae Morales 104.6

It is hardly surprising that by the end of the first century AD, Juvenal was observing that most people "anxiously hope for just two things: bread and circuses" (*Satires* 10.77–81). The "circus" referred to here, of course, consisted of gladiatorial contests in which either professional fighters or condemned criminals would fight one another to the death, or be torn apart by wild animals for the amusement of the crowds (who could be of a substantial number, judging by the size of the Colosseum in Rome, which could hold around 50,000 people).

Actually, there were several different sorts of cities in the empire. The most prestigious were those that were categorized as Roman colonies, the purpose of which was to provide a home for retired civil servants, former military commanders, and others to whom the empire owed a special debt of gratitude. Philippi was one of these, though it is not easy to know what proportion of the population would actually consist of people like this. The Roman definition of a colony was a place that, as far as was possible, aimed to replicate the life of Rome itself, which explains why Paul, in writing to the Philippian Christians, could use this terminology to affirm that a Christian's "citizenship" was not primarily defined by reference to his or her physical location. The status of other cities varied considerably. In the western empire, their governing structures tended to be modelled on life in Rome, though the role of consul (an annual appointment in Rome) was transferred to provincial governors rather than city rulers. A typical city would have two chief magistrates, whose responsibilities largely mirrored the role of the consuls in Rome and included keeping order and ensuring good governance, assisted by two other officers, known as *aediles*, who supervised the day-to-day operations of city life by taking responsibility for such things as buildings and streets. There would also typically be a local council, or *curia*, consisting of former magistrates, which operated in much the same way as the Senate in Rome itself. At least one New Testament passage refers explicitly to this structure, in the person of Erastus who is described as the "city treasurer" of Corinth and was included by Paul in a list of those sending greetings to the Roman Christians.[49] In fact, a person of that name is mentioned on an inscription in Corinth which identifies him as an *aedile*, which would be exactly the sort of position occupied by a financial manager.

With the exception of cities (such as Philippi) that were Roman colonies, the political structure of cities in Greece and Asia Minor tended to preserve traditional Greek values, which were more democratic than those of Rome, with a correspondingly larger number of civic officials and decision-making bodies whose members might be elected by the people rather than being appointed from Rome. The importance of making decisions through these structures is highlighted in the account of Paul's visit to Ephesus, when a riot was sparked off, resulting in a mass gathering of citizens in the arena, which was dispersed only when a city official insisted that the matter should be dealt with in a formal way through "the regular assembly" of citizens.[50] Interestingly, the term used to describe this "assembly" of citizens is the Greek word *ekklesia*, which is also the word conventionally translated as "church" in English versions of the New Testament. While Paul and other New Testament writers envisaged a variety of possible meanings for the term *ekklesia*, their adoption of it to describe the Christian communities highlights something that was clearly of importance to them, for the *ekklesia* as city assembly was the actual gathering of citizens when they met together rather than being some abstract entity.

All cities in the empire operated within the confines of the provinces, many of which were directly governed by the Senate in Rome itself through the agency of a local official who, in Asia Minor and Africa, had the title of "proconsul" (meaning "in the place of a consul") because his authority mirrored that of the consuls in Rome. These proconsuls often had prior experience of governance in Rome itself and were usually appointed for one year. Paul's encounter in Corinth with Gallio, the proconsul of Achaia, offers an example of the role of these individuals as a final court of appeal for matters that could not be dealt with through the local judicial systems.[51] The same structure is reflected in the advice of the town clerk to the citizens of Ephesus, that if they had "a complaint against anyone, the courts are open, and there are proconsuls".[52] Gallio's tenure of the office can be dated quite precisely from an inscription that preserves a copy of a letter sent from the emperor that shows that he was proconsul in either AD 51–52 or 52–53. That information has allowed us to establish a time-frame for the whole of Paul's life and work, something that otherwise would have been very difficult to calculate.

This structure worked well in those provinces that were happy to be a part of the Roman empire. Others, such as Syria and Judea, which had a history of resistance, were under direct rule from Rome, with local governors under strict instructions from the emperor. Their actual titles varied (in Syria it was a legate; Judea had prefects and procurators), but they always had at their disposal a sizeable military force to keep public order whenever it might become necessary. In the early period, of course, the Romans had preferred to work through local kings such as Herod the Great and then members of his family. But when such arrangements broke down, forms of direct rule from Rome were usually introduced.

9

Faiths, Philosophies, and Spiritualities

The story of Greek and Roman religious faith is at least as long and complicated as the story of the Bible, and so anything that can be said here must of necessity be somewhat abbreviated. Even the idea of treating Greek and Roman beliefs in the same chapter could be misleading if it suggested that they were more or less identical. Not only did they have their own distinctive characteristics, but each of them also changed over time. What is said here is drawn from a variety of sources and historical periods, though with the emphasis on those aspects of religious belief that would commonly be found in the New Testament period. Even then, however, there would have been significant variations in different parts of the empire.

Faiths

The fundamental focus of traditional Greek and Roman faith was not on some other world, but on everyday life in this world. The idea that belief might constitute a discrete category that could be considered in isolation from the rest of life would have made no sense to either Greeks or Romans. Belief was concerned with ensuring that the correct observances were carried out in such a way that society's ongoing security and prosperity could be assured. Matters of abstract belief, whether about God or the nature of the world and its people, were at best secondary, and certainly played nothing like the prominent role that they had in Judaism. Devotion was expressed through acts of respect directed towards the deities, with different gods or goddesses being recognized for their influence in different circumstances and at different stages of life. It is misleading, therefore, to speak of Greek or Roman religion as if it was some special sort of ritual or belief system. Religious observance, in which the intrinsic reality of the gods and goddesses was recognized, was simply an everyday part of life that was intended to preserve social stability, whether in the context of rites of passage or of legal transactions or military expeditions, or any other concern that people may have.

For all these reasons, the underlying emphasis was never on the individual, but on the community and its well-being. The notion of having a personal relationship with one of the gods would simply not have occurred to anyone as being either desirable or possible. All the practices and traditional rituals were designed to maintain the well-being of the community by ensuring the observation of the correct social forms at the right times and in the right places. This could easily be done, for example, by the head of a household acting on behalf of all members of a family, or by local magistrates as representatives of an entire community. Appropriate sites for devotion did not need to be specially designed shrines or temples; many thousands of *herms* (stone pillars with the head of the god Hermes on top and a phallic symbol in front) have been discovered at roadsides and on street corners, inviting passers-by to seek the protection of this particular deity, while recognizing the process as a way of affirming their solidarity with the community in which the herm was located.

The gods

Hellenistic religion had no organized central structure that could impose a uniform belief system at all the many local shrines. Though individual gods and goddesses had their own priests, there was no recognized professional priesthood, and being a priest was not a full-time job. Authority in religious matters generally rested with those who had secular power, which in the household meant the father, while in the city-states it would be the local magistrates or even the assembly of all citizens. The most important religious functionaries were often seers, who would deliver oracles interpreting the divine will to any who asked their opinion – which they did, on matters as diverse as personal guidance, healing, the development of national policies, or military campaigns. The oracle at Delphi was one of the most highly respected sources of such spiritual insight. Sacrifice was a common way to gain the favour of the gods; it was usually animals that were sacrificed, though corn or fruit could also be offered. Far from being a gloomy occasion, this was generally a time for festivity and celebration, for only the poorest parts of sacrificial victims were actually offered to the gods, with the best cuts of meat then being eaten in a communal banquet. There was of course a serious side to it all, and worshippers regularly made offerings in order to win some particular favour from the deity. This was understood not so much as an attempt to bribe the gods as a way of affirming that the human–divine relationship was a mutually beneficial one that operated in predictable ways in a rational and orderly universe.

The conventional framework of divinities within which all this operated was traditionally traced back to the work of Homer, a blind poet, whose life and times remain shrouded in mystery. There is no agreed consensus on either his dates or the exact location in which he flourished – or, for that matter, whether he penned the epic poems attributed to him. Insofar as answers can be given to such questions, a majority of experts would probably place him around 900 BC, while the form in which we now have his classic works, the *Iliad* and *Odyssey*, was probably settled by about the fifth or sixth century BC. A lack of certainty about matters such as date and authorship bothers today's people much more than it ever would have done in the ancient world, and such concerns to some extent betray a lack of understanding of the nature of the epic literature associated with his name. For this consists of the sort of traditional stories that can be found in the heritage of many nations, with ballads and stories of long-forgotten wars and heroes that will have been passed on orally from one generation to another long before anyone thought that they should be written down.

In these narratives, twelve gods and goddesses were identified by name as the key deities in the pantheon. They each had their own quite narrow sphere of influence, and worshippers would not only choose to follow their own favourites but would pay some homage to them all so as to ensure that every aspect of human experience might be blessed by divine attention. They were generally thought of as living in an extended family at Zeus's palace on Mt Olympus (hence the term "Olympians", by which they were often known), and they were described in very anthropomorphic terms. The way they lived was depicted in ways that closely paralleled the organization of human society, though they did have some crucial differences from ordinary people, not least in their ability to assume different shapes in different spaces and the fact that they could neither grow old nor die. So notwithstanding their many human-like qualities, ordinary mortals always had to have regard for the difference between divinity and humanity. If there had been a golden age when gods and people mingled freely with one another, that time was long since past, and for now there was a great gulf between the two modes of existence.

Though this way of looking at things had its origin in Greek culture, by the end of the third century BC the Romans had adopted the mythology as their own and were identifying the Greek deities with their own traditional gods and goddesses. There were variations from time to time with regard to those deities that might be included in the twelve most important ones, but by New Testament times there would have been general agreement, along these lines:

The twelve Olympians

- Zeus: chief god, father of other gods and patron of male authority; Roman Jupiter (Jove)
- Hera: sister and consort of Zeus, goddess of women and marriage; Roman Juno
- Athena: goddess of wisdom and the arts; Roman Minerva
- Apollo: god of sun, prophecy, music, medicine, poetry, and a model to inspire young men; he had no direct Roman equivalent
- Artemis: twin sister of Apollo, goddess of the country and of wild animals, and protector of women in childbirth; Roman Diana
- Poseidon: brother of Zeus, and god of sea and earthquakes, as well as patron of horse-riders; Roman Neptune
- Aphrodite: goddess of fertility and beauty; patron of sexuality; Roman Venus
- Hermes: god of commerce, invention, cunning, theft; messenger for the other gods; patron of travellers and rogues; conductor of the dead to Hades; Roman Mercury

- Hephaestus: disabled god of fire, and patron of craft workers; Roman Vulcan
- Ares: god of war; Roman Mars
- Demeter: goddess of agriculture; Roman Ceres
- Dionysus: god of wine, ecstasy and orgasm; Roman Bacchus

In addition to these, mention should be made of the god Hades (Roman Pluto), who was thought of as another brother of Zeus in charge of death and the underworld. He, and others like him, were known as the "chthonians" (from the Greek word *chthon*, meaning "earth"), though they were not imagined to be in opposition to the Olympians either morally or spiritually. Not all chthonians were representative of negative influences, though deities of the underworld and of death were certainly prominent among their number. But there were also positive gods within their ranks: food, for instance, grows in the earth, and even Zeus could have an earthbound, chthonic aspect to his character. Indeed, most of the leading gods had an endless list of attributes applied to them, which defy neat classification. Individual communities constantly sought to define the qualities and powers of their particular deities as being in some way distinctive and different from the wider spirituality that was shared with other people throughout the Hellenistic world. Thus, for example, the "Zeus of mountaintops" had qualities not possessed by "Zeus of the city", or (to give an example that features in the New Testament), Artemis of Ephesus[1] was capable of bestowing blessings and favours that would not be available to devotees of the manifestation of Artemis revered in other Hellenistic cities.

Though it does not feature prominently, there are traces of this traditional pantheon elsewhere in the New Testament.

When Paul and Barnabas visited Lystra, the crowd concluded that "the gods have come down to us in human form",[2] and went on to identify Barnabas as Zeus (presumably because he impressed them as being suitably regal, and silent) and Paul as Hermes (because he was the one who did all the talking on behalf of his more distinguished-looking companion). Their eagerness to connect the two apostles with the gods may have been encouraged by the story of a previous occasion when the same two deities had visited a local couple incognito, and they subsequently reaped a considerable reward for the hospitality they had unknowingly offered them (Ovid, *Metamorphoses* 8.626–630). Contrary to initial impressions, for Paul to be identified with Hermes may well have been the higher accolade, for Hermes was regarded as a lovable rogue whose mischievous antics were highly admired. An earlier episode in the book of Acts possibly reflects a similar (though less categorical) identification of a Christian with a traditional deity, when Simon Magus declared Philip to be "the power of God that is called Great".[3] Another allusion to these traditional categories of divinity may also occur in 1 Corinthians 8:5, where, in the process of an argument about whether pagan gods really existed at all, Paul refers to "so-called gods in heaven [the Olympians?] or on earth [the chthonians?]".

By New Testament times, in addition to the Olympians and chthonians (who could be traced back to the Homeric epics), there was also a third group who might be worshipped, namely the heroes. As their name implied, they were not of the same high standing as the gods, not least because they started off as humans. The first mention of them occurs in Hesiod (about 700 BC), who depicts them as deceased individuals whose lifetime accomplishments were of sufficient distinction to ensure their continued existence, which endowed them with the potential for influencing the welfare of those who were still living. In practice, they tended to be adopted as local divinities, and their relics and tombs became centres of devotion. Typical examples mentioned in the New Testament might be the twin brothers Castor and Pollux, who formed the figurehead of the ship on which Paul travelled to Rome[4], and who seem to have transcended the boundaries between humanity and divinity so as to be regarded as patrons and protectors of sailors in stormy waters.

Faith in the city

In the New Testament period, religious practices in the form of regular devotions were all directed towards affirming the stability of the political system. Roman society was built on the twin foundations of law and respect for tradition. In earlier Greek society the role of the individual had played a significant part even in civic religion, but Roman religiosity was always a corporate affair that was to be regulated by due processes of obligation and honour. The notion that state and faith might be separated would have made no sense in the Greco-Roman world, and a state without a faith would have been as meaningless as a faith without a state. The idea that the two can be held apart is a post-Enlightenment Western idea that runs contrary to the expectations of all ancient people (and can also be seen today as secular Western governments struggle to understand the more holistic mindset of the Islamic world). There was no aspect of public life that was untouched by religious duty, and the performance of appropriate ceremonies was taken for granted in every sphere of life. Each city had its own patron deity who protected it and ensured its future, and making due acknowledgment of this reality was crucial for the people's continued well-being.

Part of the genius of the Romans was their willingness to incorporate existing local deities into their own grand pantheon. This is why the Roman and Greek divinities could be so closely connected. In identifying the Greek Zeus with the Roman Jupiter, the Romans were not saying that Zeus was also Jupiter, but that they were one and the same divine entity. By the same logic, local deities could easily be incorporated into the overall picture, even though the fit might sometimes seem less than perfect. This inclusivity made good political sense, because it allowed conquered people to continue living more or less as they had before. The Jewish and Christian resistance to it was a source of constant friction and misunderstanding, for to the Roman mind there could be no harm in continuing the traditional ways, and even giving exclusive worship to one particular god, while acknowledging the existence of others.

Civic religion naturally concentrated on civic life, and shrines of various kinds were easy to find in the streets of any Hellenistic city. The main qualification for being a priest was an understanding of the ritual and legal requirements necessary to ensure that things were done properly. Priests were generally appointed by the city authorities, though in some places it was possible to purchase a priestly position. When it was available, this was considered to be a good investment, as it could secure a family's future. As well as presiding over regular rituals, a priest would also have significant administrative duties, and in large centres he might easily have several assistants. This role was especially widespread in Asia Minor, and such assistants would function in much the same way as a sacristan in a church today. When Paul visited Ephesus he learned that the entire city regarded itself as being responsible for this role.[5] We have already mentioned "Artemis of the Ephesians".[6] Her significance for the life of Ephesus provides a good example of the part played by a local deity in civic affairs. Her designation as Artemis "of the Ephesians" suggests that she started off as a local divinity and subsequently became identified with the Artemis of the classical Greek pantheon. Many statues of this particular manifestation of Artemis have been uncovered, and the Artemis temple in Ephesus was regarded as one of the seven wonders of the ancient world. In New Testament times, it was serviced by a large number of priests, both female and male, all of whom were committed to sexual abstinence for the year in which they served. In spite of the fact that she was depicted adorned with oval protrusions that look like either breasts or eggs, there is no convincing evidence to suggest that Artemis was a fertility goddess whose worship involved sexual activity. Her major function was to guard the city and ensure the ongoing stability of its life.

The most important job of a priest would have been to offer sacrifices, for he was the person who knew the right way to do this. The rationale behind sacrifice was not always the same in every place, but for the Romans it was commonly regarded as a way of sustaining the deities and ensuring that their power to help people would never be exhausted. When Paul and Barnabas were hailed as deities in Lystra, the priest of Zeus produced oxen adorned with garlands ready to be sacrificed for them.[7] This is the sort of scene that is depicted on many inscriptions and monuments of the time. To be efficacious, a sacrifice had to follow strict guidelines, which typically included offerings of wine and incense as well as the slaughter of an animal. The actual killing would usually be done by slaves, though under the supervision of a priest. He would then examine the dead animal's entrails as a way of divining a message for the worshippers, who would typically then feast on the meat once it was cooked. Frescoes depict music being played at sacrifices, perhaps to drive away hostile spirits or please the gods, but also no doubt serving the practical purpose of drowning the shrieks of the animals as they were being slaughtered.

The priests themselves were invariably rewarded by being given a portion of the meat for themselves and if they wished they could sell this to the general public. All this is reflected in the situation addressed by Paul in Corinth, where some Christians were wondering if it was permissible for them to eat meat obtained from this source. Their fear was that it might have been contaminated by the religious ceremonies in which the animals had been slaughtered. The fact that such a question could be asked at all shows that some Christians shared the widely held opinion that, even if they never worshipped them, other gods than their own did truly exist. Otherwise, how could they possibly have imagined that non-existent divinities might affect their food one way or the other?

Paul himself pointed out the inconsistency in such an idea, but still recognized that however unfounded such concerns might be, they were nevertheless very real for those he regarded as "weak believers".[8] In the course of dealing with this and related matters, he mentions all the traditional practices of a typical Greek temple: eating a meal as part of the worship[9] and buying temple meat in the market for consumption in the home;[10] he even uses the practice of priests receiving their share of the sacrificial meat as an encouragement to the Christians to support those who serve in their own communities.[11] Excavations within the city of Corinth have demonstrated that this was a particularly distinctive aspect of life in that city, with temples equipped with specially designed suites of rooms for communal eating – the ancient equivalent of a restaurant, where citizens could meet their friends and rent space for special celebrations. Animal sacrifice was not the only element of worship in the temples of the Roman empire. Vegetables and cooked food such as bread might also be sacrificed, while the pouring out of wine or water was such a widely known custom that Paul could use it metaphorically to describe how he felt towards the end of his life as he faced his own uncertain future.[12]

While sacrifices could be offered at any time on behalf of individuals or particular groups within the community, each city would have its own particular times of festive celebration that were marked by religious ceremonies. The guardian divinities of the cities all had their annual festivals, which were a time for carnivals and processions as well as athletic games and artistic exhibitions – all of them watched over by the divine patron of the city, and serving a civic function by encouraging a sense of corporate solidarity among different elements of the population and thereby affirming both the structures of city government and those who were responsible for its smooth operation.

Faith in the home

Awareness of the gods and their influence on human life was not limited to the civic sphere, and home life was also infused with a sense of the divine. Meals would start and finish with the offering of food to the gods, and the entrance to a home would be marked by a shrine that ensured the safety of the inhabitants. In this context various minor deities played a significant part: Vesta, goddess of the hearth, and Janus, god of the doorway, who had two heads so that he could look in two directions at once in order to protect the house adequately. All significant family events and rites of passage were marked by ritual and ceremonial observance within the home. It was the duty of the head of the household, acting on behalf of all other members of the family, to ensure that things were done appropriately. This included not only daily devotional observances but also the distinctive rites that marked times of birth, death, puberty, marriage and so on. The extent to which an individual's identity was subsumed in the life of the community can be gauged by reference to the way in which the dead were traditionally regarded in Roman thinking as impersonal beings, stored away in a sort of limbo world of non-being. By New Testament times, Greek ideas about the significance of the individual had started to change this, but it was some time later before any coherent view of a meaningful afterlife was to emerge, and then it was largely under Christian influence.

Funeral rites provide a good illustration of the nature of religious observance that was centred on the home. Disposal of a body was an urgent matter, not only because of the fear of ritual contamination through its presence, but also because a proper burial was important for the peace of the departed. In ancient Greece the preferred method was burial, which would be either in the ground or in an elaborate monumental tomb. Cremation was also practised, though nothing like as universally as in Rome, where it was the predominant custom until the second century AD, when burial became more fashionable simply because it lent itself to the construction of impressive grave sites to preserve an individual's memory and reputation. Meals played an important part in Greek and Roman funerals, not only at the time of death but regularly during the first year thereafter and then annually on the anniversary of the deceased's birthday. Such meals were not parties but an intrinsic aspect of the religious observances commemorating the dead, and often included the provision of food for them that would be administered through tubes that went down into the grave. This was such an important matter that rich people regularly made provision for these meals in their benefactions, while the poor often became members of funeral clubs that offered them friendship during life and the assurance that somebody would continue to care for them in death. It is likely that people in the wider culture were able to make sense of the emergence of Christian communities by regarding them as voluntary associations of this sort. There is little direct evidence for Christian funeral practices in the first century AD, but by the second century many of these Hellenistic conventions were being followed, albeit with significant alterations. The meals typically became celebrations of the eucharist and took place not on a person's birthday but on the anniversary of his or her death, which was now regarded not as the end but as the beginning of a new resurrection life. Jewish communities in the Hellenistic cities generally continued the Palestinian practice of a second burial after the decomposition of a body, when the bones would be gathered up into an ossuary, a plaster container specially designed for the purpose.

The way in which these ossuaries were decorated (or not) has revealed a great deal about the ways in which different elements within a Jewish population might either have accepted or resisted Hellenistic culture. In Rome, for instance, ossuary designs have made it possible to identify considerable diversity of opinion in the ways different sections of the Jewish community related to the wider culture. Some clearly remained faithful to the traditional ban on any sort of decoration for fear that it might transgress the first commandment on "graven images", while others happily accepted such innovations and also embraced Latin names for themselves. This sort of evidence reinforces the possibility that Claudius's expulsion of the Jews from Rome could have been due to arguments within the Jewish community about the Christian message, and it also suggests that the existence of many different home churches in that city[13] may have been due not to geographical and social factors but to differences of opinion about how Christian faith should relate to the wider culture.

The main focus of Roman society had always been on the life of the community rather than on that of the individual, though by New Testament times that had changed somewhat through the influence of the more individualistic Greek outlook. But the family unit was still all-important, something that can be seen in numerous New Testament passages. When Peter met with Cornelius, it was not a private encounter but involved his entire household becoming Christians,[14] and much the same pattern was followed with Lydia in Philippi[15] and the jailer in the same city who was encouraged by Paul and Silas to "believe on the Lord Jesus, and you will be saved, you and your household".[16] The importance of the household is everywhere taken for granted in the New Testament as being the fundamental structure on which the Christian communities were to be modelled. It is not surprising that Paul should have operated like this, for he was a Roman citizen and had a good idea of how the gospel might best be received within that culture. But he was clearly not the only one to recognize this, and when he came to write to the Christians of Rome, a place he had never visited up to that point, the greetings he sent to them clearly demonstrate that the church in that city was not some monolithic public assembly, but a network of groups meeting in different homes.[17]

The spaces outside the home were equally important in terms of traditional devotion. The ancient Greeks had always regarded nature as being alive with divine connections, and every aspect of the world had its own particular deities. Altars could be found everywhere, in fields or at the roadside just as readily as in temples or by the hearth at home. They provided spaces where homage might be paid to the many deities whose concern was the countryside and the roads and the safety of those who walked in those spaces. Augustus realized the importance of these devotional sites, and when he came to power he ordered the construction of small shrines that not only would affirm the traditional practices of the people but also, significantly, were dedicated to his own honour. Since travel, work and home were the things that concerned ordinary people every day, the religious observances of these realities were almost certainly more deeply embedded in the culture than the more elaborate civic rituals of the large temples and their ostensibly more important divinities.

Faith in the emperor

The granting of divine honours to the Roman emperor raised many questions for the early Christians, and their refusal to acknowledge his deity often led to persecution. This most often occurred locally and spontaneously, but there could also be more organized and extensive campaigns against them, such as happened in the time of Nero. The reason this became such a major issue is that faith in the emperor could never be separated out as a "religious" matter that did not impinge on a person's civic duty. To be a good citizen automatically involved giving due honour to the emperor, because he was the very embodiment of civic values and good order.

The possibility of a human becoming divine could be traced back to the story of Rome's foundation by the feral twins Romulus and Remus, who were believed to be the sons of Mars, the god of war. There are different opinions on whether these brothers were real historical persons, but regardless of that, a key factor in relation to the later cult of the emperor is the fact that after his death Romulus came to be regarded as divine and was revered as the god Quirinius. He was not the first to be so honoured in the ancient world, as it had been taken for granted in ancient Egypt and Mesopotamia that their rulers were of divine origin. Moreover, in traditional Greek thinking there was always a thin line between humanity and divinity, with the heroes being regarded as individuals who had transcended that boundary in recognition of the accomplishment of some outstanding deed, usually one that benefited other people.

This is the kind of thinking that lay at the heart of later notions of the emperor's divine status. It was based not so much on a transcendent view of him as an individual, as on an appreciation that the blessings bestowed by rulers on ordinary mortals were of such magnitude that they seemed to be the sort of thing that only the gods could accomplish. Referring to a widely accepted opinion, Aristotle noted that "men become gods by excess of virtue" (*Nicomachean Ethics* 7.1), and that was certainly the case with Alexander the Great, who would certainly not have been accorded divine status had he been less successful in his military campaigns. When Antiochus IV accepted the title "Epiphanes" and sparked off the revolt of the Maccabees in 167 BC, he was operating within this tradition. Though a strict etymology of the Greek term *epiphanes* might suggest that it implied a claim to be a divine revelation, in popular usage it was often little more than the equivalent of words like "honourable" and "royal". Similarly, the accompanying terminology of "saviour" did not necessarily imply transcendent claims but could just as easily indicate that the holder of the title had liberated a city or province from its oppressors.

The line between divine status and god-like accomplishments was always going to be easy to cross. Julius Caesar had no hesitation in agreeing to the construction of a statue of himself with the inscription *Deo Invicto* ("To the unconquerable god"), though it was only after his death that he was formally recognized as such by a decree of the Senate. But it was Augustus who embedded all this in the institutions of the state. He was well placed to do so, having been Caesar's adopted son, which logically then made him "son of god"; and from the outset of his rule he used this title in the wider empire, though not at first in Rome itself. Roman culture was always going to be more receptive to the idea that emperors attained fully divine status only at death.

Politically, of course, the notion of the emperor as divine was a masterstroke in terms of gaining the allegiance of far-flung provinces. It was always likely to be difficult to enable conquered peoples, with their own different traditions, to understand exactly what "Rome" actually stood for. Most individuals could never expect to go there to see the city, and even fewer were likely to be familiar with the intellectual values of its civilization as represented in the classics of Greek and Latin literature. People are always far more ready to give their allegiance to a person than to an idea, and identifying the empire with an individual such as the emperor made it accessible and knowable. It was possible for the emperor to be seen, through statues and other artwork displayed in the places that people regularly visited in the course of their daily lives – marketplaces, civic buildings and temples. To refuse to acknowledge the emperor was a statement of resistance to all that Rome stood for.

Christians might have had good reason to believe that Nero or Domitian had overreached his appropriate sphere of authority, but that is not how it would have looked from a Roman standpoint, because the emperor was still the embodiment of law and good order, no matter how mad he might have been as an individual. No doubt this explains why Paul, for example, went to such pains to exhort his readers to honour the emperor (Romans 13:1–7), while maintaining the position that Jesus had espoused, of giving to Caesar only those things that rightfully were his (Mark 12:13–17) – though by the time of Domitian, Christians were preferring to see Rome in a less generous light, castigating it as "Babylon the great, mother of whores and of earth's abominations" (Revelation 17:5).

Philosophies

The educated upper classes generally went along with this inherited pattern of conventional observance, but large numbers of them found their real purpose in life by embracing the teachings of the many philosophical schools of the Hellenistic world. It is no exaggeration to say that philosophy was, in effect, a religion for many such people. Mention of the word "philosophy" can conjure up images of out-of-touch eccentrics who are interested in arcane metaphysical questions and hair-splitting debates that have little connection to everyday life. But the Hellenistic philosophical schools were based on lifestyle, and offered guidance and discipline of an ethical and spiritual nature. The almost exclusive focus on observance and duty that was found in Greek and Roman religion created a need for more specific moral and spiritual advice, and this was provided not by the priests, but by the philosophers. The devotion they inspired in their followers could be experienced with all the intensity of a religious conversion. Indeed, for some devotees of the philosophers that is exactly what it was, not only demanding but also facilitating a complete and radical shift of attitude in both belief and behaviour. The most famous documented example of such a conversion was that of Polemon, who, in a drunken state, barged his way into the lecture hall of Xenocrates, a fourth-century BC Greek teacher, and was so overcome by the serenity and relevance of what he heard and saw there that he underwent a complete change of attitude, and in due course succeeded Xenocrates as leader of that particular school. The philosophical concern with behaviour gave it much in common with Judaism, which also had an ethical focus on lifestyle and personal attitudes. This was a central element in the teaching of Jesus and his early followers, too, and this range of shared interests means that the philosophical schools and their teachers are probably much more significant than traditional Greek and Roman religion as a background against which to understand the New Testament.

Paul, for one, had no hesitation in using the techniques and arguments of the philosophers when they coalesced with his Christian outlook. The most obvious example of this is his speech in Athens, as reported in Acts 17:16–31, where he found it perfectly possible to convey an accurate account of the Christian message without a single mention of the Hebrew Bible, and instead referred to the teachings of Epimenides and Aratus. He adopted much the same technique in reflecting on the nature of Hellenistic culture in Romans 1:18–2:16, and the lists of household duties that appear in Colossians 3:18–4:1, Ephesians 5:21–6:9 and 1 Peter 2:13–3:7 bear more than a passing similarity to conventional philosophical teachings. Here, though, the motivation for such behaviour is generally given a Christian orientation through references to the behaviour of Christ himself or some similar example.

The invitation to Paul in Athens to discuss his teaching with philosophical teachers also suggests that they themselves understood his message to be dealing with the sort of things they themselves were interested in.[18] On a later occasion, when Paul was denied access to the synagogue in Ephesus, the most obvious place for him to go next was into the lecture hall of Tyrannus,[19] which is another indication that he regarded the philosophical school as a more appropriate place than the local temples for his message to be heard. Likewise, the fact that he was welcomed into such places demonstrates that the philosophical fraternity viewed him in the same light, even if his message was not quite the same as their own.

By Paul's day, the philosophical schools had a long and respected history going back at least as far as the fifth century BC in Greece. Alongside their emphasis on behaviour and lifestyle they had also created a space in which monotheism (belief in only one god) might be taken seriously. Insofar as the philosophers spoke of a divine being, it tended to be a somewhat abstract and ill-defined influence not necessarily implying the existence of any transcendent realm at all, for the spiritual could often be identified with the rational, and therefore with human thought processes. But one of the by-products of this was that serious questions had been raised about the stories of the gods and their doings. Philosophers were more inclined to regard them as symbols of some first force or abstract principle that lay behind the world, rather than thinking of the gods as beings with a personal identity. But their deconstruction of traditional ideas did not invariably lead to a form of atheism, and certainly not to a discontinuation of the traditional forms of devotion, not least because of the close association between faithfulness to the gods and allegiance to the state. These beliefs disappeared only much later, when they were eventually supplanted by Christianity. Even then, though, many of their assumptions and practices were hardly displaced but came to be incorporated into Christian devotion, with things like the veneration of saints owing a good deal to the Greek belief in heroes who could transcend the boundaries between the human and the divine by virtue of their outstanding deeds.

Like many of the topics dealt with in this book, the story of the ancient philosophers is one that could easily justify an entire book to itself. By the New Testament period, it already had half a millennium of history behind it, and the philosophical teachers of the first century AD owed a great deal to those who had gone before them. There was no single way of being a philosopher, and while some advised emperors and civic rulers, others wandered through the empire as beggars, eschewing the normal comforts of civilization and going from place to place sharing their message wherever they could find a hearing. These were the Cynics, a group tracing its origins back to Diogenes of Sinope (about 400–325 BC), and the suggestion has occasionally been made that Jesus was a Cynic teacher, at least in style if not in substance. However, there is no documented evidence of any such teachers in Palestine at the time, whereas the Hebrew prophetic tradition itself offers plenty of examples of itinerant teachers who provide a more obvious model for the ministry of Jesus. Some philosophical schools, however, are specifically mentioned in the New Testament, and their teachings are more relevant to an understanding of the world in which the early church operated.

Stoics

The Stoics are named as one of the groups that Paul encountered in Athens,[20] though their influence can be traced in other New Testament passages as well. This school of thought was founded by Zeno (335–263 BC). He was a native of Cyprus, but went to Athens and eventually set up his own school in the *Stoa Poikile* (meaning a "painted portico"), from which the name "Stoic" was derived. Stoic philosophy was based on a belief that both the world and its people ultimately depend on just one principle: "Reason". Since the world itself operates by this standard, individuals who desire to enjoy a good life must "live in harmony with nature", something that was most easily accomplished through following one's conscience, for that was also inspired by "Reason". This was something people had to do for themselves, and Stoics therefore laid great emphasis on living a life of "self-sufficiency". Many of them were widely respected for their high standards of personal morality, and it was not at all uncommon for them to be prepared to commit suicide rather than lose their self-respect and dignity. It is this characteristic that motivated the application of the term "stoic" to a person who could live through hardship without flinching or allowing it to impinge on his or her inner life – though that was a much later development, and the use of the word in this way is not documented earlier than the sixteenth century.

Inevitably, this way of understanding life did not convince everyone, not least because living a life of self-sufficiency was not necessarily able to explain or address the social realities of the day. It was easy enough to assert that

> *the end of life is to act in conformity with nature, that is, at one with the nature which is in us and with the nature of the universe ... Thus the life according to nature is that virtuous and blessed flow of existence, which is*

enjoyed only by one who always acts so as to maintain the harmony between the daemon within the individual and the will of the Power that orders the universe.
Diogenes, Laertius 7.1.53

But it left unanswered some key questions in relation to everyday life. For if "Reason" filled and inspired everything, then why weren't all people the same? Why were there so many slaves, condemned to eke out a wretched existence? The Stoic could reply that, in their minds, slaves were equal to the emperor, a claim that provided very little consolation either for slaves or for those concerned for their welfare. For the socially disadvantaged, Stoicism was essentially a philosophy of hopelessness, in which most people were considered incapable of reaching any level of moral maturity.

Like all other philosophical systems of the day, Stoicism consisted of much more than merely a set of rules by which to live. It was a whole worldview that encompassed astronomy, physics and mathematics as well as ethics, and all these things were believed to be intrinsically interconnected. The definition of any sort of divinity was no more central to Stoic philosophy than it was to any of the other philosophical schools, and insofar as it was ever contemplated, the notion of "god" tended to be an ill-defined abstraction that could sometimes be associated with the whole universe, sometimes with Reason, and sometimes even with features of the natural world such as fire. In the end, though, Seneca's statement (quoting Virgil) sums up the Stoic understanding of deity: "What god we know not, yet a god there dwells" (Seneca, *Letters* 41.2).

Of the many philosophical schools of the first century AD, Stoicism is the one that has most often been compared to the

New Testament. In particular, Paul is likely to have been familiar with its teachings, since some of the most famous Stoic teachers came from his own home city of Tarsus, and Paul may well have learned something about their teachings during his early education there. More than that, though, his style of debate and argument echoes the way the Stoics presented their ideas, with regular use of rhetorical questions and short disconnected statements, the introduction of imaginary opponents to engender debates, and the frequent use of illustrations drawn from athletics, building and urban life in general. Aratus, whom Paul quoted in his speech at Athens,[21] was a well-known Stoic poet, which at least suggests that Paul did not entirely discount the possibility of finding ideas that were compatible with Christian faith in the Stoic writings. There are also phrases in his letters that are not inconsistent with Stoic doctrine, even if they do not overtly support it. One example would be the description of the cosmic Christ in Colossians 1:16–17, which says that "all things have been created through him and for him. He himself is before all things, and in him all things hold together." Another would be the way he could describe morality in terms of what is "proper" or "fitting".[22] Of course, in fundamental respects Paul's worldview was radically different from that of the Stoics, and his use of their debating techniques and terminology was all part of his conscious contextualization of his message in the culture of the day.

Epicureans

This was another popular philosophical group in the Hellenistic age, and is also specifically mentioned by Luke in relation to Paul's visit to Athens.[23] They too had an ancient pedigree, tracing their origin back to the Greek Epicurus (341–270 BC). Epicureans adopted a totally different view of life. Though many Greeks had debated what happens at death, the Epicureans believed that death was the end, and the only real way to make sense of life was to be as detached as possible from it. A good life consists in "pleasure", which for Epicurus meant a pretty abstemious lifestyle characterized by things like friendship and peace of mind, though many of his followers interpreted it differently and gained a reputation for reckless living. Unlike Stoicism, Epicureanism remained substantially unchanged from the views of its founder Epicurus. Much of its worldview was based on his understanding of the physical universe, which involved a complicated theory about the nature of atoms and space. He had a place for deities within this cosmology, though their exact significance is unclear, for they played no particular part in his philosophical system, nor were they regarded as impinging at all on human life, either here in this world or in some imaginary afterlife. Religion, for its part, was dismissed as being the source of much human unhappiness because of the judgmental attitudes which it engendered.

For all these reasons, Epicureans and Christians could often find themselves lumped together and labelled as "atheists", because both groupings were indifferent to the traditional deities of conventional civic religion, if not necessarily directly hostile to them. But whereas this aspect of the Epicurean lifestyle was generally regarded as a social curiosity, in the case of the Christians it often led to intense persecution.

Other comparisons that have been drawn between Epicureans and Christians relate to the nature of their communities. There are certainly traces of the same words being used, for instance when Paul advised the Christians of Thessalonica to "aspire to live quietly, to mind your own affairs, and to work with your hands ... so that you may behave properly towards outsiders and be dependent on no one".[24] But this was specific advice given in a particular circumstance, and in most respects the two were quite different. Far from being the sort of reclusive subculture represented by Epicureanism, the Christian communities were open to all and ready to play a full part in the life of their cities whenever they had the opportunity to do so.

These two philosophical groups were by no means the only ones to gain a following in New Testament times, and there is plenty of evidence of other teachers and systems at the time, many of them local variations of wider trends. On the whole, though, the philosophical movements found their greatest appeal among the intellectual classes, with a correspondingly diminished attraction for ordinary people. Apart from their inability to address the fears of the working classes, it was time-consuming and intellectually demanding to organize one's life in this way. As a result, philosophy had few points of contact with the mass of the people, who were not highly intellectual and had little opportunity for the leisurely pursuit of ethical debate.

Spiritualities

Although traditional religious observances were still widely practised in everyday life, the philosophers had raised enough questions about the existence of the old deities as transcendent entities to undermine any deep reliance on them as a way to discover personal meaning. At the same time, the philosophical schools failed to win the allegiance of ordinary people, partly because of their strident ethical demands, but most particularly because their systems and ideas were accessible only to the intellectual elite who had been educated to a high enough standard to be able to understand them. In addition, the establishment of easy communication routes right across the empire had helped to create an environment in which people heard of new deities who seemed to combine many of the best aspects of traditional Hellenistic beliefs with a sense of mystery, and offer personal experiences that would put their devotees in touch with the powerful realities of some other world beyond the mundane and the ordinary. In particular, international movements of trade and people had made Europeans more conscious of the existence of other gods and goddesses in the eastern part of the Roman empire, in an enchanted world filled with the sort of spiritual goodies that the over-rationalized and materialistic worldviews of Western philosophy had denied. Such deities raised their own questions, of course, foremost among which was whether they truly existed, and if they did, how could they relate to life in the great urban centres of Greece and Italy? But by the first century AD the discrediting of traditional Greco-Roman divinities, coupled with the failure of the philosophers to establish a plausible alternative that could appeal to the masses, resulted in a serious moral and spiritual vacuum that amounted to nothing less than a religious failure of nerve of the entire Hellenistic culture.

The current fascination of Western people with spiritual pathways emanating from the East is nothing new, and was a well-documented feature of the world of the New Testament. But it was not just natural curiosity that made them so attractive. What was known of them appeared to be potentially compatible with the more accessible nostrums of classic philosophy, which was another reason why they could be regarded as meaningful answers to the existential questions of people in Greece, Rome and Asia Minor. In order to explain the existence of evil in the world, philosophers had often argued that this world is neither the only world nor the best one. There is, they suggested, another world of goodness and light, which is actually the most important sphere of existence. People belong to it because they have a "soul", a spark of light that is related not to bodily existence in this world but to spiritual existence in the other world. Our brief existence here is merely an unfortunate encumbrance, and to find true meaning and fulfilment it is necessary to escape the body.

Pythagoras (c. 580–500 BC) is best known as a mathematician, but he regarded the study of mathematics less as a scientific enterprise and more as a spiritual discipline that would enable the soul to escape the confines of the material world and direct it to its true source in the world of the eternal. He went so far as to describe the body as "the prison of the soul", and in the process of doing so he espoused a form of reincarnation which envisaged the soul being transferred endlessly from one physical manifestation to another.

While much philosophical speculation denied any notion of a life beyond this one, many of the religions of the eastern empire had no hesitation in providing details of such post-mortem existence, and indeed offered to introduce their devotees to the life of some other world while they were still living here. Even those of a more narrowly scientific bent could find something to satisfy their curiosity, for philosophical thinking about mathematics and astronomy naturally provoked questions about how things work, and in particular how the sun, moon, stars and planets might affect life on earth. As Roman and Greek thinkers explored the mysteries of the universe, they found themselves speculating whether the movements of these heavenly bodies, which seemed to operate with such precision and regularity, might also hold the key to the whole of life. Traditional beliefs from the East often claimed to know the answer to such questions. Astrology and the possibility of reincarnation had been of great interest to Eastern sages for centuries, and it was perhaps inevitable that their ideas would be combined with the conclusions of Greek scientists in order to produce a new kind of hybrid spiritual movement in New Testament times.

Mystery religions

Direct and personal mystical experiences of the divine played a key role in the various mystery religions that sprang up at this time throughout the Roman empire. There had always been an interest in the mystical, even within official civic religious observance. For example, many state-sponsored shrines incorporated an oracle that could be consulted by city authorities faced with important decisions, and also by pilgrims with questions regarding the conduct of their personal lives. An oracle might be represented iconically by a figure of an animal, but was identified with the deity of a particular place, offering messages through an accredited medium. Oracles might be consulted for general advice or for specific decisions, and various formal processes might be invoked, ranging from the casting of dice to the observing of the entrails of a sacrificial animal, or messages given in a trance-like state. The story in Acts 16:16–18 seems to reflect this background, when Paul and Silas encounter "a slave-girl who had a spirit of divination". The Greek expression used by Luke here is somewhat obscured by the usual English translations, for she is described more accurately as having 'a Pythian spirit' – a term that probably refers to an episode in the establishment of the oracle of Apollo at Delphi, during which the Greek deity Apollo was said to have slain the Python (snake), a symbol of the earth goddess, in the Minoan rituals that had previously been celebrated at the same site.

Healings might also be sought through pilgrimage to the civic shrines, and these were often associated with the cult of Asclepius, who was regarded as the patron of medicine and was depicted holding a stick with a serpent coiled around it, a symbol that is still widely associated with the medical profession today.

Dreams were also widely regarded as channels through which ordinary mortals could be contacted by the gods, and Plutarch seems to imply that they were one of the main forms of divine communication, commenting that "in popular belief it is only in sleep that men receive inspiration from on high" (*On the Sign of Socrates* 20). Paul laid great store by information received in this way.[25] Luke appears to distinguish between dreams and "visions",[26] though it is not altogether clear what the difference might be.

Magic was both feared and widely practised in the first century, but it is not altogether clear what constituted "magic" in a world that regarded as supernatural many things that would now be thought of as everyday occurrences. When a truly remarkable deed (often a healing) was accomplished by someone who for other reasons was disapproved of, it might easily be dismissed as "magic", whereas a miracle performed by one's hero would be put down to genuine divine intervention. The Jewish religious authorities appear not to have questioned the reality of Jesus' healings, but instead claimed he was able to perform them only through the exercise of some malign magical forces,[27] though when the disciples asked Jesus about someone who was not part of their group, he refused to use the same tactic to condemn him.[28] Similarly, when Philip the evangelist encountered Simon the magician (Simon Magus) in Samaria, he was not condemned for being a magician[29] until he offered to buy whatever special powers he believed the apostles to possess.[30] The reality of magical powers seems to have been accepted by the early church, whether it was the insights of the Magi (the "wise men") into the circumstances of Jesus' birth[31] or the notion that fabric blessed by Paul could effect miraculous healings,[32] though there was an insistence that such accomplishments had nothing to do with the manipulation of magic spells or charms but depended on the generosity of God alone.[33] At the back of much of this was the assumption that an individual's fate was likely to be determined by unpredictable forces that were in some way connected with the movements of the planets. All of this, and more, is reflected in New Testament passages such as Galatians 4:3 and Colossians 2:8, with their insistence that Christians can be more confident of life's outcomes because they are in the care of a generous God who can be personally known.

This infrastructure of popular personal spirituality provided a ready breeding-ground for the more sophisticated mystical cults associated with the names of Demeter, Dionysus, Isis, Osiris, Serapis, Mithras, and many others – cults that together have come to be referred to as the mystery religions. Though the notion of some sort of initiation into a "mystery" was indigenous to Greek culture, it was only with the incursion of beliefs from the eastern empire that it developed into a widespread fascination and spawned the development of secret societies. Their members underwent special ceremonies that were reckoned to imbue them with knowledge of certain deities that was not accessible to all, and which in turn offered them certain advantages and benefits over others who had not been so initiated. Initiation could be an expensive business, though those involved always expected that the benefits it conferred would more than compensate for whatever the cost might be. Since these groups were *secret* societies, our specific knowledge of them is inevitably limited. Many were of only local significance and are not well documented at all, though some spread much wider and attracted an international following. A common theme in most mystery religions was concerned with the annual cycle of the seasons and with issues of fertility and power. These motifs were similar to those that had been popular for thousands of years throughout the ancient world, with mythologies and rituals that reflected the cycle of the seasons, the new life of spring following the barrenness of winter, all of it symbolized by the death and rebirth of the divinities (both male and female) of fertility.

The traditional religions of Mesopotamia and Palestine had generally celebrated this cyclical worldview in annual festivals in which priests and priestesses would act out the role of the deities, often involving ceremonies with strong sexual overtones. In the Hellenistic mysteries, such rituals became mystical experiences for the individual worshipper. Their original mythology was transferred from the ongoing life of nature and projected onto the experience of individual people, who themselves spoke of undergoing the death and rebirth that had been so important to the prosperity of the ancient farmer. The ceremonial initiations involved in this took many different forms, ranging from the orgasmic ecstasies of Dionysus (the Roman Bacchus), whose rituals became a byword for sexual promiscuity, to the more gruesome *taurobolium* involved in the cult of Attis, depicted in many inscriptions and frescoes, albeit mostly dating from the second century AD rather than the first. One of the few written accounts of this ceremony (Prudentius, *Peristephanon* 10.1011–1050) describes how the initiate would be placed in a pit in the ground, then covered over with a wicker framework on which a bull (a symbol of life and virility) would be slaughtered so that its blood would run down and soak the initiate. As the initiate emerged, those who were gathered around to witness it would go down on one knee before him in acknowledgment of the fact that he had now been elevated to a higher plane of existence through imbibing the life and energy of the bull.

Mithraism was another mystery religion in which the sacrifice of a bull played a major role, though not as a regular part of the initiation rites. This came to be one of the best-known mystery religions and was very popular among officers in the Roman army from the late first century onwards. For a long time it was believed to have roots in Zoroastrianism (an ancient Persian religion), in which Mithras appears as a divinity of trust and faithfulness on the side of Ahura Mazda, the god of light, in the cosmic battle against the forces of darkness that are personified as Ahriman. But others connect it with Greco-Roman astrological speculations about the planets. Mithraic initiation had seven degrees, each one conferring increasingly significant rights on the initiate. The precise meaning attached to these stages can only be deduced from frescoes depicting them, but it would appear that they variously involved trial by water and fire, including perhaps some ritual branding, along with beatings with whips and other actions – all of them conducted while the initiate was naked and blindfolded. Unlike most other mystery religions, women were not allowed to participate, and its initiates were committed to upholding a strong moral code of behaviour.

These mysteries – and many others – offered hope and security to their initiates, in both personal and social terms. Individuals gained a sense of personal meaning and purpose in life. They also became members of a distinctive group that shared the same secret experiences and often operated as a mutual aid society in times of difficulty or hardship. In the centuries following the New Testament period, some early Christian writers compared the claims of these mystery religions with their own faith, usually denouncing them as demonic imitations of Christian rituals such as baptism. While one can well understand the missionary impetus that might have provoked such comparisons, it is doubtful whether such apologists had a very clear understanding of the various cults, given that they were not easily accessible to outsiders.

In the process of doing this, they created the impression that there must have been some intrinsic connection between the mysteries and the early church, which in the late nineteenth century led to a good deal of speculation about the possibility that there might have been some more integrated relationship. It is an easy matter to identify superficial resemblances between the mystery religions and the Christian faith. Both were heavily influenced by religious traditions emanating from the eastern empire; both offered "salvation" to their followers; both used initiation rites (Christian baptism) and sacramental meals (the Christian communion); and the term "lord" could be used to refer to a divine saviour. Undoubtedly, the two often became intertwined as converts from the mysteries entered the church and (naturally enough) used the familiar categories of their mystery beliefs as a vehicle for articulating their new faith. It was probably this tendency that was the cause of much of the trouble in the church at Corinth, about which Paul wrote in his letters to the Corinthians, and there may also be traces of something similar in the background to Colossians.

Scholars in the late nineteenth and early twentieth centuries proposed that what Paul did was to change the simple ethical teaching of Jesus into a kind of mystery religion, and though the idea still surfaces occasionally in popular opinions about Paul, it is now given no credence within the academic community. The evidence is very disjointed, simply because the mystery religions themselves were many, and apart from the importance given to secrets and initiations, there is nothing else about them that suggests they were all part of some coherent religious movement. In addition, some of the alleged points of contact could have more than one possible explanation. For instance, when the title "lord" was applied to Jesus, it certainly did not come from mystery religions, but from Judaism. The Christian confession of faith, "may our Lord come" (recorded in 1 Corinthians 16:22 in its Aramaic form, *Maranatha*), shows that the very earliest church in Jerusalem, the only one to speak Aramaic, must have given Jesus that title long before Christianity expanded in the heart of the empire.

No doubt Paul and others knew of the mystery religions and their resemblances to Christianity. Some of them told of deities coming into the world in the guise of humans, and spoke of salvation as "dying" to the old life, of a god bestowing immortal life, and of the saviour god being called "lord". It is possible that Paul, who was ready to be "all things to all people",[34] sometimes deliberately used their language. But as with Stoicism, it is more likely that he used it unconsciously, with neither detailed knowledge of the mystery religions nor specific reference to any of their ceremonies.

Gnosticism

The word "Gnosticism" comes from the Greek noun *gnosis*, meaning "knowledge", and, like any label that may be attached to popular spirituality in the Hellenistic world, it requires further definition before it can be very useful. Just as the term "mystery religion" covers a variety of groups, all of which had their own distinctive attributes, so with the notion of "Gnosticism", which is more of a generic term covering a sort of spiritual environment than an accurate description of any particular belief system or way of life. Very few groups called themselves Gnostics, and the term originates from the writings of early Christians such as Irenaeus, Tertullian and Clement of Alexandria, all of whom wrote extensive works condemning the teaching of people whom they identified in this way. Even they, however, acknowledged the difficulty of pinning down exactly what and who they were writing about, and Irenaeus admitted that "there are as many systems of redemption as there are teachers of these mystical doctrines" (*Against Heresies* 1.21.1). Since these church leaders wrote about the Gnostics only in order to condemn them, their opinions regarding what constituted Gnostic belief were always couched in terms drawn from Christian theology rather than reflecting first-hand knowledge – which, of course, as in the case of the mystery religions, would have been hard for outsiders to come by. On the other hand, many Gnostic writings have come to light, and they tend to confirm at least the broad outlines of Gnosticism as depicted by its Christian opponents.

The foundational worldview of Gnosticism involves a radical demarcation between this world and some other world of the spirit, with the material world being regarded as evil and physical existence forming a significant hindrance to a person's achieving his or her true destiny in the world of spirit. A lot of this is familiar from the classic philosophical tradition, which made a similar differentiation between the body and the soul, between physical activities shared with animals and the rational reflection that seemed to make human beings unique. Matter, on this view, was so alien to the world of the spirit that it was regarded as the creation of an inferior deity, referred to as the Demiurge and sometimes identified with the God of the Hebrew Bible. The Demiurge therefore had a vested interest in preventing people from escaping from this world to discover their true home in the abode of the Supreme God, and was assisted in this enterprise by the Archons, who barred the path of individual souls as they tried to escape on their death. Some individuals had no chance of ever escaping material existence, because they had no divine spark at all – though some did, and these were the ones who could benefit from the *gnosis* that could equip them with the insight necessary to understand their imprisonment and open to them the possibility of escape. A Gnostic writing puts it like this:

> *It is not only the washing that is liberty, but the knowledge [gnosis] of who we were, and what we have become, where we were or where we were placed, whither we hasten, from what we are redeemed, what birth is, and what rebirth.*
> **Excerpta Theodotia 78.2**

In some Gnostic systems, this enlightenment is the work of a divine redeemer who descends from the spirit world and alerts those with the divine spark to their true status, which then enables them, on death, to escape from the material world to the spiritual. When Gnostics spoke of "knowledge" they did not have in mind an intellectual knowing of religious dogmas, or indeed of science. They referred to a mystical experience, a direct "knowing" of the supreme God. The Gnostics themselves evolved elaborate mythological stories to explain all this, many of them involving characters from the Hebrew Bible such as Adam or Cain, or individuals such as Simon the magician, mentioned in the New Testament book of Acts. But behind this complicated mythology was a personal existential dilemma related to the nature of human identity and purpose – features that enabled the twentieth-century Swiss psychiatrist Carl Gustav Jung to base much of his theory of human nature on an understanding of ancient Gnostic texts, one of which (the Jung Codex) is named after him.

In relation to personal behaviour, this kind of belief could lead to two quite opposite extremes. Some argued that their aim of complete liberation from the grasp of the material world could best be achieved by a rigorous asceticism that would effectively deny the reality of their bodily existence. But there were others who believed that by virtue of their mystical "knowledge" they had already been released from all material ties, and therefore what they did in their present life was totally irrelevant to their ultimate spiritual destiny. They saw it as their duty to spoil everything connected with life in the material world, including especially its standards of morality and what were regarded as conventional forms of behaviour. They might therefore promote anarchic and undisciplined behaviour as part of their spiritual quest.

It is not difficult to trace connections between this outlook and various groups mentioned in the New Testament. Paul's letters to the church in Corinth often seem to be criticizing views that would certainly be congenial to later Gnostics, while Colossians, 1 John and Revelation 1–3 also seem to be concerned with debates about people who were seeking to understand Christian faith in similar terms. Having said that, there is a good deal of uncertainty about the origins of Gnosticism, and it is far from certain that it existed in any structured form in the early first century AD. There is positive evidence of its existence in the second and third centuries

AD, from Gnostic documents as well as from the writings of those church leaders who wrote to denounce it. These later groups can hardly have constructed their systems out of nothing, though, and no doubt they adopted ideas that had been in circulation for a long time. The one thing that can be said for certain about Gnosticism is that it was highly eclectic and intensely syncretistic. It combined bits and pieces of spiritual wisdom from many sources and incorporated them into something like a coherent picture within its own dualistic worldview. It is therefore perfectly possible to trace connections with Judaism, with classical philosophical thought, and with traditional Persian religions as well as with Christianity, while acknowledging that there was little inner consistency about the ideas taken from these sources, and that what coherence they had was derived from the fact that Gnostics found them all to be serviceable in their own search for the spiritual meaning of life.

Some readers will have come across Gnosticism and its influence through the so-called Gnostic Gospels. The idea that there might have been other "Gospels" in addition to the four of the New Testament first surfaced in the writings of church leaders in the second century, and they occasionally referred to particular ideas found in them, usually dismissing them as Gnostic and therefore heretical. It was many centuries later before any actual copies of such documents came to light. It is worth recounting the story of their discovery in some detail, as it highlights many of the challenges facing anyone who wants to understand how materials from the wider cultural world of the Bible can be useful in understanding the text of the New Testament itself.

In 1769 two *Books of Jéu*, written in Coptic, turned up near the Egyptian city of Thebes, and a few years later in

1785 the British Museum acquired Coptic manuscripts of two books called *Pistis Sophia*. However, it was well into the nineteenth century before it began to dawn on anyone that these documents might have anything to do with ancient Gnosticism, and even then there was no adequate frame of reference within which they could be properly understood. In 1896, a handful of other Coptic texts were discovered in Egypt and included titles such as the *Apocryphon of John*, the *Sophia of Jesus Christ*, the *Acts of Peter,* and the *Gospel of Mary.* A German professor by the name of Carl Schmidt made plans to translate and publish them, but a burst water pipe in the printer's cellar ruined the plates just as they were about to go to press. The work was put aside, and it was well into the second half of the twentieth century before they were ready to be published, by which time their usefulness had been largely superseded.

A few fragments of papyrus manuscripts containing teachings of Jesus were discovered at the beginning of the twentieth century at Oxyrhynchus in Egypt. But it was just after the Second World War that the largest and most valuable collection of Gnostic literature came to light. Towards the end of 1945, a camel-driver by the name of Mohammed Ali El-Samman was digging for manure at the foot of the cliffs of Gebel et Tarif, not far from the modern town of Nag Hammadi in upper Egypt. In the process of scooping up the decomposed bird droppings he uncovered a large jar, inside which was a collection of papyrus leaves bound like books between leather covers. They were written in Coptic, so he naturally took them along to the priest of the local Coptic church, who was unable to read them because they were in a different dialect from the one with which he was familiar. The documents seemed to be of little immediate value, but Mohammed still set about trying to market them through an underground network of antique dealers with whom he had dealt before.

Within a year they were spotted by Togo Mina, director of the Cairo Coptic Museum, who bought some of the sheets. By chance, a letter from France landed on his desk at about the same time, written by a young scholar called Jean Doresse, who had a keen interest in the history and literature of the ancient Coptic church and was planning to visit Egypt with his wife Marianne to explore the sites of some ancient monasteries. On their arrival in Egypt in late summer 1947 they found the country in the grip of a savage cholera epidemic that made it extremely risky for them to travel anywhere except the major cities. Instead of visiting the remote areas that most interested them, they went to view the Coptic Museum's extensive collections of papyrus documents, paintings, statues, jewellery, and other objects remaining from the Coptic Christian culture of the early centuries.

On arrival they were greeted by the director and taken to his private office, where he showed them the papyrus sheets that had originally come from the dung heap at Nag Hammadi. Jean and Marianne Doresse could see that they contained, among other things, accounts of alleged conversations between Jesus and his disciples. There was also a copy of the documents that had come to light in 1896, but which had never been published. The French visitors were fascinated and persuaded Togo Mina to introduce them to Albert Eid, a well-known Belgian antique dealer living in Cairo, who was rumoured to have come into possession of some other similar manuscripts. These turned out to be less well preserved, but they included one called the *Gospel of Truth*, as well as a letter about resurrection addressed to a person by the name of Rheginos, together with other assorted materials. Eid told them of the existence of other similar documents, though it was some time later before Jean Doresse managed to get a glimpse of them. He recorded in his diary that they had "sensationally attractive titles" that included the *Gospel of Philip*, the *Gospel of Thomas*, the *Letter of Peter to Philip*, and the *Revelation of Adam to His Son Seth*. By this time, however, the dealers who held them had become aware of their real value and were concerned that the Egyptian government might confiscate them without offering compensation. They were smuggled out of the country and taken to New York, where no-one was interested, and they were smuggled back to Egypt again!

This sort of underhand dealing went on for several years. One entire document found its way to Germany, where it was presented as a gift to Carl Gustav Jung. But the majority remained in Cairo, and it was not until 1956 that the Coptic Museum managed to gather them all together, including the one from Germany that by now had been given the name "the Jung Codex". This small library turned out to consist of fifty-two separate works contained in thirteen volumes. It is not certain who first collected them, but there was no problem finding out when they were written. Bits of scrap papyrus had been stuffed inside the covers as strengthening material, and these included invoices, receipts and letters bearing dates between AD 333 and 348. That means the books were probably bound about AD 350, and hidden away not long after.

In the years since their discovery and initial publication, these documents from Nag Hammadi have been extensively studied by scholars, while their existence has provoked much popular speculation about the possibility that they contain some alternative account of Jesus and his teaching – perhaps even his "real" teaching, which had been deliberately suppressed by the leaders of the early church because it contained ideas they found uncongenial.

Another Gospel? Gnostic Texts from Nag Hammadi

It is undeniable that many aspects of Jesus' life and teaching were left out of the New Testament Gospels. John 20:30–31 explicitly says that he was offering a selective account, and Luke 1:1–4 adds the further detail that he took his material from much larger collections that were available to him at the time. There is every reason to suppose that Matthew and Mark did the same, and so in principle there is no particular reason why some of this other material should not have been preserved elsewhere. It would be surprising if it had not. The *Gospel of Thomas* contains 114 sayings of Jesus. The vast majority of them are very similar to well-known New Testament passages, but they are not the same. Does Thomas contain expansions and additions? Or is it the New Testament Gospels that have serious omissions? If we could be sure that Thomas was compiled as early as some of the New Testament Gospels, then that would be a genuine question. As it is, however, Thomas in its present form seems to date from about the fourth century – and no-one doubts that it is a thoroughly Gnostic text. It was probably translated into Coptic from Greek, and by coincidence different versions of some of its sayings are found not only in the New Testament, but also (in Greek) in the papyrus documents discovered previously at Oxyrhynchus. When we compare these three versions of Jesus' teaching, it becomes obvious that the sayings in Thomas are a development based on the New Testament, and not some form of independent Gospel – much less a more reliable one. Consider the following statements that are found in all three sources:

Search, and you will find ... everyone who searches finds.
Matthew 7:7–8

Come to me ... and I will give you rest.
Matthew 11:28

*Let him who seeks not cease seeking until he finds; and
when he finds he will be astounded, and having been
astounded he will reign; and reigning, he will rest.*
Oxyrhychus Papyrus 654.5–9

*He who seeks should not stop seeking until he finds; and
when he finds, he will be bewildered; and when he is
bewildered, he will marvel, and will reign over the All.*
Gospel of Thomas Saying 2

You do not need to be a Coptic scholar to see how the
relatively simple New Testament sayings have developed
through the halfway house of Oxyrhynchus into the Gnostic
version found in Thomas. At those points where it can be
tested, Thomas has clearly imposed an interpretation on
the sayings it contains, in order to give them a meaning
congenial to the members of the sect that preserved it.
The other Gnostic Gospels are the same. Moreover, this
understanding coincides with the relative dates at which the
various documents were written: the New Testament in the
first century, the Oxyrhynchus finds at the end of the second,
and Thomas (at least in its Nag Hammadi version) about the
beginning of the fourth.

Judaism

It may come as a surprise to see Judaism mentioned again here in this context. But from the perspective of someone living in the western cities of the Roman empire, Judaism could also be thought of as an eastern religion, and for that reason alone it held all the attractions of mystery and intrigue that such an origin implied. Unlike the esoteric mystery cults with connections to Egypt or Mesopotamia, however, Judaism was not a secret affair, and both its teachings and its rituals were accessible to any outsiders who may be interested. Its focus on everyday practical morality meant that it shared some of the best aspects of the philosophical schools, while also being rooted in ancient scriptural texts that, being written originally in Hebrew, had an aura of mystery about them – though the fact that they were readily available in Greek meant that anyone in the empire could read them. In addition, the presence of significant Jewish communities in almost every city made it possible to see how all this worked out in practice just by observing the lifestyle of one's Jewish neighbours. Moreover, Jewish religious leaders were aware of this and recognized it as an opportunity to gain converts. Even in the time of Jesus, the persistence and enthusiasm of Jewish rabbis in sharing their faith with others, crossing land and sea to do so, were legendary[35] – and we have already noted the example of Cornelius, who was typical of the sort of Roman among whom Jewish standards of personal and social morality found a warm reception.

Epilogue

The journey through the world of the Bible has taken in something like 2,000 years of history, not to mention the prehistoric beliefs of ancient Mesopotamians and Egyptians that helped set the scene for understanding the Bible's own approach to primeval times. Culturally, it has introduced us to some of the greatest and richest cities of the ancient world as well as to more ordinary dwellings in rural settlements and nomadic encampments. Over the course of the ages, languages changed, and lifestyles were never the same for long. But throughout all this, one thing remained constant, and that was faith in some sort of divine being. In most of the Bible lands, life was precariously balanced on the vicissitudes of the natural world. The climate and geography played a major role in the lives of people in all the biblical civilizations, and because these people had no sense of a division between what we would call the secular and the sacred, it was natural that religious faith would be intimately bound up with everyday survival. In Mesopotamia the stability of life depended to a considerable degree on harnessing the resources of the two great rivers, the Tigris and the Euphrates, which brought fertility to the fields and food to the people, and provided a ready means of transport. There was a similar story further to the west in Egypt. Here too the meaning of life could never be detached from the river, which was the source of economic prosperity. As the Nile rose and fell in an annual cycle, it left in its wake a great covering of rich and fertile soil.

Between these two ancient superpowers, in Palestine itself, survival also depended on the smooth operation of the natural world, this time on the rains coming at the right time in the year, and in the correct quantities. No matter how you look at it, the Hebrew Bible cannot be fully understood without some knowledge of the history of the surrounding nations and the religious beliefs that undergirded their self-understanding and identity. The most creative thinkers of the time – the Hebrew prophets – adopted a sophisticated approach to this wider culture. They knew that their understanding of God was quite different from that of other nations, but they also knew that no-one can ever live in a cultural vacuum. So they sought to affirm and recognize the cultural context while seeking to contextualize their own different worldview within the ideological frame of reference that people would understand. In many ways this was fundamentally opposed to the spirituality of Mesopotamia, Egypt and Canaan. Instead of seeing God as a manifestation of the forces of nature, they traced their own understanding back to the revelation entrusted to Moses on Mt Sinai, in which God was presented as a personal being whose actions and attitudes were formed not in the random unpredictability of nature but in a moral universe where standards never changed.

More than a thousand years later, even in Rome – one of the most urbanized empires ever known – daily life still found its meaning with reference to respect for the forces of nature. Elements such as rain, thunder and the sun were personified and became the objects of devotion. Traditional Greek culture had a similar underpinning, which is why it was a relatively simple matter for the pantheons of Greece and Rome to be identified with one another. Everything found its true meaning by reference to the actions of the gods and goddesses. If things went wrong and the crops failed to mature, or if brave warriors were defeated in battle, then inappropriate religious devotion was seen as the most likely cause. Even simple everyday things like rain were given a religious explanation. In *The Cloud*, a comic play by Aristophanes (456–386 BC), the hero Strepsiades reflects the common view that rain was produced by Zeus pissing through a sieve! The same play also offers evidence for rising tensions between such traditional beliefs and the growth of more sophisticated philosophical ideas, while cynically poking fun at both of them. By the start of the Christian era, pressure for change was irresistible as the old certainties of the past were questioned and people were less willing to believe in the old stories that had sustained previous generations. In the process they questioned the long-established rules of morality and religion and sought to replace what was now regarded as unfounded superstition with a reasoned explanation of things. This endeavour led to a great expansion of knowledge, not only about human behaviour but also about the natural world. Some of their ideas sound comical today, and scientists would laugh at the idea that the world's primary constituent might be fire or water. But this new spirit of inquiry widened the horizons of many people and led to a growing confidence in the power of human reason to resolve some, if not all, of the big questions of human existence.

By the time the Roman empire was fully established, most educated people had been trained in this way of thinking, though others who never went to school struggled to understand such ideas. But they knew enough to understand that things could never be quite the same again. The thinkers had apparently disproved the existence of the old traditional gods, and alongside that, new movements of trade and people were introducing the people of Europe to other, apparently more exotic, deities from further east. Did they really exist?

And if they did, how might they relate to life in the great urban centres of Greece and Italy?

These uncertainties conspired together to induce a religious crisis in the Roman world. The philosophers had discredited traditional ways of explaining life, but had failed to establish a readily accessible alternative. As a result, many people found themselves in a moral and spiritual vacuum. New ideas soon came rushing in to fill the void, especially from the East, among them the mystery religions as well as longer-established faiths such as Judaism – and Christianity. Though Jesus never travelled beyond his own native land of Palestine, within twenty years of his death there were thriving Christian communities in all the major cities of the Mediterranean lands. This is another phenomenon that cannot be understood apart from the cultural upheavals that were taking place at the time. Knowing something about the world of the Bible might not be the same thing as understanding its core message. But the message cannot be fully appreciated without taking into account the historical, social, cultural, and spiritual circumstances in which it was first articulated.

Endnotes

Chapter 1

1. Matthew 5:38–48
2. Joshua 15:62
3. Genesis 19:26
4. Luke 1:1–4
5. John 20:31
6. Hebrews 13:21–25
7. Revelation 1:4–3:22
8. 1 Kings 14:19
9. 1 Kings 14:29
10. Joshua 10:13; 2 Samuel 1:18
11. Numbers 21:14
12. Luke 1:1–4
13. John 20:31; 21:25
14. e.g. Galatians 1:7–9
15. 2 Peter 3:16

Chapter 2

1. Genesis 6:1–9:29
2. Genesis 5:27
3. Genesis 6:1–4
4. Genesis 1:1–2
5. Genesis 1:21
6. Genesis 1:14–19
7. Genesis 1:26–27
8. Genesis 1:29
9. Genesis 3:1–13
10. Genesis 11:1–9
11. 1 Samuel 9:1–10:24
12. 1 Kings 8:1–66
13. Genesis 13:1–14:16
14. Genesis 16:1–16; 21:8–21
15. Genesis 10:22; Ezra 4:9;
    Jeremiah 49:34–39; Acts 2:9
16. Genesis 10:16; Exodus 3:8; 1
    Chronicles 1:14
17. Deuteronomy 26:5
18. Genesis 32:38
19. Joshua 24:2
20. Exodus 3:13–15
21. Genesis 18:6–8
22. Genesis 12:6–9; 13:12–18;
    33:18–20
23. Genesis 26:12
24. Genesis 12:10–20; 20:1–18;
    26:6–11
25. Genesis 46:28 – 47:12
26. Genesis 14:1–24
27. Genesis 16:1–14
28. Genesis 21:9–13
29. Genesis 15:1–4
30. Leviticus 18:18
31. Genesis 29:15–30
32. Genesis 20:12; Leviticus 18:9,
    11; 20:17; Deuteronomy 27:22
33. Exodus 20:1–21
34. Genesis 4:23

Chapter 3

1. Exodus 12:1–14:31
2. Genesis 37:1–50:26
3. Deuteronomy 34:1–4
4. Genesis 37:1–50:26
5. Genesis 41:14
6. Genesis 43:32
7. Genesis 50:26
8. Exodus 1:8
9. Exodus 2:1 – 14:31
10. Exodus 5:6–19
11. Exodus 12:38
12. 1 Kings 9:16
13. Jeremiah 44:17

Chapter 4

1. Exodus 12:38
2. Joshua 8:33–35
3. Joshua 24:14–15
4. Joshua 6:25
5. Matthew 1:5
6. Joshua 9:1–27
7. 1 Samuel 28:3–25

8. Isaiah 14:9–11
9. Jeremiah 16:6
10. Leviticus 10:8–11; Isaiah 28:7–8
11. 1 Kings 18:20–40
12. Psalms 47:9; 99:1
13. Leviticus 16:8, 10, 26
14. 1 Samuel 8:5
15. 2 Kings 18:26; Isaiah 36:11
16. Deuteronomy 22:8
17. 2 Kings 4:10
18. 1 Samuel 9:25
19. Joshua 2:1–9
20. Judges 19:15–21
21. Judges 19:22 – 20:48
22. 1 Samuel 9:1–2
23. Ruth 2:1–23
24. Judges 6:25–32
25. 1 Kings 7:13–14
26. 2 Samuel 5:11
27. 1 Kings 5:20
28. 2 Kings 12:11–12
29. Amos 5:12
30. Psalm 18:42; Isaiah 57:20; Micah 7:10
31. Zechariah 9:3
32. Zechariah10:5
33. Leviticus 23:12–13
34. 2 Kings 9:37, Jeremiah 8:2; 9:22; 16:4
35. Joshua 2:15
36. 2 Samuel 8:15–18; 20:23–26; 1 Kings 4:1–28
37. Jeremiah 37:21
38. Isaiah 44:19
39. Leviticus 26:26
40. Isaiah 7:3; 36:2
41. Isaiah 5:8
42. Jeremiah 5:27–28
43. Amos 2:6–8; 5:7–12
44. 1 Kings 10:26–29
45. 1 Kings 9:26–28
46. 1 Kings 11:3
47. 1 Kings 4:29–34; 10:1–7
48. 1 Kings 11:5–8
49. 1 Kings 12:25–33
50. 1 Kings 18:17–19

51. Jeremiah 7:18
52. Ecclesiastes 3:1–8
53. Exodus 15:20–21
54. Judges 11:34
55. 1 Samuel 18:6; 30:16
56. 2 Samuel 6:14–15
57. Solomon 2:8; 6:13; 7:1ff; Psalm 45:15–16
58. 1 Samuel 10:5–7
59. Psalm 22:3
60. Psalm 63:5
61. Psalm 42:4
62. 1 Chronicles 15:16–24; 16:4–7; Ezra 2:40–42
63. 2 Samuel 6:5; Psalms 43:4; 68:25; 81:1–3; 98:4–6; 150:3–5; Isaiah 30:29; 1 Chronicles 25:1–5
64. Psalms 42:5, 11; 43:5; 46:7, 11
65. Psalm 26:6
66. Psalms 149:3; 150:4
67. Psalm 42:4; 48:12–14
68. Psalm 118:19, 26–7
69. Psalms 46; 66; 74
70. Exodus 12:21–28
71. Ezekiel 3:26
72. Ezekiel 4:1–3
73. Ezekiel 4:4–8
74. Ezekiel 5:1–4
75. Jeremiah 13:1–14
76. Jeremiah 18:1–19:15
77. Jeremiah 25:15–36
78. Jeremiah 43:6–13
79. Jeremiah 51:62–64
80. 2 Kings 13:14–19; Ezekiel 4:1–7:27
81. Exodus 20:4
82. 1 Kings 22:39
83. Amos 6:4
84. Amos 3:15
85. 1 Kings 10:18
86. 1 Kings 11:41
87. Numbers 21:14

Chapter 5

1. 1 Kings 14:25–28

2. 1 Kings 14:30; 15:16–22
3. Kings 16:31
4. 2 Kings 13:1–9, 22–23
5. 2 Kings 12:17–18
6. 2 Kings 15:17–22
7. Isaiah 7:10–25
8. 2 Kings 16:5–9
9. 2 Kings 15:29
10. 2 Kings 17:1–4
11. 2 Chronicles 32:5; Isaiah 22:9–11
12. 2 Chronicles 32:5–6, 27–29
13. 2 Chronicles 35:25
14. Ezra 6:3–5
15. Isaiah 45:1 (the Hebrew word is *mashiach*, usually translated "messiah").

Chapter 6

1. Matthew 2:1
2. Matthew 2:16
3. Exodus 20:4
4. Mark 6:17–29
5. Luke 23:6–12
6. Acts 26:28–32
7. Matthew 27:19
8. Luke 23:12

Chapter 7

1. John 8:2–11
2. Matthew 1:18–19
3. John 4:17–18
4. Acts 22:3
5. Acts 4:13
6. Luke 4:16–30
7. Luke 2:41–51
8. Luke 12:15–21
9. Luke 1:14, 57–58; 2:13–14
10. Matthew 1:21
11. Luke 1:31
12. Luke 2:21
13. Acts 15:1–21
14. Luke 2:41–52
15. For example Mark 5:38–39; John 19:39–40; Acts 9:36–37
16. John 19:31–32
17. John 19:28–29
18. John 19:25–27
19. Mark 2:23–28; 3:1–6
20. Exodus 20:11
21. Mark 3:4
22. Mark 2:27
23. Luke 12:41
24. Mark:12–25
25. Acts 2:41
26. Colossians 2:16–19
27. Acts 6:8 – 8:1
28. Acts 15:1–21; 21:17–26; Galatians 2:11–12
29. Matthew 19:3–12; Mark 10:2–9
30. John 7:53–8:11
31. Deuteronomy 18:18–19
32. Acts 7:41–53
33. Hebrews 5:6–10; 6:20; 7:1–19
34. Luke 6:15
35. Matthew 10:4
36. Mark 3:18
37. Mark 3:19
38. Mark 15:6–15
39. Acts 21:37–39
40. Acts 6:1; 9:29
41. 1 Corinthians 9:5
42. Matthew 13:55
43. Matthew 5:14
44. Matthew 6:2
45. John 6:23
46. John 6:1; 21:1
47. Luke 1:1–4; John 20:30–31
48. Matthew 11:19
49. Acts 23:23–33
50. Acts 25:1 – 27:2
51. Acts 10:1

Chapter 8

1. Matthew 22:20; Mark 12:17
2. Acts 18:24; 19:1; 1 Corinthians 1:12; 3:4–6
3. Acts 18:2
4. Romans 13:1–7
5. Acts 18:12–17
6. 1 Peter 1:7
7. 1 Peter 5:8

8. Acts 13:7
9. Acts 18:12–17
10. Galatians 4:5; Romans 8:15, 23; 9:4; Ephesians 1:5
11. Acts 21:39
12. Acts 22:26–27
13. Philippians 3:20
14. Ephesians 2:19
15. Acts 22:28
16. See for instance, Ephesians 5:26–7; Revelation 21:2
17. 1 Timothy 5:14; Titus 2:3–5
18. Colossians 3:18 – 4:1; 1 Peter 3:1–7
19. 1 Corinthians 11:2–16
20. Philippians 4:2–3
21. Romans 16:7
22. Mark 9:33–37; 10:13–16
23. Acts 20:7–12
24. Romans 2–4; 1 Corinthians 6:12–20; 15:29–35
25. James 2:14–26
26. Galatians 3:23–25
27. Galatians 1:1–5
28. For example Philippians 1:3–11
29. Philippians 1:6–4:31
30. Philippians 5:1–6:10
31. Galatians 6:11–17
32. Galatians 6:18
33. Luke 1:1–4; John 20:30–31
34. Acts 17:21
35. Thessalonians 5:27
36. 2 Peter 3:15–16
37. See, among many examples, Romans 16:23; 1 Peter 4:9; 3 John 5–8; Hebrews 13:2
38. Acts 18:8
39. 1 Corinthians 11:20–22
40. 1Corinthians 8:1–13
41. 1 Corinthians 5:1–5; 7:1–16
42. 1 Corinthians 1:10–17
43. 1 Corinthians 14:26–40
44. 1 Corinthians 13:1–3
45. 1 Corinthians 14:7–8
46. Acts 19:29–41
47. Acts 12:20–23

48. 1 Corinthians 9:24–27; Philippians 3:14; Hebrews 12:1; 2 Timothy 2:5
49. Romans 16:23
50. Acts 19:39–41
51. Acts 18:12–17
52. Acts 19:38

Chapter 9

1. Acts 19:28
2. Acts 14:11
3. Acts 8:10
4. Acts 28:11
5. Acts 19:35
6. Acts 19:28
7. Acts 14:13
8. 1 Corinthians 8:11
9. 1 Corinthians 8:10
10. 1 Corinthians 10:25
11. 1 Corinthians 9:13
12. Philippians 2:17; 2 Timothy 4:6
13. As documented in Romans 16:1–16
14. Acts 10:2, 33, 44–48
15. Acts 16:14–15
16. Acts 16:31–34
17. Romans 16:1–16
18. Acts 17:16–34
19. Acts 19:9–10
20. Acts 17:18
21. Acts 17:28
22. Ephesians 5:3–4; Colossians 3:18
23. Acts 17:18
24. 1 Thessalonians 4:11–12
25. Acts 23:11; 27:23–24
26. For examples of visions see Acts 10:10–16; 16:9–10
27. Mark 3:19–22
28. Mark 9:38–41
29. Acts 8:11–13
30. Acts 8:14–24
31. Matthew 2:1–12
32. Acts 19:11–12
33. Acts 19:13–19
34. 1 Corinthians 9:22
35. Matthew 23:15

Bibliography

Ackroyd, Peter R., *Israel under Babylon and Persia*, Oxford University Press, 1970

Aling, Charles F., *Egypt and Bible History: From Earliest Times to 1000 BC*, Baker Book House, 1981

Ara, Rami, *Cities Through the Looking Glass: Essays on the History and Archaeology of Biblical Urbanism*, Eisenbrauns, 2007

Arnold, Bill T. and Beyer, Bryan E. (eds.), *Readings from the Ancient Near East: Primary Sources for Old Testament Study*, Baker Academic, 2002

Aufrecht, Walter E.; Mirau, Neil A. and Gauley, Steven W. (eds.), *Urbanism in Antiquity: from Mesopotamia to Crete*, Sheffield Academic Press, 1997

Austin, M. M., *The Hellenistic World from Alexander to the Roman Conquest: A Selection of Ancient Sources in Translation*, Cambridge University Press, 1981

Avalos, Hector, *Illness and Health Care in the Ancient Near East: The Role of the Temple in Greece, Mesopotamia, and Israel*, Scholars Press, 1995

Barrett, C. K., *The New Testament Background*, Harper, 1961

Batey, Richard A., *Jesus and the Forgotten City: New Light on Sepphoris and the Urban World of Jesus*, Baker Book House, 1991

Beckman, Gary and Lewis, Theodore J., *Text, Artifact and Image: Revealing Ancient Israelite Religion*, Brown University Press, 2006

Bell, H. Idris, *Cults and Creeds in Graeco-Roman Egypt*, Ares Publishers, 1975

Beyerlin, Walter (ed.), *Near Eastern Religious Texts Relating to the Old Testament*, SCM Press, 1978

Block, Daniel I., *The Gods of the Nations: Studies in Ancient Near Eastern National Theology*, Baker Books, 2000

Borowski, Oded, *Daily Life in Biblical Times*, Society of Biblical Luterature, 2003

Bottéro, Jean, *Religion in ancient Mesopotamia*, Lavender Fagan, Teresa (trans.), University of Chicago Press, 2001

Bricault, Laurent; Versluys, Miguel John and Meyboom, Paul G. P. (eds.), *Nile into Tiber: Egypt in the Roman world: Proceedings of the IIIrd International Conference of Isis Studies, Faculty of Archaeology, Leiden University, May 11–14, 2005*, Brill, 2007

Brooke, G. J.; Curtis A. H. W. and Healy, J. F. (eds.), *Ugarit and the Bible*, Ugarit-Verlag, 1994

Caquot, André and Sznycer, Maurice, *Ugaritic Religion*, Brill, 1980

Casson, Lionel, *Libraries in the Ancient World*, Yale University Press, 2001

Charlesworth, James H. (ed.), *Jesus and Archaeology* Eerdmans, 2006

——, *The Bible and the Dead Sea Scrolls: The Second Princeton Symposium on Judaism and Christian Origins*, Baylor University Press, 2006

Chavalas, Mark W. and Younger, Jr., K. Lawson (eds.), *Mesopotamia and the Bible: Comparative Explorations*, Sheffield Academic Press, 2002

Chirichigno, Gregory C., *Debt-Slavery in Israel and the Ancient Near East*, JSOT Press, 1993

Clemens, David M., *Sources for Ugaritic Ritual and Sacrifice*, Ugarit-Verlag, 2001

Collins, John J. and Kugler, Robert A., *Religion in the Dead Sea Scrolls*, 2000

Contenau, Georges, *Everyday Life in Babylon and Assyria*, Maxwell-Hyslop, K. R. & A. R. (trans.), E. Arnold, 1954

Coogan, Michael D., *The Oxford History of the Biblical World*, Oxford University Press, 2001

Coogan, Michael D., (ed. and trans.), *Stories from Ancient Canaan*, Westminster Press, 1978

Cooper, Jerrold S., *Reconstructing History from Ancient Inscriptions: The Lagash-Umma Border Conflict*, Undena Publications, 1983

Craigie, Peter C., *Ugarit and the Old Testament*, Eerdmans, 1983

Cross, Frank Moore, *The Ancient Library of Qumran*, Fortress, 1995

Currid, John D. *Ancient Egypt and the Old Testament*, Baker, 1997

Curtis, Adrian, *Ugarit*, Eerdmans, 1985

Dalley, Stephanie, *Myths From Mesopotamia: Creation, The Flood, Gilgamesh and Others*, Oxford University Press, 2000

Daviau, P. M. M.; Wevers, J. W. and Weigl, M. (eds.), *The World of the Aramaeans*, Sheffield Academic Press, 2001

David, A. Rosalie, *The Ancient Egyptians: Religious Beliefs and Practices*, Routledge & Kegan Paul, 1982

Davis, John J., *Moses and the Gods of Egypt: Studies in Exodus*, Baker Book House, 1986

Day, John *Yahweh and the Gods and Goddesses of Canaan*, Sheffield Academic Press, 2000

Dearman, J. A. and Graham, M. P., *The Land That I Will Show You: Essays on the History and Archaeology of the Ancient Near East*, Sheffield Academic Press, 2001

Driver, Godfrey Rolles and Mills, John C. (eds.), *The Assyrian Laws*, Clarendon Press, 1935

Eddy, Samuel K., *The King is Dead: Studies in the Near Eastern resistance to Hellenism, 334–31 BC*, University of Nebraska Press, 1961

Edwards, Douglas R. (ed.), *Religion and Society in Roman*

Palestine: Old Questions, New Approaches, Routledge, 2004

Eph'al, Israel (ed.), *The City Besieged: Siege and its Manifestations in the Ancient Near East*, Brill, 2009

Epzstein, Leon, *Social Justice in the Ancient Near East and the People of the Bible*, SCM Press 1986

Falkenstein, Adam, *The Sumerian Temple City*, Undena Publications, 1974

Ferguson, Everett, *Backgrounds of Early Christianity*, third edition, Eerdmans, 2003

Fisher, Loren R., *The Claremont Ras Shamra Tablets* , Pontifical Biblical Institute, 1972

Fleming, Daniel E.,*The Installation of Baal's High Priestess at Emar: A Window on Ancient Syrian Religion*, Scholars Press, 1992

Flusser, David, *Judaism of the Second Temple period*, Yadin, Azzan (trans.), The Hebrew University Magnes Press: Jerusalem Perspective, 2007

Foster, Benjamin R., *Before the Muses: An Anthology of Akkadian Literature*, CDL Press, 2005

Freedman, David Noel and Kuhlken, Pam Fox, *What are the Dead Sea Scrolls and Why Do they Matter?* Eerdmans, 2007

Galil, Gershon, *The Lower Stratum Families in the Neo-Assyrian Period*, Brill, 2007.

Galinsky, Karl (ed.), *The Cambridge Companion to the Age of Augustus*, Cambridge University Press, 2005

Gallagher, William R., *Sennacherib's Campaign to Judah*, Brill, 1999

Gammie, John G. and Perdue, Leo G., *The Sage in Israel and the Ancient Near East*, Eisenbrauns, 1990

García Martínez, Florentino and Luttikhuizen, Gerard P., *Interpretations of the Flood*, Brill, 1999

George, Andrew, *The Epic of Gilgamesh*, Penguin, 1999

Gibson, J. C. L., *Canaanite Myths and Legends*, T & T Clark, 1978

Goedicke, Hans and Roberts, J. J. M., (eds.), *Unity and Diversity: Essays in the History, Literature and Religion of the Ancient Near East*, Johns Hopkins University Press, 1975

Gordon, Cyrus H., *The Ancient Near East*, Norton, 1965

Grant, Michael, *Atlas of Classical History*, Oxford University Press, 1994

Grayson, Albert K., *Assyrian Rulers of Early First Millennia BC (1114–859 BC)*, University of Toronto Press, 1991

——, *Assyrian & Babylonian Chronicles*, Eisenbrauns, 2000

Grimal, Nicolas-Christophe, *A History of Ancient Egypt*, Blackwell, 1993

Grootkerk, Salomon E., *Ancient Sites in Galilee: A Toponymic Gazetteer*, Brill, 2000

Harris, John Richard (ed.), *The Legacy of Egypt*, Clarendon Press, 1971

Harris, W. V. (ed.), *Ancient Alexandria Between Egypt and Greece*, Brill, 2004

Heimpel, Wolfgang, *Letters to the King of Mari*, Eisenbrauns, 2003

Heinz, Marlies and Feldman, Marian H., *Representations of Political Power: Case Histories from Times of Change and Dissolving Order in the Ancient Near East*, Eisenbrauns, 2007

Hess, Richard S., *Israelite Religions: An Archaeological and Biblical Survey*, Baker Academic, 2007

Hillel, Daniel, *The Natural History of the Bible*, Columbia University Press, 2006

Hinnells, John R. (ed), *A Handbook of Ancient Religions*, Cambridge University Press, 2007

Higginbotham, Carolyn R., *Egyptianization and Elite Emulation in Ramesside Palestine: Governance and Accommodation on the Imperial Periphery*, Brill, 2000

Hirschfeld, Yizhar, *Qumran in Context: Reassessing the Archaeological Evidence*, Hendrickson Publishers, 2004

Hoerth, Alfred J. et al (eds.), *Peoples of the Old Testament World*, Baker, 1994

Hoffman, Michael A., *Egypt Before the Pharaohs: The Prehistoric Foundations of Egyptian Civilization*, Knopf, 1979

Hoffmeier, James K., *Ancient Israel in Sinai*, Oxford University Press, 2005

Hopkins, David C., *The Highlands of Canaan: Agricultural Life in the Early Iron Age*, Almond Press, 1985

Hopkins Hawkes, Jacquetta, *The First Great Civilizations: Life in Mesopotamia, the Indus Valley, and Egypt*, Knopf, 1973

Horowitz, Wayne, *Mesopotamian Cosmic Geography*, Eisenbrauns, 1998

Houston, Mary Galway, *Ancient Egyptian, Mesopotamian & Persian Costume and Decoration*, A & C Black, 1954

James, E. O., *The Ancient Gods: The History and Diffusion of Religion in the Ancient Near East and the Eastern Mediterranean*, Weidenfeld & Nicholson, 1960

James, T. G. H., *Pharaoh's People: Scenes from Life in Imperial Egypt*, University of Chicago Press, 1984

Johnston, Sarah Iles, *Religions of the Ancient World: A Guide*, Belknap Press, 2004

Judge, E.A., *The First Christians in the Roman World*, Mohr Siebeck, 2008

Kapelrud, Arvid S., *The Ras Shamra Discoveries and the Old Testament*, Blackwell, 1965

Keresztes, Paul, *Imperial Rome and the Christians: From Herod the Great to about 200 AD*, University Press of America, 1989

Kessler, Rainer, *The Social History of Ancient Israel: An Introduction*, Maloney, Linda M. (trans.), Fortress Press, 2008

King, L. W., *Babylonian Religion and Mythology*, AMS Press, 1976.

Bibliography

——, *The Letters and Inscriptions of Hammurabi, King of Babylon*, AMS Press, 1976

——, *The Seven Tablets of Creation*, AMS Press, 1976

Kotkin, Joel, *The City: A Global History*, Modern Library, 2005.

Kramer, S. N. and Maier, John (eds.), *Myths of Enki, the Crafty God*, Oxford University Press, 1989

Kurht, Amelie, *The Ancient Near East, c. 3000–330 BC*, Routledge, 1995)

Læssøe, Jørgen, *People of Ancient Assyria: Their Inscriptions and Correspondence*, Leigh-Browne, F. S. (trans.), Barnes & Noble, 1963

Lambert, W. G., *Babylonian Oracle Questions*, Eisenbrauns, 2007

Lichtheim, Miriam, *Moral Values in Ancient Egypt*, Vandenhoeck & Ruprecht, 1997

Lim, Timothy H., (ed.) with Hurtado, Larry W.; Auld, A.; Graeme and Jack, Alison, *The Dead Sea Scrolls in Their Historical Context*, T & T Clark International, 2004.

Lloyd, Seton, *The Art of the Ancient Near East*, Thames and Hudson, 1961

Loewenstamm, Samuel E., *From Babylon to Canaan: Studies in the Bible and its Oriental Background*, Magnes Press, Hebrew University, 1992.

MacDonald, Alasdair A. et al (eds.), *Learned Antiquity: Scholarship and Society in the Near East, the Greco-Roman World, and the Early Medieval West*, Peeters, 2003

MacKenzie, Donald A., *Mythology of the Babylonian People*, Bracken Books, 1996

Magness, Jodi, *The Archaeology of Qumran and the Dead Sea Scrolls*, Eerdmans, 2002

Manning, J. G. and Morris, Ian M (eds.), *The Ancient Economy: Evidence and Models*, Stanford University Press, 2005

Mason, Steve, *Josephus, Judea, and Christian Origins: Methods and Categories*, Hendrickson Publishers, Inc., 2009

Matthews, Victor H. and Benjamin, Don C., *Old Testament Parallels: Laws and Stories from the Ancient Near East*, Paulist Press, 1997

Meeks, Dimitri and Favard-Meeks, Christine, *Daily life of the Egyptian Gods*, Cornell University Press, 1996

Mertz, Barbara, *Temples, Tombs & Hieroglyphs: A Popular History of Ancient Egypt*, Brockhampton Press, 1999

Meyers, Eric M. (ed.), *Galilee Through the Centuries: Confluence of Cultures*, Eisenbrauns, 1999

——; Netzer, Ehud and Meyers, Carol L., *Sepphoris*, Eisenbrauns; Joint Sepphoris Project, 1992

Michalowski, Piotr, *Letters from early Mesopotamia*, Scholars Press, 1993

Moor, Johannes C. de, *An Anthology of Religious Texts from Ugarit*, Brill, 1987

Moran, William L.,*The Amarna Letters.* Johns Hopkins University Press, 1992

Morenz, Siegfried, *Egyptian Religion*, Keep, Ann E. (trans.), Cornell University Press, 1973

Morrison, Martha A., *The Eastern Archives of Nuzi*, Eisenbrauns, 1993

Nash, Ronald H., *Christianity and the Hellenistic World*, Probe Ministries International, 1984

Nemet-Nejat, Karen Rhea, *Daily Life in Ancient Mesopotamia*, Greenwood Press, 1998

Netzer, Ehud with the assistance of Laureys-Chachy, Rachel, *The Architecture of Herod, the Great Builder* Mohr Siebeck, 2006

Nibbi, Alessandra, *The Sea Peoples and Egypt*, Noyes Press, 1975

Niehaus, Jeffrey Jay, *Ancient Near Eastern Themes in Biblical Theology*, Kregel, 2008

Nissen, Hans J., *The Early History of the Ancient Near East, 9000–2000 BC,* University of Chicago Press, 1988

Nissinen, Martii (ed.), *Prophets and Prophecy in the Ancient Near East*, Society of Biblical Literature, 2003

Noll, K. L., *Canaan and Israel in Antiquity: An Introduction*, Sheffield Academic Press, 2001

O'Brien, Joan and Major, Wilfred, *In the Beginning: Creation Myths From Ancient Mesopotamia, Israel, and Greece*, Scholars Press, 1982

Olmo Lete, Gregorio del, *Canaanite Religion According to the Liturgical Texts of Ugarit*, Eisenbrauns, 2004

Oppenheim, A. Leo, *Ancient Mesopotamia, Portrait of a Dead Civilization* University of Chicago Press, 1964

Pardee, Dennis, *Ritual and Cult at Ugarit*, Society of Biblical Literature, 2002

Parkinson, R. B. (trans. and ed.), *Voices from Ancient Egypt: An Anthology of Middle Kingdom Writings*, University of Oklahoma Press, 1991

Pearson, Birger A., *Gnosticism, Judaism, and Egyptian Christianity*, Fortress Press, 1990

Peden, A. J.,*The Graffiti of Pharaonic Egypt: Scope and Roles of Informal Writings (c. 3100–332 BC)*, Brill, 2001

Perdue, Leo G., *Scribes, Sages and Seers,* Vandenhoeck & Ruprecht, 2008

Polin, Claire C. J., *Music of the Ancient Near East*, Vantage Press, 1954

Postgate, J. N., *Taxation and Conscription in the Assyrian Empire*, Biblical Institute Press, 1974

James Putnam, *Egyptology: An Introduction to the History, Art, and Culture of Ancient Egypt* , Quantum Books, 1990

Rainey, Anson F. and Notley, R. Steven, *The Sacred Bridge: Carta's Atlas of the Biblical World*, Carta, 2006

Redford, Donald B. (ed.), *The Oxford Encyclopedia of Ancient Egypt,* Oxford University Press, 2001

——, *The Wars in Syria and Palestine of Thurmose III*, Brill, 2003

Bibliography

Rice, Michael, *Who's Who in Ancient Egypt*, Routledge, 2003

Richard, Suzanne (ed.), *Near Eastern Archaeology: A Reader*, Eisenbrauns, 2003

Richardson, Peter, *Herod: King of the Jews and Friend of the Romans*, University of South Carolina Press, 1996

Roaf, Michael, *Cultural Atlas of Mesopotamia and the Ancient Near East*, Facts on File, 1990

Rocca, Samuel, *Herod's Judaea: A Mediterranean State in the Classical World*, Mohr Siebeck, 2008

Russell, John M. *The Writing on the Wall: Studies in the Architectural Context of Late Assyrian Palace Inscriptions*, Eisenbrauns, 1999

Saad El-Din, Morsi et al (eds.), *Alexandria: The Site & the History, Essays* New York University Press, 1993

Sack, Ronald H., *Cuneiform Documents from the Chaldean and Persian Periods* Susquehanna University Press, 1994

Saggs, H. W. F., *The Greatness That Was Babylon: A Sketch of the Ancient Civilization of the Tigris-Euphrates Valley*, Sidwick and Jackson, 1962

——, *The Might that Was Assyria*, St. Martin's Press, 1989.

Sasson, Jack M., *The Treatment of Criminals in the Ancient Near East*, Brill, 1977

Sasson, Jack M. et al (eds.), *Civilizations of the Ancient Near East in 4 vols*, Scribner, 1995

Schiffman, Lawrence H., (ed.), *Semitic Papyrology in Context: A Climate of Creativity*, Brill, 2003

Schloen. J. D. (ed.), *The House of the Father As Fact and Symbol: Patrimonialism in Ugarit and the Ancient Near East*, Eisenbrauns, 2001

Schreiber, Nicola, *The Cypro-Phoenician Pottery of the Iron Age*, Brill, 2002

Schwantes, Siegfried J., *A Short History of the Ancient Near East*, Baker, 1965

Seton-Williams, M. V., *Egyptian Legends and Stories*, Barnes & Noble, 1999

Shafer, Bryon E., (ed.), *Temples of Ancient Egypt*, Cornell University Press, 1997

Silberman, Neil A. and Small, David (eds.), *The Archaeology of Israel: Constructing the Past, Interpreting the Present*, Sheffield Academic Press, 1997

Slater, Elizabeth A., Mee, C. B. and Bienkowski, Piotr (eds.), *Writing and Ancient Near Eastern Society*, T & T Clark, 2005

Snell, Daniel C., *Life in the Ancient Near East 3100–332 BCE*, Yale University Press, 1997

——, *Flight and Freedom in the Ancient Near East*, Brill, 2001

Steinkeller, Piotr, *Third-Millennium Legal and Administrative Texts in the Iraq Museum*, Eisenbrauns, 1991

Stol, M. and Vleeming, S. P. (eds.), *The Care of the Elderly in the ancient Near East*, Brill, 1998

Time-Life Books (eds.), *What Life Was Like on the Banks of the Nile: Egypt, 3050–30 BC* Time-Life Books, 1996

Trigger, Bruce G., *Early Civilizations: Ancient Egypt in Context*, American University in Cairo Press, 1993

Uehlinger, Christoph (ed.), *Images as Media: Sources for the Cultural History of the Near East and the Eastern Mediterranean*, University Press 2000

van de Mieroop, Marc, *A History of the Ancient Near East*, 2nd ed, Blackwell, 2007

van der Deijl, Aarnoud *Protest or Propaganda: War in the Old Testament Book of Kings and in Contemporaneous Ancient Near Eastern Texts*, Brill, 2008

van der Toorn, Karel, *Family Religion in Babylonia, Syria, and Israel*, Brill, 1996

van Henten, Jan Willem, *Food and Drink in the Biblical worlds*, Society of Biblical Literature, 1999

VanderKam, James C. and Flint, Peter, *The Meaning of the Dead Sea Scrolls: Their Significance for Understanding the Bible, Judaism, Jesus, and Christianity*, HarperSanFrancisco, 2002

Vermes, Geza, *An Introduction to the Complete Dead Sea Scrolls*, Fortress Press, 2000

——, *Jesus In His Jewish Context*, Fortress Press, 2003.

von Soden, Wolfram, *The Ancient Orient An Introduction to the Study of the Ancient Near East*, Schley, Donald G.(trans.), Eerdmans, 1994.

Walton, John H. *Ancient Near Eastern thought and the Old Testament*, Apollos, 2007

Warburton, David A. *State and Economy in Ancient Egypt: Fiscal Vocabulary of the New Kingdom*, Vandenhoeck & Ruprecht, 1997

Watson, W. G. E. and Wyatt, N., *Handbook of Ugaritic Studies*, Brill, 1999

Watterson, Barbara, *Gods of Ancient Egypt*, Bramley Books, 1996

Westbrook, Raymond and Jasnow, Richard (eds.), *Security for Debt In Ancient Near Eastern Law*, Brill, 2001

Williamson, H. G. M., *Understanding the History of Ancient Israel*, Oxford University Press, 2007

Wyatt, Nick, *Religious Texts from Ugarit*, Sheffield Academic Press, 2002

Yamada, Shigeo, *The Construction of the Assyrian Empire*, Brill, 2000

Yon, Marguerite, *The City of Ugarit at Tell Ras Shamra*, Eisenbrauns, 2006

Younger, K. Lawson, *Ancient Conquest Accounts: A Study in Near Eastern and Biblical History Writing*, JSOT Press, 1990

Index

Index

Index